THE PURSUIT OF THE SOUL

Books by Peter Tyler:

Teresa of Avila: Doctor of the Soul
The Return to the Mystical: Ludwig Wittgenstein, Teresa of Avila and the Western Mystical Tradition
St John of the Cross: Outstanding Christian Thinker
Picturing the Soul: Revisioning Psychotherapy and Spiritual Direction
The Way of Ecstasy: Praying with St Teresa of Avila
The Bloomsbury Guide to Christian Spirituality (with Richard Woods)
Sources of Transformation: Revitilizing Christian Spirituality (with Edward Howells)

THE PURSUIT OF THE SOUL

PSYCHOANALYSIS, SOUL-MAKING AND THE CHRISTIAN TRADITION

Peter Tyler

Bloomsbury T&T Clark
An imprint of Bloomsbury Publishing Plc

B L O O M S B U R Y
LONDON · OXFORD · NEW YORK · NEW DELHI · SYDNEY

Bloomsbury T&T Clark

An imprint of Bloomsbury Publishing Plc

Imprint previously known as T&T Clark

50 Bedford Square   1385 Broadway
London   New York
WC1B 3DP   NY 10018
UK   USA

www.bloomsbury.com

**BLOOMSBURY, T&T CLARK and the Diana logo are trademarks of
Bloomsbury Publishing Plc**

First published 2016

© Peter Tyler, 2016

British Library Cataloguing-in-Publication Data
A catalogue record for this book is available from the British Library.

ISBN: HB: 978-0-56727-442-7
         PB: 978-0-56714-077-7
         ePDF: 978-0-56720-454-7
         ePub: 978-0-56761-109-3

Library of Congress Cataloging-in-Publication Data
Tyler, Peter, 1963–
The pursuit of the soul : psychoanalysis, soul-making, and the Christian
tradition / by Peter Tyler.
pages cm
ISBN 978-0-567-27442-7 (hardback)-- ISBN 978-0-567-14077-7 (pbk.)
1. Soul–Christianity. 2. Christianity–Psychology. 3. Psychoanalysis and
religion. I. Title.
BT741.3.T95 2016
233'.5–dc23
2015024316

Typeset by Fakenham Prepress Solutions, Fakenham, Norfolk NR21 8NN
Printed and bound in India

CONTENTS

PART I
ORIGINS OF THE SOUL

PROLOGUE: A NIGHT-DREAM

Qui enim se cognoscit, in se omnia cognoscet.
(*Whoever knows their self, knows all things in their self.*)

Giovanni Pico Della Mirandola, *Oratio de hominis dignitate/Oration on the Dignity of Man*, 118

It is night. A taxi has come to take me from London to my home in Worcestershire. As we drive I slowly realize that my driver is the celebrated American composer, Philip Glass. He is rather silent and soon I fall asleep. When I awake it is still dark but just before dawn – we are parked in a strange housing estate and my driver is asleep. I shake him awake and ask him where we are. He neither knows nor seems concerned – all he can say is that we got lost during the night. Despite my anxiety (I am due to teach at the university that morning), he seems implacable. In fact, the more agitated I become the more unconcerned he appears. Eventually I go to seek help: first from a woman in an office and then a man on the street. From both I plead for a GPS or satnav in order to find our position. As I am negotiating the loan of these, Philip Glass returns, this time with a group of followers. He tells me, as the sun is rising we now need to pray. I think to myself: 'Hmmm, this guy would make a good spiritual director, he is so relaxed and easy-going ...'

This dream came to me during a stormy night in southern Italy whilst I was thinking about the shape this book would take. At first I was somewhat surprised. My working hours were preoccupied with 'the mind of Christ' as it is described by St Paul, the early mental constructs of Christianity and how they relate to the last 150 years of psychoanalysis. Yet, whenever I receive a dream such as this from the ever-resourceful unconscious I first of all essay my reactions as I was taught during my analytical training. I immediately knew that this was an important dream – it was an 'opening dream' that was opening my perceptions and heart. I looked at the images and the shape of the dream. First of all there was the choice of my 'dream-guide': the somewhat taciturn figure of the great American minimalist maestro, Philip Glass. *Where did he come from?* I asked myself. This slightly new-age eclectic composer was not what my conscious mind had been seeking. I had spent Easter in the southern Italian town dodging showers and downpours whilst participating in the fervent devotions of Holy Week in the little hill-top villages and, like the southern storm, my unconscious had blown away my conscious musings on Freud, Jung and the great Christian tradition. As I struggled with the conscious forms – the London of my psychological training as an adult and the Worcestershire of my childhood and religious upbringing – here sat the 'composer' of the unconscious, quite happy in the gathering dawn simply to pray. As Novalis wrote in the *Hymns to the Night*, the night is darkest just before dawn, and in the deepest unknowing a simple light was being shed over my thoughts. The ego had been hijacked by the 'taxi driver' unconscious and taken to a new place, what I will end up calling in this book, a 'third position of the soul': a position that the medievals termed the 'knowing unknowing'. The unconscious had presented the whole book to me in such an elegant and simple fashion that my conscious mind could not have arranged. For, as with all books, there is the desire to communicate and share ideas with you, the reader, but also there is the desire to work on a problem that besets the author. In my case it was how to reconcile two halves of my adult life: working as a psychological analyst in the Jungian and Freudian tradition on the one hand, and working as a theologian and spiritual director in the Christian Catholic tradition on the other. For in our own lifetimes these two great streams of interpretation of the *psyche* – that glittering, fragile axis of our existence which the Greeks termed *iridescent, breath, life, spirit* and even *butterfly* – have met. Once sworn enemies, in the past few decades psychologists and theologians have once again begun to talk to each other, and I offer this book as a contribution to that dialogue – a dialogue between thought-traditions, ideas and experiences of the self and the world.

On an academic level, many of the arguments of this book will be between the realms of the Old World and the New – the pre-modern and the postmodern. It is no coincidence, I believe, that my 'dream-guide' came from the New World and we shall throughout these pages see how the Old World ideas and pictures of Plato, Aristotle, St Paul, St Augustine, Evagrius and the other founders of Christianity will enter into dialogue with those who have shaped our modern conceptions of self: Sigmund Freud, Carl Jung, Ludwig Wittgenstein, Edith Stein and Otto Rank.

As my work proceeded it seemed that the narrative of my account reflected the place where Christians find themselves today: with old attachments to ancient and venerable concepts and attitudes fading away before new ones have arisen. Consequently, my hope for this book is that it will contribute to this contemporary phenomenon of a newly emerging consciousness that is genuinely respectful of the ancient Christian categories but will allow those categories to transform and rejuvenate into the new forms needed for the demands of the emerging era. As St Paul wrote 2,000 years ago, 'be transformed by the renewing of your mind so that you may discern what is the will of God' (Rom. 12.2).

As we explore these concepts together in this book – those of the classical Christian tradition and those of contemporary psychology – my aim will be to create a space where new pictures of self may emerge for you the reader. As Wittgenstein once wrote, we 'make pictures' of the world before us. Thus throughout this book pictures and arguments will be presented and it is my sincere hope that by engaging with them you too may experience something of that 'transformation of mind' that St Paul so fervently wished for all as Christianity first emerged into the classical world. For one of the main aims of this book is to remind us all of the 'iridescent, subtle and fleeting' nature of the *psyche* and how any attempt to 'pin it down' will leave it inert and lifeless.

In the psychology faculty, discourse on the soul (as we shall see later) dropped out of respectable circles some decades ago and those who persisted in using the old-fashioned term (often as not following the usage of the 'founding fathers' of analysis, Carl Jung and Sigmund Freud) were either excluded or sidelined from mainstream discourse. Yet, against all the odds, the term persists in contemporary discourse. Not only that, as we shall see, an increasing number of contemporary and original thinkers have seen that 'soul-discourse' offers a plausible narrative of the self in postmodern times. This, then, is where our journey begins – in contemporary discourse and the rediscovery of soul language in psychoanalysis, counselling and pastoral care. Yet to focus on this discourse alone (as we shall do in Part II of this book), would, I think, be a misrepresentation of the tradition of soul-discourse in the West.

Soul-discourse has a long and lively history in Western thought (and I apologize that I will not cover much of the Eastern tradition in the present volume; I hope to pursue these ideas in a later volume) and this discourse continues to cast its long shadow over contemporary discourse of the self. Accordingly, in Part I of this book we shall engage in some intellectual archaeology as we survey some of the key forces shaping the Western, and in particular the Christian, view of the soul as it emerges from the crucible of the late classical/early medieval period. I have chosen for the purposes of clarity to concentrate on the narrative that emerges from the Platonic corpus and its interpretation, integration, assimilation and rejection by the emerging Christian consciousness. As many contemporary writers on the soul, such as James Hillman, have likewise taken their bearings from the interaction of the Platonic and Christian traditions in these early centuries, it will not be unhelpful to retrace again some of the key arguments and debates of this period. Out of this cauldron I will suggest that two or three dominating 'pictures of the soul' emerge that will then play their parts in the evolution of the soul discourse through the medieval and early modern periods.

Those seeking a comprehensive and all-embracing history of the soul in Western culture will be disappointed. Even if such a book could be written (and I doubt whether it could, although see Charles Taylor's *Sources of the Self* for the nearest thing to this), this is not my purpose here. Rather, as I expressed in my earlier 'mystical trilogy' of *St John of the Cross: Outstanding Christian Thinker, The Return to the Mystical* and *Teresa of Avila: Doctor of the Soul* (Tyler 2010a, 2011, 2013a), my growing contention has been that *reflection on the pre-modern gives answers to postmodern questions.*[1] Accordingly, in the final chapters of the present book I shall do exactly that, by bringing the discussion up to date with the solutions I see proposed to the problems of the self explored in this volume by two great German-speaking masters of the discourse: Ludwig Wittgenstein and Edith Stein.[2] With their presentation of the self I shall conclude this odyssey by proposing some answers to the fundamental question of our times: 'Whither the soul?'

As with all such undertakings this one presented many logistical and intellectual challenges, all of which could not have been faced without the help of a committed army of friends, colleagues, advisors and family, so it is with many thanks I address this book to them. T&T Clark/Bloomsbury have been their usual outstandingly professional and kind selves in getting this manuscript ready for publication and I would in particular like to thank Anna Turton, my editor, Miriam Cantwell, Ronnie Hanna and Kim Storry. My colleagues and students at St Mary's University have been their usual kind selves and have helped me in so many ways. I particularly

---

[1] What is presented here might best be described in Foucault's terms as a 'genealogy' rather than a 'history' of the soul (See Foucault, M. *Nietzsche, Genealogy, History* in Foucault 1991).

[2] I have explored the late medieval period not covered in the present volume in the earlier books where I looked at soul discourse through the eyes of Dionysius the Areopagite, the Victorines, Jean Gerson and the Spanish mystics and I refer the interested reader to those volumes. Of course these volumes themselves are by no means an exhaustive treatment of the subject and I look forward in future works to tackling Thomas Aquinas, the Rhineland mystics and other medieval giants on the subject of psychological selfhood.

thank Professor Chris Keith, Dr John McDade, Steph Modak, Dr Tarcisius Mukuka and Dr Eugenia Russell for looking over early drafts of various chapters, and Dr Maureen Glackin for supporting the writing process. Colleagues from other institutions have been immensely supportive and I particularly thank Professor Chris Cook, Archbishop Kevin McDonald, Professor Bernard McGinn, Fr Ronald Rolheiser OMI, Professor Jane Shaw and Dr Rowan Williams for kindly agreeing to read the manuscript and comment on it. Logistical support (e.g. cups of tea and glasses of wine) has been provided by such devoted family and friends as Allyson Davies, Dr Ashish Deved, Dr Mary Eaton, Julienne McLean, Br Patrick Moore and Gill and Hymie Wyse. Their kindness is unending.

This was the first book I have written whilst keeping a blog (http://insoulpursuit.blogspot.co.uk). I have enjoyed the interaction of this and it has helped sustain me during some of the lonesome writing periods. So I thank all who have read and interacted in the blogosphere (surely a modern day equivalent of Plotinus' World Mind?). Some of the research for the book was carried out at the excellent facilities of the Oblate School of Theology in San Antonio, Texas. I would like in particular to thank Cliff Knighten, Fr John Markey OP, Fr Ronald Rolheiser OMI and Greg Zuschlag for all their kindnesses and help there. The final stages of the book came together whilst staying with friends in India connected with the Carmelites of Mary Immaculate. Professor Jose Nandhikkara CMI (an impressive Wittgensteinian himself) did sterling work in getting me around India and making introductions. I am very indebted to him and all the fathers and brothers of the CMI, especially Fr Anto Vattakuzhy CMI for the kind hospitality at Vidyavanam Ashram. The book is dedicated to all who seek the soul, especially my students, spiritual pilgrims and therapeutic clients, past, present and future. I thank them all for all they have taught me.

CHAPTER 1
WHAT'S IN A NAME?

The identity crisis of psychology

We live in a time of crisis for psychology, or so at least some of the authors we shall deal with in this book will contend. As Professor Glen Slater suggests:

> Today psychology rarely inspires … Materialism and numbers have eclipsed interiority. Cognitive-behaviourism and neuroscience dominate the landscape – flatlands where subjects are quantified, therapies are determined economically, and pills are given before anyone asks, 'what's wrong?' Functionality reigns …
>
> Psychology has placed itself inside a Skinner box – a place with an empty interior where psychologists map the brain and observe activity. (Slater 2005)

Or as James Hillman suggested in 1975, psychology is often reduced to 'statistics, physical anthropology, cultural journalism or animal breeding' (Hillman RVP: xii). Statistics show that Americans spend more than 55 billion dollars a year on therapy and medication and in 2005 one out of ten Americans was on antidepressants (Russell 2013: 2). The tragic death of Robin Williams by his own hand in summer 2014 raised many questions to the general public as to the nature, purpose and ambit of 'mental health' and psychological intervention.[1] As already stated above one of the interesting developments from a Christian perspective has been the appropriation and re-examination of 'soul-language' by some psychologists seeking an escape from the impasse that much contemporary psychology seems trapped in.

At the time of writing the largest school in the British Royal College of Psychiatrists is the spirituality section and the recent creation of the British Association for the Study of Spirituality has given many healthcare professionals in the UK the intellectual space to explore that which had previously

---

[1] For a recent forensic examination of the travails and challenges of the contemporary psychological scene see the final chapter of Scull 2015.

been off-limits: 'the spiritual'.[2] Yet even in the somewhat calmer meadows of theological enquiry there seemed to be something approaching embarrassment regarding 'the soul' such that discussion of its nature, origins and implications (especially when this might imply a dangerous neo-Platonic spiritualizing of the self) had slipped into abeyance. Within the void left by the two spheres of psychoanalysis and theology a new form of 'soul-language' has developed in the past few decades. Jungian psychology had always had an eye on the transcendent and Carl Jung himself was entirely comfortable in his own version of neo-Gnostic spirituality. However it took his successor, James Hillman, to grasp the metaphor of soul by the horns and lead it into some new and surprising places. Considered at best maverick, at worst heretical (and we shall meet many heretics over the coming pages) by his fellow analysts, Hillman, in a colourful and varied career, was able to develop his own understanding of soul-language. In one of his last interviews before his death in 2011 he stated that:

> I am critical of the whole analytic discipline ... It has become a kind of New Age substitute for life, on the one hand; a substitute for rigorous education in culture, philosophy and religion, on the other; and third, a 'helping profession' ... the whole thing has lost its way. Something is deeply missing.[3]

Thus 'soul' and 'soul-language' for Hillman became a coded reference not only to that 'which is deeply missing' in the helping professions, but in wider Western society as a whole, including the religions and churches. In a world whose increasing desire seemed to conquer, codify and classify the infinitely resourceful and unknown realms of the psyche, Hillman saw 'soul-language' as a way of guarding the essential poetic ambiguity that lies close to the sources of human wonder and discovery. Although my own views differ in many respects from Hillman's (as I will demonstrate later in this book), it is from this same place of wonder and poetic astonishment that this book was conceived. I am myself a registered psychotherapist (albeit one who has not parted company with the Catholic Christian tradition). As I sit week after week listening to the torments, joys and wonders that my contemporaries struggle with I see more and more that the poetic wonder of the unknowing soul is ultimately the kindest light to lead through an often devastating and

---

[2] For more on these developments see Cook, Powell and Sims (2009) and Cook (2013).
[3] Interview with Jan Marlan, IAAP Newsletter 26: 2006.

all-consuming gloom. From this perspective I look back and see certain key moments that have shaped our contemporary understanding of the soul and psyche. As is consonant with the approach I have employed over the past couple of decades in books and lectures, I do not see a necessary conflict between the psychological and the theological. Nor do I see it necessary to create a cosy 'spiritual mush' from collapsing the one into the other (for more on this see Tyler 2014). Rather, I aim to demonstrate in this book, that if we stare long and hard at the origins of analysis and the origins of Christianity we see a comparable ambiguity within the creation of soul-language by each discipline – a comparable ambiguity that both traditions would later seek to 'tidy up' as they moved into less ambiguous dominating narratives of the nature of the human psyche and its astonishing apophasis.

Accordingly, in this text I will investigate the origins of both soul-narratives within Christianity and psychoanalysis before returning at the end of the book to our current day preoccupations in these disciplines and how the contemporary 'return of the soul' may be navigated for the revitalization of not only Christian but also psychoanalytic traditions (and, one would hope, wider society).

As already stated, one of the leading voices in this reappraisal has been the late James Hillman whose theories and ideas we shall explore later in the book. Hillman (I will suggest wrongly) ultimately saw Christianity as the source of the malaise in contemporary conceptions of the self and insisted on resurrecting a Platonic multivalency of self as opposed to the monovalent Christian soul that he saw as having such a pernicious influence. As he wrote in *Revisioning Psychology*:

> Religion in our culture derives from spirit rather than from soul, and so our culture does not have a religion that reflects psychology or is mainly concerned with soul-making. Instead we have psychology that reflects religion. Since the religion in our culture has been monotheistic, our psychologies are monotheistic. (Hillman RVP: 4)

Hillman is not the only 'soul-maker' who takes issue with Christianity. The Italian psychologist Luigi Zoja, writing in 1998, lamented the role that Christian 'ethics and education' have played in placing guilt at the centre of the Western psyche, preferring 'unilateral goodness' to the ambiguous profundity of either Judaism or Greek polytheism (Zoja 1998: 35).

Yet it will be my argument in this book that Christian 'soul-making' is far more complicated and multi-layered than critics such as Hillman and Zoja give credit for and one of the chief aims of this volume will be to present this Christian soul-making in all its complexity and ambiguity as a means to reinvigorate the contemporary discourse of the self; this we shall do through the eyes of two great twentieth century theorists: Ludwig Wittgenstein and Edith Stein, both working in the Christian tradition yet able to transcend it by their bold and perceptive insights into the wider European philosophical climate within which they found themselves immersed.[4]

Therefore the present work arises as a response to the growth of soul-language removed from its Christian context. In the first part of the book I will demonstrate how the early Christian church overcame its Platonic legacy to construct a soul-work that could present an image of self that held the positive Platonic notion with the birth of the transcendent in Christ. Although the pursuit of the soul has preoccupied Christians for 2,000 years, official pronouncements of the Church on the subject have been rather reticent. As we shall see in Chapter 3, the Church has perhaps wisely refrained from delineating rigidly the language of the soul and seems to have recognized that several competing pictures have at times emerged (and continue to emerge).

Just as a discourse of the soul has returned to the world of psychology in the last few decades, so, too, in the Church we have seen a return to soul-talk. In 2012 the Roman Catholic Church, under the aegis of Pope Benedict XVI, decided to introduce a new English translation of its liturgy. Amongst all the changes one addition to the wording took many people by surprise. Before the communicant receives the Blessed Sacrament of Christ's body at the Eucharist it had been the custom to whisper 'Lord, I am not worthy to receive you, but only say the word and I shall be healed'. Wanting to bring the words closer in line with the older Latin rite and following the description of the healing of the Centurion's servant in Luke 7.6 the translators now added the more intriguing: 'Lord, I am not *worthy that you should* enter under my roof, but only say the word and *my soul* shall be healed.' It was the use of the word 'soul' that struck some commentators as somewhat old-fashioned and atavistic. Why start using the term

---

[4] Already we have a problem with terminology – to hyphenate or not to hyphenate? Much of my discourse in this volume will explore terms that exist in German for which there is no straightforward English translation. I shall attempt English versions of *Seelsorge, seelische* and *Seele* itself. The word 'soul', if not irrevocably associated with southern Blues musicians, has accrued the religious connotations in English denied its German equivalent. 'Soulmaking' or 'Soul-making'? I shall leave it to the reader to decide but will stay with the more English hyphen for now …

'soul' again, especially after it seemed to have been quietly forgotten for the past thirty years? As an unashamed observer of religious words and their usage I found this return of the soul fascinating. To understand how the contemporary Catholic church uses the term we can do worse than survey the use of the term in the last official Catholic document on the subject, the *Catechism of the Roman Catholic Church*, promulgated in 1994 in order to map Catholic doctrine and dogma in the after-shock of the Second Vatican Council (1962–5).

Within its text we can discover the *Catechism* using the term 'soul' in at least ten differing ways. In this respect it is merely reproducing the many and varied ways in which *animus* and *psyche* have been used in the 2,000 years of Western Christianity, as we shall see shortly.[5] To begin it may be worth reviewing these different usages as they will throw light on much of the discussion that will come later. In this respect, the *Catechesis* can be seen as a primer of all the disputes and arguments that have categorized the Western 'pursuit of the soul' for the past 2,000 years. It will also act as a primer for some of the key aspects of 'soul' that we shall discuss during this book, in particular:

The philosophical perspective

We shall see throughout this book how our description of soul reflects our deeper metaphysical views on the nature of the cosmos. Soul-language implicitly betrays our perspective on the universe (even the refusal to use the term 'soul' betrays a metaphysical perspective in itself). From Plato onwards speculation about the nature of self has automatically been connected with speculation as to the nature of the cosmos.

---

[5] An etymological note. The English *soul,* like the German *Seele,* has roots in the Gothic *saiwala* and Old German *saiwalô,* which for Jung can be linked with the Greek Αἴολος/*aiolos*: mobile, coloured, iridescent (see Tyler 1997), also the mythical keeper of the Winds. Other commentators (for example Barnhart 1988 and Klein 1971) link it to the Proto-Germanic, *saiwaz,* literally 'coming from or connected with the sea or lake', an alleged reference to the dwelling place of the soul in ancient Northern European cultures (the numerous cultic objects and indeed human and animal sacrifices found in Northern bogs and mires may attest to this). As well as *soul/Seele,* I shall in this book spend a certain amount of time exploring the origins and various uses of the Greek *psyche*/ψυχή and the Latin *animus*. *Psyche*, as we shall see, has links with the Greek *psykhein* 'to blow, cool' as well as various terms for life-force, ghost, spirit and even butterfly (we shall essay these uses as we move through the book). The Latin *animus,* on the other hand (often in the early centuries a translation for *psyche*), again has a variety of meanings connected with rationality, mental life, personhood etc. It in its turn is related to the Greek *anemos*/ἄνεμος, 'wind or breeze', and possibly the Sanskrit अनिल (ánila/'air, wind') and is cognate with the Welsh *anadl*/'breath' and Old Irish *animm*/'soul'.

The psychological/anthropological perspective

The word pictures we use in our soul-language reveal too how we understand our human personhood. Throughout the book we shall observe the use of the terms 'psyche', 'soul' and 'self'. As we review the various pictures of our soul-makers we shall have recourse to these terms and varying perspectives on the nature of self, in contemporary terms, what we can call the 'psychological' or 'anthropological'.

The theological perspective

How we use soul-language also reflects our understanding of how we stand in relation to the *theos*. Soul-language is the *telos*-orientated language *par excellence*.

Therefore, as we review the use of the term in the *Catechesis* we shall also introduce the first theoretical design that shall form a central part of this book: what Wittgenstein termed the *Übersichtliche Blick* and to which we shall return in Chapter 7 – that is, a way of seeing that looks for connections rather than analytical or conceptual clarity. It is a way of 'unknowing' as much as knowing and one that we shall return to throughout these pages (see also Tyler 2011). Essentially we shall observe the use of the 'soul-language' as a nexus of meanings rather than being in pursuit of an entity or essence – 'the soul'. Thus, in this volume we shall concentrate on the term 'soul' as a locus for performative discourse, especially of a transcendental nature, rather than as referent to any particular part of self.

Philosophical uses of soul-language in the Catechesis

As the heir to the great Graeco-Roman traditions within which it was gestated (see St John Paul II, *Fides et Ratio,* 1994 and *Crossing the Threshold of Hope,* 1998) it is perhaps no surprise that 2,000 years later Latin Christianity still takes its guiding philosophical models in the *Catechesis* from the key shapers of antique soul-language, in particular Plato and Aristotle. From its inception Christianity, as we shall see shortly, has had an often troubled relationship with the classical matrix within which it was born. Plato, in particular, dominates the rules of early Christian soul-language and at many times the Church itself becomes deeply uneasy with this platonizing tendency, especially when soul-language begins to be pushed into the wider cosmo-hieratical spheres of Gnosticism in the late second and early third centuries. It is only really with the baptism of Aristotle by Thomas Aquinas in the thirteenth century Latin West that this collective platonization can be held in check by the equally dominant later tendency towards the Aristotelian. Yet, as we shall see, the Platonic terminology is never really lost and will continue to exert its influence. In the *Catechesis* itself the legacy of both scholars is clearly apparent. Thus in CCC: 364 we read that: 'the human body shares in the dignity of "the image of God": it is a human body *precisely because it is animated by a spiritual soul,* and it is the whole human person that is intended to become, in the body of Christ, a temple of the Spirit.' The notion of human bodies 'animated' by a 'spiritual soul' is, we shall see, a constant in the Western language of the soul. As CCC: 364 puts it: 'man, though made of body and soul, is a unity. Through his very bodily condition he sums up in himself the elements of the material world. Through him they are thus brought to their highest perfection and can raise their voice in praise freely given to the Creator.' If it was not for the little word 'unity' this view might appear heavily dualist, yet the writers of this passage are clearly struggling to offset the inherent dualism towards which these passages are creeping with something else. That something else is the Aristotelian tradition inherited from the scholastics, in particular Aquinas.[6] This dualist tendency is at its strongest in its final pages when it discusses the destiny of the human being after death. In CCC: 1005, for example, it is stated that 'to rise with Christ, we must die with Christ: we must "be away from the body and at home with the Lord" (2 Cor. 5.8). In that "departure" which is death the soul is separated from the body (Phil. 1.23). It will be reunited with the body on the day of resurrection of the dead.' The clear message is that 'soul' as an entity will be separated from body at death (CCC: 1016), only to be reunited at the resurrection of the 'last day'.

To counter these stronger more dualist views, the authors of the *Catechism* refer to the major Western teaching on the soul that arises after Aquinas: that of the Council of Vienne from 1312.[7] Here we have a clear statement of the Aristotelian view to counteract the supposed platonizing dualism:

---

[6] See also CCC: 360 which quotes Augustine: 'O wondrous vision, which makes us contemplate the human race in the unity of its origin in God … in the unity of its nature, composed equally in all men of a material body and a spiritual soul; in the unity of its immediate end and its mission in the world; in the unity of its dwelling, the earth, whose benefits all men, by right of nature, may use to sustain and develop life; in the unity of its supernatural end: God himself, to whom all ought to tend; in the unity of the means for attaining this end; … in the unity of the redemption wrought by Christ for all.' And CCC: 362 'The human person, created in the image of God, is a being at once corporeal and spiritual. The biblical account expresses this reality in symbolic language when it affirms that "then the LORD God formed man of dust from the ground, and breathed into his nostrils the breath of life; and man became a living being".'

[7] As noted, it is striking how few official church pronouncements there are on the nature of the soul – we shall review them in Chapter 3.

> The unity of soul and body is so profound that one has to consider the soul to be the 'form' of the body (Council of Vienne, 1312): i.e., it is because of its spiritual soul that the body made of matter becomes a living, human body; spirit and matter, in man, are not two natures united, but rather their union forms a single nature. (CCC: 365)

We have, then, two clear philosophical underpinnings to the soul-discourse used in the *Catechesis*:

1. A philosophical position where 'soul' is determined as 'that which is not material', indeed, as the 'animating principle' to the merely lifeless material,

   and

2. The essentially Aristotelian perspective (as adapted by Aquinas and promulgated at the Council of Vienne) that the soul is the 'form of the body', the entelechy of the body.

Thus, in summary, what we find philosophically in the *Catechesis* are not just the bare bones of Plato and Aristotle – those two ancient masters of soul-language who will so shape what comes after them – but the essence of the philosophical discourse that has shaped 2,000 years of Western soul-discourse with all its concomitant contradictions and tensions. We shall examine these in more detail shortly.

Psychological/anthropological uses of soul-language in the Catechesis

As stated at the outset, soul-language is often used to determine the anthropological or psychological view of a particular discourse. In this respect it is no surprise then that the majority of the uses of the term (five) in the *Catechesis* relate to how the *Catechesis* itself understands the human person, beginning with:

Soul as unity of self: type of person or individual (CCC: Prol. 24, 1.1.363)

In this respect one of the key determinates of soul-discourse in the *Catechesis* is the need to emphasize the *unity* of the locus of soul-discourse.

From a twenty-first century Western perspective (post-Descartes), this may seem so blindingly obvious as to not need stating. Yet, arising from its Platonic roots, the universal Christian church felt very early on the necessity to affirm this unity in the Council of Constantinople IV in 870 (referenced in the *Catechism* in CCC: 367). We shall refer back to the debates of Constantinople shortly, for now it is worth mentioning that one of the striking themes in contemporary re-appropriation of soul-language by contemporary psychologists such as Hillman is precisely the insistence that the soul is *not* a unified whole. Hillman would like to maintain the distinctive 'voices' of the self that soul-discourse introduces – a multi-discourse, he believes, that is excluded by the mono-maniacal insistences of the empirico-critical scientist methodologies of contemporary psychologies. However in contrast to Hillman's 'multi-soul' the Roman Catholic Church in its catechism insists on the unity of what Kant would call the 'manifold of apperception' for all true believers:

> Sometimes the soul is distinguished from the spirit: St. Paul for instance prays that God may sanctify his people 'wholly', with 'spirit and soul and body' kept sound and blameless at the Lord's coming (1 Th 5:23). The Church teaches that this distinction does not introduce a duality into the soul. (CCC: 367)

Having affirmed the necessity of unity in soul-language, the Church then prescribes the fourth perspective on its use of soul-language, that:

The soul is seen as animating principle

Following the unity of the self, the second psychological principle the soul-language of the *Catechism* would like to assert is that soul-language refers to that which animates the self. Here the *Catechism* draws heavily on the writings of Augustine, another figure we shall return to shortly. For Augustine, soul-language is nothing less than that which connects us with *theos*. Thus, the principle of soul is also the principle of life/animation in the self, that which distinguishes us from the inarticulate or insensate:

> The Beatitudes respond to the natural desire for happiness. This desire is of divine origin: God has placed it in the human heart in order to draw man to the One who alone can fulfill it: 'How is it, then, that I seek you, Lord? Since in seeking you, my God, I seek a happy life, let me seek you so that my soul may live, for my body draws life from my

soul and my soul draws life from you.' (St. Augustine, Conf. 10, 20: PL
32, 791). (CCC: 1718)[8]

Although I shall refer shortly to the theological aspects of the soul-talk of
the *Catechism* I include this dimension of its discussion within the 'psychological' as the principle that is being referred to here by Augustine and
the *Catechism* would probably be closer in modern psychological/philo-
sophical terms to 'consciousness' than anything else. Just as contemporary
philosophy of mind seeks the animating principle that distinguishes mind
from matter (what distinguishes us from computers) so Augustine (true as
always to his Platonic/Gnostic roots) invests this animating principle, this
consciousness, with the 'spark of the divine' within us. Just to be conscious,
suggests Augustine, is to touch the divine, which is a key claim of any
Christian Catholic soul-language:

> The human body shares in the dignity of 'the image of God': it is a
> human body precisely because it is animated by a spiritual soul, and
> it is the whole human person that is intended to become, in the body
> of Christ, a temple of the Spirit. (CCC: 364)

Which brings us to the fifth psychological dimension of the soul as defined
by the *Catechism*:

Soul as 'rational', 'willing' part of self

Connected with the notion of soul-speech as referring to animation of the
self another ancient part of the tradition reiterated in the *Catechism* is the
notion that soul-speech relates to the 'rationality' or 'will' of the self. Here
again the ghost of Augustine stretches with his tripartite division of the soul
into the three aspects of memory, will and understanding. But again, as with
so much to do with soul-language, we find that his shadow mingles with
that of Descartes' *cogito* and the urge to create the modern *rational* self. Like
us, Christ was early declared to have a 'rational' soul that would distinguish
his solidarity with the human race:

> The fourth ecumenical council, at Chalcedon in 451, confessed:
> 'Following the holy Fathers, we unanimously teach and confess

---

[8]Cf. Aristotle in the *Nicomachean Ethics* (1102a.5) who states that *eudemonia* (happiness)
corresponds to the action of virtue in the soul (I am indebted to Dr Eugenia Russell for drawing
this to my attention).

one and the same Son, our Lord Jesus Christ: the same perfect in divinity and perfect in humanity, the same truly God and truly man, composed of rational soul and body; consubstantial with the Father as to his divinity and consubstantial with us as to his humanity.' (CCC: 467)

The rational component of the intellectual soul is also for the Church the willing component that shall determine our *choice* to choose God in all things (CCC: 1711). As we shall see in the next chapter, soul-language, from its Platonic roots, has stressed the link between rationality and soul-discourse. For the Catholic Church such rationality is clearly confined to our souls, Christ and God. Yet, as we shall see, for many of Plato's followers (including some early Christians) such rationality extended far beyond the personal to all corners of the cosmos. The *Nous*, or 'World Soul', contained a rationality spreading like a world-wide-web throughout the cosmos. Such notions of rationality and will within the soul-language will create their own issues that we shall have to discuss as we journey. Following its inspiration from Augustine (and the conciliar decrees on the human nature of Christ's soul) it is perhaps unsurprising to find the *Catechism*'s emphasis on the rational and willing power of the soul. What is perhaps more intriguing is the next psychological category of soul introduced into the text:

'Modern' soul as 'innermost aspect of man'
In CCC: 363 we read that:

In Sacred Scripture the term 'soul' often refers to human life or the entire human person. But 'soul' also refers to the innermost aspect of man, that which is of greatest value in him, (Mt 10:28; 26:38; Jn 12:27; 2 Macc 6:30) that by which he is most especially in God's image: 'soul' signifies the spiritual principle in man.

The use of the term 'innermost' is perhaps the most surprising here. This is a picture that it not quite so endemic to the Christian tradition as we would think. Plato and Aristotle rarely referred to the soul as the 'innermost' quality of self and even in the late medieval Teresa of Avila whose 'mansions' are often referred to as 'the interior castle', an argument can be made that Teresa is advocating a decentred self to which interiority cannot strictly be applied (see Tyler 2013). As Charles Taylor has demonstrated (Taylor 1989), it is to Descartes we have to turn for the truly modern 'interior turn' (aided and abetted, as we shall see in a later chapter, by Augustine and Plotinus). As we shall see towards the end of the book, under the critique of Wittgenstein, such notions of interiority have a questionable basis in the picture of the soul.

Finally, we come to the last psychological perspective as presented in the *Catechesis*:

The soul as the whole self

As we have seen, the picture of human personhood presented to us in the catechetical soul-discourse is one characterized by unity, rationality, will and interiority. Yet it would be misleading to finish this survey of the psychological pictures of the *Catechesis* without mentioning its emphasis that soul-language points towards the connectivity of the self. The self, for the catechists, is a web of interactions, a holistic locus:

> In Sacred Scripture the term 'soul' often refers to human life or the entire human person (Mt 16:25-26; Jn 15:13; Acts 2:41). (CCC: 363)

This is demonstrated in particular in the pastoral orientation of the *Catechism* and the reminder that it (as a Christian document) is a clear call to ministry and pastoral action rather than solely philosophical speculation:

> Christ's compassion toward the sick and his many healings of every kind of infirmity are a resplendent sign that 'God has visited his people' and that the Kingdom of God is close at hand. Jesus has the power not only to heal, but also to forgive sins; he has come to heal the whole man, soul and body; he is the physician the sick have need of (Mk 2:17). (CCC: 1503)

Such 'wholeness' of self as defined by the catechists also includes very modern (or even postmodern) notions of sexuality:

> Sexuality affects all aspects of the human person in the unity of his body and soul. It especially concerns affectivity, the capacity to love and to procreate, and in a more general way the aptitude for forming bonds of communion with others. (CCC: 2332)

As we shall see in the following chapter and throughout this book, *eros* has long had an intimate connection with *psyche* and it is therefore perhaps unsurprising that the authors of the *Catechism* feel the need to reference this ancient tradition. For if we take the holistic language of the *Catechism*'s anthropology seriously we also have to include the sexual dimension within the soulful definition of self.

So, in summary, in its psychological perspective the *Catechism* is a bit like the householder doing her spring cleaning described in the Gospels: unsurprisingly, she brings out both old and new. We have the old Augustinian orthodoxies of the wilful and rational nature of the self, along with the ancient determination to emphasize the unity of soul-language, with what are in many ways, striking modern characteristics of self: the interiority at the heart of self and the holistic view that must by necessity include the sexual dimension of the person.

Theological use of soul-language in the Catechism

The final aspect of the *Catechism* that concerns us here is how its soul-language uses a distinctly teleological turn to inscribe within itself what it sees as the end or purpose of human life. For the Catholic Church this will of course point to soul-language as that language of the self that characterizes our need to develop in relationship to the *theos* of the teleological turn. Thus, the eighth, theological, perspective of the *Catechism*'s soul-language emphasizes:

'Soul-language' as a way of coming to know God catechetically and apologetically

The *Catechism* is of course a polemical work that is seeking to move the reader into action. Here the catechetical role of soul-language is particularly apt, such as in the passage that it quotes from St John Damascene:

> 'The beauty of the images moves me to contemplation, as a meadow delights the eyes and subtly infuses the soul with the glory of God.' (St John Damascene, De imag. 1, 27: PG 94, 1268A, B). Similarly, the contemplation of sacred icons, united with meditation on the Word of God and the singing of liturgical hymns, enters into the harmony of the signs of celebration so that the mystery celebrated is imprinted in the heart's memory and is then expressed in the new life of the faithful. (CCC: 1162)

Soul-language is for the catechists one that involves beauty, harmony and praise as much as cool rational dissection. In this the unknowing at the heart of God is mirrored in the unknowing that we possess in our own selves:

> With his openness to truth and beauty, his sense of moral goodness, his freedom and the voice of his conscience, with his longings for the infinite and for happiness, man questions himself about God's existence. In all this he discerns signs of his spiritual soul. The soul, the 'seed of eternity we bear in ourselves, irreducible to the merely material' (GS 18 # 1; cf. 14 # 2), can have its origin only in God. (CCC: 33)

Thus, claims the *Catechism*, by opening ourselves to the possibility of talk about beauty or *telos* we have automatically engaged in soul-discourse (see also CCC: 32). As with the connection between *psyche* and *eros*, the *Catechism* makes a necessary link between our search for the *psyche* and our search for the *telos* of the cosmos. The one will inevitably, it suggests, lead to the other, especially through the media of art, beauty and creativity. I shall refer to this later as the 'symbolic' nature of the soul and shall return to it throughout the book.

The final two soul-aspects of the *Catechism* are:

The scriptural soul – soul as Pauline contrast to spirit

As well as its references to the Jewish *ruach* the *Catechism* (aside from the scattered references to *psyche* from the Gospels) devotes its longest scriptural meditation on the soul to St Paul's tripartite division of the self in his epistles into *psyche, soma* and *pneuma*. In keeping with its earlier insistence on the unity of the self, the *Catechesis* is at pains to emphasize that St Paul's division cannot possibly lead to a breach of that unity so carefully won at the Council of Constantinople:

> Sometimes the soul is distinguished from the spirit: St. Paul for instance prays that God may sanctify his people 'wholly', with 'spirit and soul and body' kept sound and blameless at the Lord's coming (1 Th 5:23). The Church teaches that this distinction does not introduce a duality into the soul (Council of Constantinople IV [870]: DS 657). 'Spirit' signifies that from creation man is ordered to a supernatural end and that his soul can gratuitously be raised beyond all it deserves to communion with God. (CCC: 367)

Again, if we are to understand the subsequent history of Christian soul-language we need to look carefully at St Paul's own topography of the soul and how this will be interpreted by later commentators. We shall explore this in more depth in Chapter 2 below. However, as with its insistence on unity and wholeness in terms of its psychological dimension, the *Catechism* is adamant that at the heart of its soul-discourse there must be *theos*: its soul-language is as much *theos-logos* as *psyche-logos*. In this respect, one of the chief and determining aspects of soul-language in the *Catechism* is that, as stated in Genesis, we are made 'in the image and likeness of God':

Soul as *imago dei*
The *Catechism* repeats the teaching of one of the key Second Vatican Council documents to reference the soul, *Gaudium et Spes*:

> 'Christ, ... in the very revelation of the mystery of the Father and of his love, makes man fully manifest to himself and brings to light his exalted vocation' (GS 22). It is in Christ, 'the image of the invisible God,' (Col 1:15; cf. 2 Cor 4:4) that man has been created 'in the image and likeness' of the Creator. It is in Christ, Redeemer and Savior, that the divine image, disfigured in man by the first sin, has been restored to its original beauty and ennobled by the grace of God (GS 22). (CCC: 1701)

Again, in a tradition as old as Augustine, the catechists suggest that in contemplation of the self, we are drawn to contemplation of God and in so far as any of the psychological qualities have meaning they derive it from the underlying theological basis of the self. As they state:

> The divine image is present in every man. It shines forth in the communion of persons, in the likeness of the union of the divine persons among themselves. (CCC: 1702)

As we shall see throughout this book, because of the triune nature of the Christian God, this reflection of the Christian *theos* within the human *psyche* will raise particular issues that will require the philosophical and psychological subtlety of writers such as St Augustine and St Teresa Benedicta a Cruce (Edith Stein) to harmonize the two visions.

Summary

I began this chapter by suggesting that a 'crisis in psychology' had caused some psychologists to search out a contemporary 'language of the soul' to offset some of the deficiencies perceived in contemporary talk of the self. By analysing the soul-language of the *Catechism* of the Roman Catholic Church I have aimed to demonstrate that even within a body of thinking where one would expect a rigid conformity (or so it is often presumed), it is surprising just how multi-layered and multi-textual is its soul-referencing. Within the *Catechism* itself we have found at least ten distinctive uses of its soul-discourse highlighting the three perspectives of the philosophical, psychological and theological:

Philosophical Perspective (the metaphysics of the self):

1. Contrast with that which is material
2. 'Form of the body'

Psychological/Anthropological Perspective (the study of the self):

3. Unity
4. Animating principle
5. Rational will
6. Interiority
7. Wholeness

Theological Perspective (the end or *telos* of the self):

8. Way of coming to know God: catechetical and apologetic
9. Based in revelation and Scripture
10. *Imago dei*

Although the division of the discourse into the three categories of philosophical, psychological and theological may seem unnecessarily laboured and artificial I think it serves the purpose of revealing how understanding of the methodological perspective within which soul-language is deployed can give us a good insight into the pitfalls hidden within the language itself. Most of this book will be concerned with determining how far that discourse has been determined by the intersection of these three loci and I think that the *Catechism* makes a good test case of what happens when these three loci mingle. If we also assume, as I will throughout this book, that 'the soul' is not some small furry beast lurking in the hinterland of ourselves but a linguistic signifier that is there to serve a performative function, then I think many of the prior questions that have tightened our discourse will be loosened. As already stated, in this analysis I am bringing traditional theological Christian discourse into dialogue with post-analytic and linguistic philosophical analysis, particularly of the Wittgensteinian type. For the purposes of the present volume my Wittgensteinian perspective has been enhanced by one from the post-Freudian stable of contemporary psychoanalysis. As we explore the origins, and more importantly the future, of our soul-discourse throughout this book I will be arguing that this discourse, loosened by the perspectives of Wittgenstein and Freud, can now be released in new ways that will fructify and enhance the very religious traditions from which the terms originally derive. For if we find in the *Catechism*, that yardstick of contemporary Catholic voice, at least ten overlapping versions of soul-discourse, then we are likely to find equally complicated soul-discourse wherever the 'soul word' occurs.

This should be no surprise. As we shall see in the following pages over the past 2,000 years the Christian church has adapted to and 'borrowed' from many currents and streams in the Western mindset.[9] However, throughout I would ask you the reader to hold in mind the three interweaving strands of philosophy, psychology and theology that have made Western soul-discourse so rich. If we are finding this in contemporary Christian (and increasingly in contemporary psychological) discourse this should be no surprise, as the three strands are interwoven from the very inception of soul-discourse into the West by Our Father in Faith, Plato, to whom we turn next.

---

[9] As already stated, my emphasis here will be on the West, however I will be especially concerned with Orthodox developments in the early history of the Church. I am afraid that constrictions of space forbid me to go into later developments in Orthodoxy; perhaps this can be the subject of a later work or further scholarship by others.

CHAPTER 2
PLATO: OUR FATHER IN FAITH?

As we have already seen, the ghost of Plato haunts the Christian conception of the soul/*psyche*. Before we turn to the nature of that inheritance it is worth spending some time investigating the chief narratives of the soul in the Platonic corpus and sketching their general outlines. These narratives, of course, lay the foundations not only for the Christian inheritance but the wider Western discourse on the nature of self. In surveying this inheritance I will concentrate on four 'stories of the *psyche*' that Plato presents to us in the four key dialogues (roughly in chronological order) of the *Phaedo, Republic, Phaedrus* and *Timaeus*.[1] Let us now look at each in turn.

Phaedo

As we come to the Platonic discourses afresh what is striking from the contemporary psychological perspective is Plato's insistence that the personal life of the individual *psyche* is intimately connected with the wider order and unity of the cosmos as manifest in the transcendent order. Fate, previous lives and the intervention of other-worldly helpers all play a part in Plato's construction of the self, which will have clear consequences for the future story of the soul in Western discourse. *Phaedo*, Plato's narration of the last hours of Socrates and his meditations on the nature of life after death, has always been regarded as one of the earliest dialogues and within it Plato delineates clearly the conception of self that will later be referred to as 'Platonic dualism' – essentially that the human self comprises two components: the immortal, indivisible, slightly mysterious *psyche* – ψυχή – and the earthly, divisible, all too fallible *somatos* – σώματος. As we shall see, later dialogues present nuances and variations on this essential division, yet throughout Plato there lies an overriding distrust of the body/*soma* and its influence. At various times it is described as untrustworthy, inconsistent,

---

[1] I shall not deal here with *The Symposium, Apology* and other minor works. I hope to explore these in a later volume where I shall investigate the links between *eros* and *psyche* in greater depth.

fallible and generally seems to strive to thwart the 'nobler' and 'higher' aspirations of the *psyche*. This, of course, is Platonic dualism as generally understood in the eyes of later (often hostile) interpreters. However, if we listen to the words of the Platonic discourses carefully we can hear, as I will argue here, a slightly more nuanced view of the nature of self. What emerges from this interrogation of Plato's discourse is a story of the soul that will thread its way, as we shall see, through later Christian doctrine to the images and figures of emergent psychoanalysis and the present day retrieval of the 'story of the soul' in writers such as James Hillman and Thomas Moore.

Phaedo begins with questions of life and death and the nature of personality and human selfhood at the impending moment of the dissolution of Socrates' body at his execution. Very early on in the dialogue Plato (via his mouthpiece Socrates) is insistent that ψυχή will be separated from the σώματος at death:

> Is death nothing more or less than this, the separate condition of the body by itself when it is released from the ψυχή, and the separate condition by itself of the ψυχή when it is released from the body? (*Phaedo* 64c)

Therefore, argues Socrates, the philosopher should not concern themselves with bodily pleasures such as food, drink and sex (64d) (literally, 'that belonging to Aphrodite'), smart clothes, shoes and bodily ornaments, for the *psyche* is that which is not any of these 'worldly' things. It is a denial of matter, flesh, presence, the everyday, for 'the true philosopher despises these ... In matters of this sort philosophers, above all other men, may be observed in every sort of way to dissever the soul from the body' (64e). Therefore the philosopher is the one who is defined by the turning away from the body to the *psyche*. In this argument *soma* equates to matter which equates to death and unreality whilst *psyche* equates to life and reality. The body itself becomes a 'hinderer' to the pursuit of knowledge, to the pursuit of the philosopher:

> The body fills us with passions and desires and fears, and all sorts of fancies and foolishness, so that, as they say, it really and truly makes it impossible for us to think at all ... We are slaves to its service. And so, because of all these things, we have no leisure for philosophy ... and all experience shows that if we would have pure knowledge of anything we must be free of the body, and thus through the soul in herself behold

reality ... For if while in company with the body the soul cannot have pure knowledge, one of two things seems to follow – either knowledge is not to be attained at all, or, if at all, after death. For then, and not till then, the soul will be in herself alone and without the body. (66c–e)

The separation of the two, body and soul, is what Plato terms a *katharsis/* κάθαρσις[2] (67c) – it is essentially the will/decision/desire to separate *psyche* from *soma*:

And what is *katharsis* but the separation of the *psyche* from the body, as I was saying before; the habit of the *psyche* gathering and collecting herself into herself, out of all the courses of the body; the dwelling in her own place alone, as in another life, so also in this, as far as she can; the release of the *psyche* from the chains of the body? (67c)

For as Socrates rather pithily puts it: 'true philosophers make dying their profession' (67e). Thus the aim of philosophy is this *katharsis,* this separation of *psyche* from *soma.* To aid them in this task Plato proposes three qualities of the philosopher which we shall see reoccurring throughout his narratives (68). First there is the disposition of *sophrosyne/σωφροσύνη* (68c). A disposition later discussed in the *Charmides* which we can translate as moderation, temperance, discretion or self-control, it is essentially 'the middle-way'. Secondly, there is *andreia/ἀνδρεία* – manly spirit/courage, and finally δικαιοσύνη/righteousness or justice (fulfilment of the law). *Katharsis,* and thereby wisdom, thus derives from the deft employment of these three virtues by the philosopher during their life (69c). As Socrates puts it: 'Many carry the thyrsus but few enter the Bacchic frenzy' (69d).

The nature of the soul

What then happens to the *psyche* after it is separated from the body at the *katharsis* of death? Cebes, in his speech to Socrates, suggests that it is dispersed like 'breath or smoke' and 'vanishes away':

In what relates to the soul, men are apt to be incredulous; they fear that when she leaves the body her place may be nowhere, and that on

---

[2] As Liddell and Scott (1996) define it: 'a cleansing from guilt or defilement, purification, Latin *lustratio*, also, a pruning of trees, a winnowing of grain.'

the very day of death she may be destroyed and perish immediately on her release from the body, issuing forth like smoke or air and vanishing away into nothingness. (70a)

In contrast to this notion of *psyche* as a wafting vapour (which lies close to its original etymological derivation in Greek; see footnote on page 13). Socrates would rather argue for *psyche* to be an entity that is somehow passed from somatic existence to the next. For each person can 'recollect'/'ἀνάμνησις' their previous existences through learning/*mathein*/ μάθησις (72e–73b). For at birth, as Wordsworth was later to remind us, we forget the knowledge we held before (75e).[3] Therefore, claims Socrates, our souls (*psyche*) must have existed before birth:

> Then, Simmias, our souls must have existed before they were in human form, without bodies, and must have had intelligence/understanding (*phroneis*/ φρονέω). (*Phaedo* 76c/d)

Having proved to his satisfaction the pre-existence of *psyche* before the *soma*, Plato now needs to prove that it exists after death (77c). The argument he uses here is an epistemological argument: that to have knowledge we must recall other forms of knowledge. Therefore to have any knowledge at all there must be a pre-existing framework. There is no end to the recession of links of the chain, therefore it pre-exists us. Following this reasoning, Socrates argues that because the soul does not break up or scatter at death it must be a non-composite object (78) and in this respect resembles the divine (80a). For *psyche* is *theios*, literally 'from the gods, sent by the gods', the implications of which Plato will draw out in the later dialogues:

> *Psyche* is in the very likeness of the divine, and immortal, and intelligible, and uniform, and indissoluble, and unchangeable; and the body is in the very likeness of the human, and mortal, and unintelligible, and multiform, and dissoluble, and changeable. Can this, my dear Cebes, be denied? (80b)

---

[3] 'Our birth is but a sleep and a forgetting: The Soul that rises with us, our life's Star, Hath had elsewhere its setting, And cometh from afar' (William Wordsworth, *Ode: Intimations of Immortality from Recollections of Early Childhood*, 5: 58–62).

To summarize then, so far Plato has given us a soul narrative which includes the following:

a) *Psyche* is an entity – it is not a gas or vapour that is dispersed at death but rather it can exist without dependence on *soma*. In this respect it is indivisible and unchanging. **It is utterly other than body and often opposes its 'passions'** (94). In this respect Plato gives the famous example of Odysseus suppressing his rage:

> As Homer in the *Odyssey* when he says of Odysseus:
> 'He beat his breast, and thus reproached his heart: Endure, my heart; far worse hast thou endured!'
> Do you think that Homer wrote this under the idea that the soul is a harmony capable of being led by the affections of the body, and not rather of a nature which should lead and master them: and itself a far more divine thing than any harmony? (94d/e)

b) In which case it has pre-existence and post-existence to that of each individual somatic dwelling. This pre-existence also brings with it a certain knowledge for **the *psyche* is capable of passing in and out of several births, deaths and reincarnations:**

> For granting even more than you affirm to be possible, and acknowledging not only that the soul existed before birth, but also that the souls of some exist, and will continue to exist after death, and will be born and die again and again, and that there is a natural strength in the soul allowing it to be born several times. Nevertheless, we may be still inclined to think that it will weary in the labours of successive births, and may at last succumb in one of its deaths and utterly perish. But we might say that no one knows beforehand the particular death and particular dissolution of the body which brings destruction to the soul, for none of us can have had any experience of it. (*Phaedo* 88a/b)[4]

For in this dialogue Plato does not claim that the soul is immortal – even the soul can wear out after several of these reincarnations.

---

[4] Cf. Homer's *Iliad* 23.72 where Patroclus speaks of the *psyche* as the souls or likenesses of the dead.

c) **Psyche comes from the *theos***: after separation from the *soma* it will return to the presence of *theos*, if it is the soul of a just philosopher who has striven to avoid material things (80e/82c). The souls of the unjust after death 'hang around tombs and graveyards' (81c/d) after which they are then attracted to bodies that 'agree with their disposition' (81e).

Therefore, for Plato, the aim of philosophy is to prepare the *psyche* for its journey after death and release from the 'prison' of *soma*:

> The lovers of knowledge are conscious that their souls, when philosophy receives them, are simply fastened and glued to their bodies: the soul is only able to view existence through the bars of a prison, and not in her own nature; she is wallowing in the mire of all ignorance; and philosophy, seeing the terrible nature of her confinement, and that the captive through desire is led to conspire in her own captivity. (82e–83a)

For each pleasure and pain becomes 'a sort of nail which nails and rivets the soul to the body, and engrosses her and makes her believe that to be true which the body affirms to be true' (83d).

d) Therefore **the philosopher must cultivate the reasoning (*logismos*/λογισμός) component of the *psyche*** which will allow this release to happen (84a, 107c). Philosophy itself is a praxis that will allow this to happen. However, this last element where Plato suggests a divide in the *psyche* between a logical 'calm'[5] component and a troubled one of desire and passion suggests a divided or bifurcated soul – not quite the indivisible entity he had begun by suggesting. This problem is one that is left unresolved in the *Phaedo* and requires further modification and exploration in the later dialogues to which we will turn shortly.

e) **Mind (*Nous*/νόος)[6] produces all order in the cosmos.** What is striking to modern ears is how Plato does not set a limit on soul/*psyche* to the individual person. *Nous*/mind can permeate all the cosmos and in many respects our individual soul is but an aspect of the larger 'World Soul':

---

[5] γαλήνη, literally 'the calmness of a still sea'.
[6] It is difficult to get all the nuances of *Nous* in contemporary English: mind, perception, apprehension, purpose, intention all give a flavour of its meaning ... *mindfulness* (see Tyler 2013) or *attentiveness* may also allude to its meaning.

Then I heard someone reading, as he said, from a book of Anaxagoras, that mind was the disposer and cause of all, and I was delighted at this notion, which appeared quite admirable, and I said to myself: If mind is the disposer, mind will dispose all for the best, and put each particular in the best place. (97c–98b)

f) **Within the cosmos there are *daimones*/δαίμωνες that protect and guide the soul.** Not only is there a concept of the World Soul in Plato but entities or individuals, *daimones* as he refers to them, who take an active part in the construction and manipulation of that cosmos, ourselves included:

> For after death, as they say, the genius of each individual, to whom he belonged in life, leads him to a certain place in which the dead are gathered together, whence after judgment has been given they pass into the world below, following the guide, who is appointed to conduct them from this world to the other: and when they have there received their due and remained their time, another guide brings them back again after many revolutions of ages … And when it (the *psyche*) arrives at the place where the other souls are gathered, if it is impure and had done impure deeds, whether foul murders or other crimes which are the brothers of these, and the works of brothers in crime – from that soul every one flees and turns away; no one will be its companion or guide. (107d/e)

As we shall see these semi-divine beings, a link between the gods and humans, will continue to be referenced in the emerging soul-consciousness of early Christianity and will even play a role in the later postmodern re-emergence of soul-language.

The Republic

As we have seen, the picture of the soul presented by Plato in the *Phaedo* raises as many questions as it answers. First, there is the relationship between the different components of the self: is *psyche* all of them or only part of them? Secondly, there is the relationship between the individual *psyche* and the overall ordering *Nous* of the cosmos (let alone with the gods themselves). Third, there are still questions remaining about the goal and ultimate end of the *psyche*, despite the poetic descriptions given in the

Phaedo. Finally, there is the role of the *daimones* – where do they come from, what are they, how do they act? In *The Republic* and the other later dialogues we see Plato reiterating elements of the basic scheme from the *Phaedo* but also trying to elaborate and resolve some of the dilemmas presented in the original picture. *The Republic* is notable for codifying and describing the threefold nature of *psyche* – the tripartite soul – the description of which, we already saw in the previous chapter, was to cast such a long shadow over Western language of the self.

The tripartite soul

Once again Plato begins the psycho-discussion of the *Republic* with the conflict of desire that exists within a person, in this case the desire for food and drink and the repression of that desire (*Republic* 4: 439c). For, suggests Socrates reiterating positions taken in the *Phaedo*, appetites such as these are controlled by the 'calculations of reason', *logismos*/λογισμός, rather than the movements of passion/*pathein*/πάθημα:

> And the forbidding principle is derived from reason, and that which bids and attracts proceeds from passion and disease? ... Then we may fairly assume that they are two, and that they differ from one another; the one with which a man reasons, we may call the rational principle of the soul, the other, with which he loves and hungers and thirsts and feels the flutterings of any other desire, may be termed the irrational or appetitive, the ally of sundry pleasures and satisfactions? (*Republic* 4: 439d)

Thus we have the first basic division in Plato's soul between the *logismos*/λογισμός (the reasoning faculty) and *epithumia*/ἐπιθυμία (the desiring faculty). Plato further refines the distinction by introducing a third level, the *thumos*/θυμός (439e), variously translated into English as passion, spirit, will, courage or 'high spirit', anger or 'noble wrath'. Socrates illustrates its occurrence by giving the famous example of Leontius being torn whether to look at the corpses outside Piraeus or not:

> The story is that Leontius, the son of Aglaion, coming up one day from the Piraeus, under the north wall on the outside, observed some dead bodies lying on the ground at the place of execution. He felt a desire to see them, and also a dread and abhorrence of them; for a

time he struggled and covered his eyes, but at length the desire got the better of him; and forcing them open, he ran up to the dead bodies, saying: Look, ye wretches, take your fill of the fair sight. (4: 440a)

Thumos, therefore, sometimes sides with the *logismos* and at other times with *epithumia* 'When a man believes himself to be wronged does not his spirit in that case seethe and grow fierce?':

But a further question arises: Is passion different from reason also, or only a kind of reason; in which latter case, instead of three principles in the soul, there will only be two, the rational *logistikon* and the appetitive *epithumitikon*; or rather, as the State was composed of three classes, traders, auxiliaries, counsellors, so may there not be in the individual soul a third element which is high spirit (*thumos*), and when not corrupted by bad education is the natural auxiliary of reason? (*Republic* 4: 440e/441a)

In the *Republic* the internal invariably reflects the external and vice versa. Thus, the predominant part of the soul of the individual citizens will shape the nature of the *polis* they end up creating: the ideal democracy will be peopled with those who have *logiston* in the ascendancy, oligarchy by those in whom *epithumia* prevails and finally tyranny with those overwhelmed by *thumos* (Book 9: 571b–572b). Thus, he concludes, there are three classes of people:

Then we may begin by assuming that there are three classes of men – lovers of wisdom φιλόσοφος, lovers of honour, lovers of gain. (9: 582c)

As we would expect from Plato, the philosopher is in the advantage of having 'always known the taste of the other pleasures from his childhood' (9: 582b), whereas the epithumial person is 'always busy with gluttony and sensuality' (6: 586b) and the thumotic person always 'carrying his passion into action' being 'envious and ambitious, or violent and contentious, or angry and discontented, if he be seeking to attain honour and victory and the satisfaction of his anger without reason or sense' (9: 586c).

In summary, then, the self/soul/*psyche* of the *Republic* is a 'many headed beast' (9: 588c) where some heads are gentle, others savage. *Logismos*, unsurprisingly, is the 'natural ruler of the soul' (4: 441c) for it controls *thumos* and *epithumia*. It is always wanting to lead the other two parts, sometimes, as we shall see in the next dialogue *Phaedrus*, successfully, often not so. It is the 'learning-loving' and 'philosophical' part of the *psyche* (9: 581b). Plato's view is therefore a generally optimistic one about human nature – people, Plato says, have an essentially refined and noble nature. Yes, *epithumia,* uncontrolled desire for pleasure, is there but ultimately, he suggests, *logiston* will overcome it. *Thumos,* on the other hand, the high spirited part, changes its allegiance from *epithumia* to *logiston* and back again for it is essentially vacillating and unreliable. As Lorenz puts it:

> It is a character trait or psychological tendency that includes as a central aspect eagerness to distinguish oneself and to gain and maintain the esteem and respect of others in one's community. It crucially involves an awareness of one's social position and of one's merits. It also involves solicitude that one's status be duly noted and respected by others and that such merits as one might have be recognised and honoured. (Lorenz 2008: 259)

This, therefore, is the part of the *psyche* that is sensitive to slights and insults and therefore gives *thumos* proximity to anger and pride: that is, deriving from our need for respect and honour.

The charioteer: *Phaedrus*

The *Republic*, therefore, refines the insights of the *Phaedo* but as with the earlier dialogue creates new problems and tensions that have to be explored. Although Plato has isolated three aspects of the *psyche* – *logismos, thumos* and *epithumia* – he still does not show us how the three will or should relate to each other. For if the *logiston* is meant to be in control how then do we explain all the manifest problems where this clearly is not the case? *Phaedo* had also introduced the notion of the connection between the individual *psyche* and the 'World Soul', the *Nous*. Although links had been made between the individual *psyche* and the political composition of the *polis* in the *Republic* these larger metaphysical questions remained untouched in the second dialogue. We shall return to them shortly when we consider the last dialogue that concerns us here – *Timaeus*. Although the *Phaedrus* does not dwell on these more metaphysical aspects to the soul it introduces another important element into Plato's vocabulary of the soul which will be destined to play a significant role in Western discourse – the role of *eros* and its connection to the other parts of the self. For of the four dialogues under consideration here, the *Phaedrus* is the one most concerned with interpersonal love and its relationship to the development of what we would today call 'character' or 'personality'. The dialogue begins with the encounter between Socrates and Phaedrus and the ominous words: 'Where are you coming from, Phaedrus my friend, and where do you go?' (227a). The two meet on a hot summer's day (the apex of life) as they choose to paddle in the stream (of life), gently flowing past as they speculate on what has happened and what will occur. Early on, Socrates states the over-arching Platonic manifesto that we shall return to throughout this book, the message of the Delphic oracle: 'know thyself' (229e) as the Delphic oracle states γνῶναι ἐμαυτόν:

> I must first know myself, as the Delphic inscription says; to be curious about that which is not my concern, while I am still in ignorance of my own self, would be ridiculous. (230a)

What is notable in the *Phaedrus* is that from the beginning the gods, and their inspiration, are not far away. We are close to that world of the *daimones* mentioned in the *Phaedo*, whose watchful presence is forever around us. Thus, as Phaedrus talks Socrates becomes 'inspired with a phrenzy' (234d, to use Jowett's rather wonderful translation) and, in reaction to Lysias' speech, 'something wells up' in Socrates' breast 'not from his own mind' but as a reaction perhaps to the rhetorical 'heady' polish of Lysias' presentation:

> I am sure that I must have heard; but at this moment I do not remember from whom; perhaps from Sappho the fair, or Anacreon the wise; or, possibly, from a prose writer. Why do I say so? Why, because I perceive that my bosom is full, and that I could make another speech as good as that of Lysias, and different. Now I am certain that this is not an invention of my own, who am well aware that I know nothing, and therefore I can only infer that I have been filled through the ears, like a pitcher, from the waters of another, though I have actually forgotten in my stupidity who was my informant. (*Phaedrus* 235c)

Such a speech comes from divine inspiration. In this atmosphere heightened by the presence of the gods (the stream where they sit is itself sacred to the deities) it is no wonder that the crude *epithumia* of the *Republic* is now blithed by the presence of *eros*, the presence of divine love in the soul:

Every one sees that love/ἔρως is a desire/ἐπιθυμία, and we know also that non-lovers desire the beautiful and good. (237d)

As in the *Republic* Plato reiterates that we have two desires working within the soul: *epithumia* and *thumos*:

Let us note that in every one of us there are two guiding and ruling principles which lead us whither they will; one is the natural desire of pleasure, the other is an acquired opinion which aspires after the best; and these two are sometimes in harmony and then again at war, and sometimes the one, sometimes the other conquers. (237d)

And once again we have the reiteration of the need for *sophrosyne*/temperance/σωφροσύνη to control these desires (237e). We shall return in a later chapter to the role of saying and unsaying in the therapeutic relationship. At this point it is worth noting how for Plato the *saying* of *logos* will introduce the *sophrosyne* to moderate the demands of *epithumia* and *thumos*. When *epithumia* is in control, on the other hand, it leads to excess, wantonness and *hubris*/ὕβρις. Yet while this discourse is proceeding, much of which is a reiteration of what has occurred in the earlier dialogues, Socrates tells Phaedrus to be silent as he becomes dithyrambic[7] in this holy place:

Listen to me, then, in silence; for surely the place is holy; so that you must not wonder, if, as I proceed, I appear to be in a divine frenzy, for already I am getting into dithyrambics. (238d)

For having given a long speech on how even holy *eros* can be corrupted by base *epithumia* (240/241), he relents as he hears a new voice from the gods telling him to forgo such impiety:

I mean to say that as I was about to cross the stream the usual sign was given to me, – that sign which always forbids, but never bids, me to do anything which I am going to do; and I thought that I heard a voice saying in my ear that I had been guilty of impiety, and that I must not go away until I had made an atonement. Now I am a diviner, though not a very good one, but I have enough religion for my own

---

[7] Poetic speech inspired by the presence of Dionysius.

use, as you might say of a bad writer – his writing is good enough for
him; and I am beginning to see that I was in error. O my friend, how
prophetic (*mantikos*/μαντικός) is the human soul! (242c)

Eros, as the son of the god Aphrodite, has divinity in it and cannot be led
to impiety (242e) therefore Socrates now calls for a *katharsis* to wipe away
the bad effects of his impious speech. In reaction to Lysias' speech which
stressed the importance of the non-lover over the lover and belittled the role
of the lover, Socrates must now reverse this and make a new speech stressing
the importance of the lover (243b). And at this point a subtle shift occurs
in the narrative. It is as though Plato has realized the limits of the *logiston/
thumos/epithumia* model elaborated in the earlier dialogue. Wisdom, states
Socrates, is a kind of divine madness/*mania* and the *psyche* must be aware
of its irrational powers (244a). The *cordon sanitaire* between the powers of
the *psyche* begins to weaken and we have a glimpse of a far more disturbing,
dangerous even, image of the *psyche*. It is a *psyche* that can touch the divine
mania of the gods and at this point be inspired by prophecy:

> It might be so if madness/μανία were simply an evil; but there is also
> a madness which is a divine gift, and the source of the chief blessings
> granted to men. For prophecy is a madness, and the prophetess at
> Delphi and the priestesses at Dodona when out of their senses have
> conferred great benefits on Hellas, both in public and private life, but
> when in their senses few or none. (244a)

Or as he elaborates it, playing on the similarity of the words *Mantike* and
Manike, there is a divine connection between the two states:

> There will be more reason in appealing to the ancient inventors of
> names, who would never have connected prophecy (*mantike*) which
> foretells the future and is the noblest of arts, with madness (*manike*),
> or called them both by the same name, if they had deemed madness
> to be a disgrace or dishonour; – they must have thought that there
> was an inspired madness which was a noble thing; for the two words,
> *mantike* and *manike*, are really the same, and the letter *tau* is only a
> modern and tasteless insertion. (244c)

Therefore, the madness of *eros* is 'the greatest of heaven's blessings' (245c)
and from this point arises Socrates' justly famous discourse on the nature

of the *psyche* which is to be compared to that of a winged charioteer with *thumos* and *epithumia* being the two errant horses that the *logiston* tries to control using *sophrosyne* to reign in the hubris of excess that exists when either of the subordinate powers is in control:

> Of the nature of the soul, though her true form be ever a theme of large and more than mortal discourse, let me speak briefly, and in a figure. And let the figure be composite – a pair of winged horses and a charioteer. Now the winged horses and the charioteers of the gods are all of them noble and of noble descent, but those of other races are mixed; the human charioteer drives his in a pair; and one of them is noble and of noble breed, and the other is ignoble and of ignoble breed; and the driving of them of necessity gives a great deal of trouble to him. I will endeavour to explain to you in what way the mortal differs from the immortal creature. The soul in her totality has the care of inanimate being everywhere, and traverses the whole heaven in divers forms appearing – when perfect and fully winged she soars upward, and orders the whole world; whereas the imperfect soul, losing her wings and drooping in her flight at last settles on the solid ground – there, finding a home, she receives an earthly frame which appears to be self-moved, but is really moved by her power; and this composition of soul and body is called a living and mortal creature. For immortal no such union can be reasonably believed to be; although fancy, not having seen nor surely known the nature of God, may imagine an immortal creature having both a body and also a soul which are united throughout all time. Let that, however, be as God wills, and be spoken of acceptably to him. And now let us ask the reason why the soul loses her wings. (246a/b)

This image of the *psyche* as connected with the winged plume or feather is one that we shall see returning within the early Christian discourse in the following chapters where this passage is often referenced:

> The wing is the corporeal element which is most akin to the divine, and which by nature tends to soar aloft and carry that which gravitates downwards into the upper region, which is the habitation of the gods. The divine is beauty, wisdom, goodness, and the like; and by these the wing of the soul is nourished, and grows apace; but when fed upon evil and foulness and the opposite of good, wastes and falls away. Zeus,

the mighty lord, holding the reins of a winged chariot, leads the way in heaven, ordering all and taking care of all; and there follows him the array of gods and demi-gods, marshalled in eleven bands. (246d/e)

But the picture presented here is one that must allow access to the divine phrenzy. Unlike the rationally ordered *polis* portrayed in the *Republic* this new picture of *psyche* must have space for the *psyche* to interact with the divine *dianoia* (thought, intelligence, intention), through its *Nous*, and return to it:

The divine intelligence (διάνοια) being nurtured upon mind and pure knowledge, and the intelligence of every soul which is capable of receiving the food proper to it, rejoices at beholding reality, and once more gazing upon truth, is replenished and made glad, until the revolution of the worlds brings her round again to the same place. (*Phaedrus* 247d)

And now, for the first time, we find Plato's elaboration of the metaphysical connection of the human *psyche* to the divine spheres – a theme which will preoccupy his last diversion into the realm of the *psyche*, the *Timaeus*:

The reason why the souls exhibit this exceeding eagerness to behold the plain of truth is that pasturage is found there, which is suited to the highest part of the soul; and the wing on which the soul soars is nourished with this … and the soul which has seen most of truth shall come to the birth as a philosopher, or artist, or some musical and loving nature; that which has seen truth in the second degree shall be some righteous king or warrior chief; the soul which is of the third class shall be a politician, or economist, or trader; the fourth shall be a lover of gymnastic toils, or a physician; the fifth shall lead the life of a prophet or hierophant; to the sixth the character of poet or some other imitative artist will be assigned; to the seventh the life of an artisan or husbandman; to the eighth that of a sophist or demagogue; to the ninth that of a tyrant – all these are states of probation, in which he who does righteously improves, and he who does unrighteously, deteriorates his lot. (248d/e)

Thus, through its attachment to the extra-terrestrial spheres, the soul's future reincarnations will be determined, as 'ten thousand years must elapse before the soul of each one can return to the place from whence she came, for she cannot grow her wings in less; only the soul of a philosopher, guileless and true, or the soul of a lover, who is not devoid of philosophy, may acquire wings in the third of the recurring periods of a thousand years' (249). The phrenzy of the lover thus recalls the former existences and the higher world within which the *psyche* once dwelt (249c/250c), for all human beings have had a vision of the divine, and have fallen by degrees from it:

> For, as has been already said, every soul of man has in the way of nature beheld true being; this was the condition of her passing into the form of man. But all souls do not easily recall the things of the other world; they may have seen them for a short time only, or they may have been unfortunate in their earthly lot, and, having had their hearts turned to unrighteousness through some corrupting influence. (249e/250e)

And to achieve this remembrance beauty, especially the beauty of the lover, will play a significant and central role (250b/c). And thus falling in love is a remembrance of this state, but mixed with the confusion of *epithumia* (251a/b, 253c–254e). Therefore, Socrates ends his discourse by urging us not to forgo or renounce *eros*, but rejoice in it as a heaven sent gift to lead us back to the divine:

> And when this feeling continues and he is nearer to him and embraces him, in gymnastic exercises and at other times of meeting, then the fountain of that stream, which Zeus when he was in love with Ganymede named *eros*, overflows upon the lover, and some enters into his soul ... He wants to see him, touch him, kiss him, embrace him, and probably not long afterwards his desire is accomplished ... For those who have once begun the heavenward pilgrimage may not go down again to darkness and the journey beneath the earth, but they live in light always; happy companions in their pilgrimage, and when the time comes at which they receive their wings they have the same plumage because of their love. (255c–256e)

Therefore *eros* is a type of madness, but this is not a madness that is *alogiston* but a madness that enables us to touch upon the divine, for there are 'four types of divine madness' according to Plato: prophetic/inspirational presided over by Apollo; initiatory presided over by Dionysius; poetic presided over by the Muses; and erotic, presided over by Aphrodite and Eros (265b). Thus Plato has further refined his picture of the soul and given it in a stroke not only more psychological verisimilitude but made it possible for the individual *psyche* to be connected to the divine *Nous*, a theme hinted at in the earlier dialogues but not elaborated. This will come about in the final dialogue concerning the *psyche* that we shall consider here, the *Timaeus*.

Timaeus

Of all the dialogues of Plato *Timaeus* could arguably be said to be the one that would have the most influence upon the early Christian era, not least because of the sophisticated elaboration of the metaphysics of the relationship of the individual *psyche* to the World Soul. These characteristics make it equally one of the strangest to contemporary readers as the metaphysical world described is so alien to that of our post-scientific outlook. In contrast to the other dialogues, *Timaeus* starts from a clear theological perspective: that *Nous* and *logos*/λόγος are the determining principles of creation (29a). Following the developments of the *Phaedrus* where we saw greater room being made for the divine expression within the *psyche*, this is perhaps not surprising. For the later Plato 'intelligence could not be present in anything which was devoid of soul':

> For which reason, when he was framing the universe, he put intelligence/*logos* in soul, and soul in body, that he might be the creator of a work which was by nature fairest and best. Wherefore, using the language of probability, we may say that the world became a living creature truly endowed with soul and intelligence by the providence of God. (*Timaeus* 30b)

Just as we saw in the *Phaedrus* the individual *psyche* being divinized by the intrusion of the divine madness, so now the whole world becomes a living soul and we reflect the intelligence of the universe in our own *psyche*. The cosmos, therefore, is made from a 'compound' of soul and body and it is from this that the seven spheres of the planets are created – Sun, Mercury, Venus, Moon, Saturn, Mars and Jupiter (36d) – and within this cosmos 'the soul, interfused everywhere from the centre to the circumference of heaven, of which also she is the external envelopment, herself turning in herself, began a divine beginning of never-ceasing and rational life enduring throughout all time' (36e) making the cosmos like a 'perfect and intelligent animal' (39e). Thus, the divine Creator creates the chief gods and planets and the world *psyche* but the creation of humans is then left to these lesser deities, who use the left over parts of the cosmos for this work, a fact that we shall see will have great significance for the neo-Platonic thinkers who interacted with the early rise of Christianity. Each human soul in the *Timaeus* derives from a star (41d/e) and if we live well in this life (following the philosopher's path of *sophrosyne*) then on death our *psyche* will return to its appointed star (42b/c). As the gods create us they put the *psyche* within the head, 'being the most divine part of us and the lord of all that is in us' (*Timaeus* 44; see also Onians 1951: 118), whereas the lower parts go into the rest of the body; these elements will contain the *thumos* and *epithumia* (69c/d): the *thumos* in the thorax (69e) and the *epithumia* in the abdomen (70e). The fluidity with which Plato speaks of the location of the parts of *psyche*, and *psyche* itself, throughout his dialogues is reflected in much contemporary Greek literature. Onians in his extensive discussion of the topic (1951) remarks how *thumos*, on the one hand is 'constantly spoken of as feeling and thinking, as active in the lungs, or chest of the living person, and as departing at death, but is not spoken of in connection with the succeeding states' (Onians 1951: 94). *Psyche*, in contrast, is referred to as 'a life principle or soul not concerned in ordinary consciousness and to be what persists' (after death); in this respect *psyche* is more associated with the head than the chest. As we stated at the beginning of this chapter, many contemporary writers have wanted to emphasize the role of the *logismos* in Plato's writings as the seat of order over the passions of the *thumos* and *epithumia* (as graphically depicted in the *Phaedrus* charioteer). Taylor is indicative of this trend when he states that within Plato's dialogues, 'we are good when reason rules and bad when we are dominated by our desires' (Taylor 1989: 115). 'Thought/Reason' is the location for moral resource in Plato, according to Taylor, which allows us self-mastery. The higher part of the self 'rules' over the lower part of the self – reason (*logismos*) over desires (*epithumia*). The realm of reason is that of order, and that of desire one of chaos. The desiring element for Plato is 'by nature insatiable', whereas reason is controlled and bounded. To deal with these two extremes of reason and passion, writes Taylor, in *The Republic* Plato therefore introduces the notion of *thumos* whose proper role is to support reason, so that, according to him (Taylor 1989: 117) we end up with 'a sort of containment of the ethic of action and glory, uneasily held in the hegemony of a higher morality of reason or purity'.

There is no doubt that Taylor is correct here. Yet his account notably downplays the role of the phrenzies, *daimones* and the supernatural world of the gods we have already encountered. As Taylor states, for Plato reason *is* connected with order, yet there is also the divine madness inspired by the gods (as manifest in the *Phaedrus* and the *Timaeus*). This too is part of the cosmic order to which the *psyche* bears witness, and especially at the time of the madness of love/*eros* so graphically described in the *Phaedrus*. Yes, Plato has given the ordering and controlling role of the *logismos*, but he has also allowed space for the divine phrenzy of the *psyche* in its link to *eros*.

Conclusion: The Platonic soul

The psychological landscape left after Plato was one, as we have seen, that was full of contradictions, unfollowed paths and unexplored potentials. His writings were to dominate the thought processes of the ancient world and created the milieu into which early Christianity emerged as it sought to articulate itself and its faith in the God-man Jesus Christ. Plato had left as his legacy a divided self with the possibility of an immortal *psyche* that could transcend the earthbound and deathly *soma*. This *psyche* was somehow connected with the unseen order of the divinities and *daimones*. As we shall see in the next chapter, as early Christianity struggles to articulate the human self and the personality of *psyche*, the language and inheritance of Plato will play a vital, if ultimately suppressed, role.

CHAPTER 3
JESUS AMONGST THE PLATONISTS:
PLOTINUS AND AUGUSTINE

410

The world changed forever in 410. In the last hot days of the Roman summer the army of Alaric the Visigoth, *magister militum per Illyricum,* entered the Roman capital at the Salarian Gate by the northern wall. A devout (Arian) Christian himself, Alaric commanded that churches and shrines be spared the worst effects of the looting but, nevertheless, the city that had controlled most of the Western world for so many centuries had fallen to a foreign military commander. From the comparative safety of Palestine St Jerome wrote:

> A dreadful rumour comes from the West. Rome had been besieged and its citizens had been forced to buy their lives with gold. Then thus despoiled they had been besieged again and having already lost their goods, they must now lose their lives as well. My voice is choked with sobs as I dictate these words. The city that has conquered the whole world is now herself conquered. (St Jerome, Letter 127: 12)

As St Jerome tried to make sense of this new altered state of world affairs in Bethlehem his contemporary, St Augustine, in the relative security of North Africa (although Augustine would himself live to see his beloved Hippo fall to Vandal hands at the end of his life), simultaneously struggled with twilight questions at the *finis* of the Roman world. Although his magisterial *City of God* would later tackle the questions that arose for him concerning the earthly *polis* and its relationship to the Heavenly City, in 410 the 56-year-old Bishop of Hippo Regius was preoccupied with another question, the question that has preoccupied us throughout this book, that is, how can we talk of human personhood with respect to its relationship to the divine?

These questions were of course not new to Augustine, nor to his contemporaries, and they represent a life-long struggle for the African to come to terms with what it means to be a human in relationship to the divine – so eloquently expressed in his most famous work, *The Confessions*. In this *Ur*-text of Western selfhood, Augustine surfs the currents and eddies of the late Roman world in his attempt to find a satisfactory answer to his perennial question – *Who Am I?* And all the possible solutions are presented before us: the ancient pagan philosophies of Plato and the Neo-Platonists; esoteric Eastern practices as lived by Augustine in his Manichean phase; the scepticism and cynicism of the late Roman intellectual milieu and the ultimate resting place for his questioning – in the ideas and theories of salvation presented by the rapidly evolving early Christian church. As well as reflecting these currents, Augustine would of course go on to shape a 'picture of the soul' that would cast such a long shadow on the next millennium of Western psychological development. Thus, Augustine will stand for us in this chapter as a representative of that era of Christian intellectual engagement that sought to meld the insights of the Gospels with the older classical patrimony and I will seek to trace the success or otherwise of this attempt to pursue the soul by Platonic means within emerging Christian consciousness. To this end I propose to examine three pictures of the soul that emerge in the late classical/early medieval world. The first will be in the inheritors of the Platonic tradition that we explored in the previous chapter – the so-called neo-Platonists and in particular the work of the man who so influenced Augustine, Plotinus of Egypt. Secondly, I shall describe the picture of the soul that Augustine worked with throughout his life before concluding by looking at how these two late classical pictures of the soul, the Augustinian and the Plotinian, fare within the emerging Christian world, especially concentrating on their relationship to the emerging psychological world of the Desert Fathers and Mothers which we shall explore in the following chapter.

Uses of psyche

We saw in the previous chapter how the Platonic *corpus* opened up enormous possibilities as to how the ancient world could understand *psyche*, and ultimately itself. The early picture of *psyche* in the *Phaedo* as a simple unity connected with the divine and able to reincarnate was, as we saw, elaborated and developed in the later dialogues to take into account the warring elements within the self as perceived by Plato and how they could be reconciled with the ultimate 'moral' end of the self – restoration of the self with the Divine soul and harmony with the cosmos.[1] This was accompanied by an increasing interest in the cosmology of the *psyche* and how it may relate to *Nous* as a cosmic principle – the famous metaphysical speculation of the *Timaeus*. If Plato's system had been straightforward and coherent then there would have been little scope for disagreement or multiple interpretations amongst his followers. Fortunately this was not the case and the brilliant metaphysical possibilities essayed by Plato begin to unwind and spread their influences across the ancient world until well into the Common Era. This, then, was the Western context for understanding the self, *psyche* and soul within which nascent Christianity emerged during this time.

Yet despite the influence that Plato will have on emerging Christianity's understanding of itself it would be wrong, I suggest, to see the Platonic conception of the *psyche* as the only Greek interpretation of the term. Homer used ψυχή, in common with later writers such as Aristotle, to denote 'life in the distinctiveness of individual existence, especially of man' (Cremer 1895: 582) and occasionally of animals too. For both Homer and Aristotle the body is considered essential for the full functioning of the ψυχή and Platonic notions of the perfection of *psyche* without *soma*/body seem alien. For Homer, too, the various constituent passions are distributed amongst the parts of the body (see Onians 1951, e.g. Homer's connection of *psyche* with blood). Although as we saw this is still implied in Plato, especially the later dialogues, we can observe in his writings a marked concentration of the willing and desiring parts of the self amongst the constituent parts of *psyche* – *logismos, epithumia* and *thumos*. In fact it is possible to interpret Plato as offering a compromise tension, or perhaps a developmental stage, in the evolution between the more divided *psyche* of the earlier writers such as Homer and the unified notion of self that will emerge rapidly in the early Christian centuries.[2] From Aristotle onwards we have an increased emphasis upon the notion of *psychikos* as that which denotes life generally rather than the Platonic notion of *psyche* as an entity

---

[1] Note Armstrong here: 'For a pagan Greek, to say that the soul was not merely *theios*, divine, but *theos*, a god, did not necessarily mean more than that it was an immortal being. *Theos* is a word of very vague and various meaning, and certainly no pagan Platonist thought that all beings called *theoi* were identical with or parts of the Absolute Good, the Supreme Body, the Creator of heaven and earth (in the Christian sense)' (Armstrong 1967: 6).

[2] This tension between the unified and distributed self is one that we shall have occasion to return to throughout the book. In Chapter 5 we shall return to James Hillman and his contemporary attempt to return to the multifaceted self of the pre-Platonic authors.

in itself, often in contrast to *somatikos*. In addition to these usages (some of which Plato had already alluded to) we can trace uses of *psyche* referring to breath and butterfly (see previous footnote on page 13 above).

Thus, by the time we come to the first documents of emerging Christianity – the New Testament – we find fifty uses of ψυχή within the four Gospels and fifty-four within the Epistles, Acts and Book of Revelation. Of these hundred or so uses there is again the variety that we have already seen in the wider Greek context, yet we can trace a clear shift in the movement of the sense of the term, especially from the Platonic sense. We can thus see seven major uses of *psyche* in the New Testament, some of which are on a continuum from these early Greek senses, but some that are strikingly new and frame the emerging Christian perspective:

1. Old Greek sense of animating life-force
We find certain passages which reflect the old Greek sense of *psyche* as the life-force that is animating dead matter or the body, for example in Mt. 2.20, Acts 20.10, Rev. 8.9 and 1 Cor. 14.7. Matter, we are told, will be 'ensouled' by the dwelling of the *psyche* as will humans:

Get up, take the child and his mother, and go to the land of Israel, for those who were seeking the child's life (*psyche*/ψυχὴν) are dead. (Mt. 2.20)

It is the same way with lifeless (*a-psychic*/ἄψυχα) instruments that produce sound, such as the flute or the harp. (1 Cor. 14.7)

2. *Psyche* as personality/individuality
At other times *psyche* is interchangeable with the individual, it being the equivalent expression, as in Mt. 11.29 ('find rest for your *psyche*/soul') or Lk. 1.45 ('My *psyche*/soul magnifies the Lord'). The soul/*psyche* is what makes us an individual. It can also be the equivalent of the first person pronoun – suggesting a more dramatic emphasis on personal existence. An equivalent to this would be in modern news reports when after a disaster the news reporter intones gravely '300 souls were lost in the crash'. For example: 'three thousand *psyches*/souls (ψυχαὶ) were added that day' (Acts 2.41).

3. Soul/*psyche* as contrast to body/*soma*
Here we see shades of the Platonic dualistic sense of *psyche* we were exploring in the previous chapter. *Psyche* is that which is clearly not *soma/*

body, and in fact may be a hindrance to the development of *psyche*. For example: 'For the *psyche*/soul is more than food and the *soma* more than clothing' (Lk. 12.22) and:

> And do not fear the ones that kill the *soma* but are unable to kill the *psyche*/soul, but rather fear the one who can destroy both *psyche*/soul and *soma* in Gehenna. (Mt. 10.28)

4. *Psyche*/soul as that which will be judged in heaven or hell and survives death

In this respect the *psyche*/soul thus becomes a signifier for that element of the personality that shall be judged and survives death: 'When he opened the fifth seal, I saw under the altar the souls/*psyches* of those who had been slaughtered for the word of God and for the testimony they had given' (Rev. 6.9). And: 'You should know that whoever brings back a sinner from wandering will save the sinner's soul/*psyche* from death' (Jas 5.20).

5. 'Psychological' sense of psyche in the sense of one element that constitutes a part of the whole

Again, as in Plato, we have an ambiguity as to whether *psyche* constitutes the whole person or is a part or element of the psychological make up. Sometimes it is contrasted with heart and other times with *epithumia*: 'Beloved, I urge you as aliens and exiles to abstain from the desires of the flesh (*epithumion* of the *sarx*/σαρκικῶν ἐπιθυμιῶν) that wage war against the soul/*psyche*(ψυχῆς)' (1 Pet. 2.11). Or, in Mt. 22.37 where *psyche* is contrasted with heart/καρδία and mind/διανοίᾳ: 'You shall love the Lord your God with all your heart, and with all your soul, and with all your mind.'

6. *Psyche, pneuma* and the *daimones*

Just as *psyche* in these passages contrasts with *kardia* and *dianoia*, so in several of the Epistles (especially St Paul) *psyche* is contrasted with *pneuma*/Spirit. In Romans 8.10 *pneuma* is the 'divine life principle' (Cremer 1895: 585) whereas *psyche* is 'the individual life in which *pneuma* is manifested'. Thus *psychikos* in the New Testament often stands in contrast to *pneuma* rather than *soma*, i.e. the 'person in Christ' receives *pneuma* which then alters the *psyche*. Thus the reception of *pneuma* will change the individual *psyche* and St Paul in particular emphasizes the difference of a person ruled by themselves (and presumably selfish) and the person who has been acted upon by the *pneuma* and is thus more selfless in their lives and actions.

This, as several commentators point out, is a new way of understanding *psyche* different from that in Plato or the Greeks generally. In James 3, for example, *pneuma* and *psyche* are contrasted where *pneuma* is 'the wisdom from above' as opposed to that of the *psyche* which is 'earthly'. Thus, in James 3.14 jealousy and rivalry is from the knowledge that is 'earthly, *psychical/ ψυχική* and *daimonical/δαιμονιώδης*' where *daimones* and *psyche* are placed together. Plato's *daimones*, which we saw in the last chapter were helpers of the soul, have now become enemies to the seeker. In the coming chapters we shall see the mixed fate of the *daimones* from the Desert Fathers to the contemporary reappropriation of soul-language by writers such as Hillman where they stand for different poles of the *psyche*. In Jude 19 the mockers and scorners are '*psychikoi/ψυχικοί*' (usually translated as 'worldly') for they have given themselves up to their *epithumia/ἐπιθυμίας*.

Again, in 1 Corinthians 2.14, the '*psychikos*' person 'does not receive the things of the *pneuma* of God', as opposed to the person centred on *pneuma* who can 'discern spiritual things'. Such a pneumatic person will have the *Nous* of Christ and of God and in 1 Corinthians 15.44 we read that Adam was sown in the psychical body which will become a pneumatic one by God's grace. In these passages we can discern a clear shift away from the Platonic sense of *psyche* as the undisputed gateway to the secrets of the World of Forms to one where *psyche* has a more subordinate role to play in the personal journey to the Divine and possibly even a negative connotation where it is a hindrance to our understanding of the true *pneuma* that comes from Christ. In this respect the *daimones* are no longer our helpers on the road to enlightenment but rather can conspire to detract us from the true sense of *pneuma*.

7. Christ as ethical charge to the *psyche*
In these passages, then, Christ becomes the lodestone of the movement of the *psyche* that leads to *pneuma*. In itself, therefore, *psyche* is morally neutral for these New Testament writers, but by attaching itself to Christ it becomes ethically charged. Christ, as it were, produces an ethical field that surrounds *psyche*, so that *psyche* now has a moral or ethical life: 'the one finding his *psyche* will lose it, and the one losing the *psyche* for the sake of me will find it' (Mt. 10.39; see also Mt. 16.25, Mk 8.35 and Lk. 9.24).

8. Not to seek the *psyche* in itself (separate from Christ)
Therefore, again in contrast to Plato, we have the exhortation not to seek *psyche* as an end in itself, but rather only in so far as it helps us find Christ and the *pneuma*: 'Those who try to make their *psyche* secure will lose it, but

those who lose their *psyche* will keep it' (Lk. 17.33; see also Lk. 9.24, Mt. 10.39 and Jn 12.25). Or in John 10.15 where Christ says he will 'lay down my *psyche* for the sheep'.

Thus, as the first generations of Christians came to understand how to define their identity in terms of ψυχή they had a problem. Not only were they faced with the contrasting New Testament uses of the term (to say nothing of the different emphases within the Jewish scriptures), but, philosophically, they had to incorporate the varying perspectives of the Greek philosophical schools (including varying perspectives within the differing schools themselves). From the perspective of our contemporary understanding of *psyche*/soul, then, these first Christian centuries are fascinating. For what we find here is a veritable battleground for the soul resulting in schools and interpretations that, in a way, have never gone away from the Christian and Western sense of self. For, as we saw in Chapter 1, and as we shall return to throughout this book, resonances and echoes of these varying schools and battles persist right up to the present day. In the rest of this chapter and the following, then, I intend to trace some of these strands of interpretation and how successful, or otherwise, they will ultimately be in shaping Christian self-identity or, better still, soul-identity. In this respect we shall find ourselves returning to the person and thought of St Augustine who in so many ways embodies this early Christian struggle to 'pin down' the *psyche*.

'The books of the Platonists'

In Chapter Seven of the *Confessions*, Augustine tells us that as a young man he read 'the books of the Platonists/*lectis platonicorum illis libris*' from whom he learnt to 'seek the truth beyond corporeal forms (*incorpoream veritatem*)' (Conf 7.20). From these books, he says, he learnt to turn his gaze 'towards invisible reality' away from 'the darkness of my soul/*tenebras animae meae*'. As Kenney points out (Kenney 2013: 37–8), the account in the *Confessions* accords with that in two other sources: the account to Romanianus (still at that time a Manichee) in the *Contra Academicos* and the later account to Manlius Theodorus in the *De Beata Vita*. In both Augustine describes how the 'books of the Platonists' or 'the books of Plotinus'[3] rekindled in him the love

---

[3] Kenney here takes the Latin *Plotini* from the *Corpus Christianorum* Series (Latin Vol. 29) rather than the *Platonis* that we find in Migne's PL.

'for that religion which had been grafted into us as boys' and led him back to the writings of St Paul and the Christianity he had been brought up in. From these accounts two important aspects of Augustine's theological and spiritual development emerge: first, the importance of Platonism and neo-Platonist thought, especially Plotinus, in the development of his later views on God, the self and the cosmos, and secondly, how much he wants to distinguish his own position from that of the Platonists. Thus we have in microcosm here the early Christian dilemma of how much the language of *psyche* can draw on the old Platonic sources and how much it must be a break or rupture from it. Both facets of this are important to the argument I will develop here – first the importance of the Platonic background to Augustine, and secondly, his desire (using the scriptural passages we have just explored) to distinguish his 'Christian' conception of self from the Platonic milieu within which his intellectual development occurred. We shall turn first to this milieu.

Plotinus and the Platonists

Kenney, reflecting O'Donnell (1992) and Crouse (2000), agrees that Augustine's *Libri Platonicorum* (or *libri Plotini*) comprised a selection of treatises collected in Rome from the neo-Platonists Plotinus and Porphyry.[4] Porphyry had been a pupil of the famous Plotinus in Rome and had edited his works with an account of Plotinus' life in theses of nine chapters – the famous *Enneads*. Who was Plotinus and how does his writing fit into our account of the soul? This, as with so much of the period, divides critics. What is clear is that the varying conceptions of self and the cosmos outlined by Plato in the previous chapter left sufficient room for differing schools of interpretation to arise that would form the background not only to the late classical neo-Platonic paganism that Augustine encountered, but also to the nascent Christian understandings of self that arose contemporaneously. As Berchman writes:

> Jewish and Christian Platonism in the first three centuries A.D. are kindred conceptual frameworks which can be compared to Hellenic

---

[4] In the same work Crouse wisely counsels against drawing too strong a contrast between Augustinian and Platonic perspectives: 'Faith is, for Augustine, not a distinct faculty, nor a substitute for intellect, but the salvation of intellect. It is not the contradiction or the destruction of Platonism, but its conversion and redemption' (Crouse 2000: 42). See also Lamb 2007 for an elaboration of Crouse's position.

Platonism in the same period. They share a common conceptual framework which organizes the world and the experience of the world, through synthesizing forms of thought that are elemental components of Graeco-Roman civilisation. (Berchman 1984: 16)

Born around 204/205 CE in Alexandria, at the age of about twenty-eight in 232, according to his biographer Porphyry he 'converted to philosophy' in the Alexandrian schools. Here he studied with Ammonius Saccas (who also apparently taught the Christian Origen, more of whom in the next chapter) for about eleven years before setting off for, and failing to reach, India. Afterwards Plotinus ended up travelling to Rome where he taught, wrote and eventually died in 270 (see Porphyry's *Life of Plotinus*), thus bringing the Hellenistic traditions of Platonic and neo-Platonic interpretation to the heart of the Roman Empire and consequently to the emerging Christian sense of self. The importance of Plotinus to Augustine (and to subsequent Christian understanding of the self) is that he summarizes many of the strands of neo-Platonic interpretation that are swirling around the late classical world and presents them in a digestible fashion not only for Augustine but for us today.

Thus, within his work, we find the influences of Aristotle, Plato, the Stoics, neo-Pythagoreans and the earlier middle Platonists. Essentially his cosmology (following *Timaeus*) envisages a 'great chain of being' (which will become so important in the later medieval period) manifest in three *hypostases*/principles of the cosmos: at the beginning is the first principle which is absolutely transcendent (*To en*). It is beyond all description:

It is 'beyond being'. The phrase 'beyond being' does not mean that it is a particular thing – for it makes no positive statement about it – and it does not say its name, but all it implies is that it is 'not this' … But this 'what it is like' must indicate that it is 'not like': for there is no 'being like' in what is not a 'something' … even the term 'One' is inadequate, but is the best term available. (Enn 5.5.6)

Such transcendence is ineffable and unknowing:

Once more, we must be patient with language; we are forced to apply to the Supreme terms which strictly are ruled out; everywhere we must read 'So to speak'. (Enn 6.8.13)

From this Transcendent Other comes the great outpouring – the emanation 'like the outpouring of the sun' (Enn 1.7.1; 5.1.6; 6.8.18). For the nature of the One is 'generative of all, Unity is none of all; neither thing nor quality nor intellect nor soul; not in motion, not at rest, not in place, not in time; it is the self-defined, unique in form, or better, formless' (Enn 6.9.3).

The first manifestation of the outpouring of the One is Universal Intelligence/*Nous*. It is the higher and most perfect form of being, 'It is *Nous* that contains, or rather is, the totality of all being, the Forms and Ideas of all things in the universe, of all individuals and all classes of living things.' *Nous* proceeds from the One, then contemplates the One through *theoria* (Enn 5.3.11). In Louth's words: 'Here knower and known are one, here knowledge is intuitive, it is not the result of seeking and finding, with the possibility of error, but a possession, marked by infallibility' (Louth 2007: 38).

From *Nous* comes the World Soul (*psyche ton pantos*) as described in *Timaeus,* ultimately being able to turn back and contemplate the *Nous* as *Nous* in itself contemplates the One.[5] Thus Plotinus expounds a three-fold hierarchy in the universe where *Nous* proceeds from the One and *psyche* (including our individual *psyche*) from *Nous*:

> There is the One beyond being, of such a kind as our argument wanted to show, so far as demonstration was possible in these matters, and next in order there is Being, that is *Nous*, and the nature of *psyche* is the third place. (Enn 5.1.10)

Our individual soul will thus replicate and reflect this hierarchy in its structure:

> He who intends to know what *Nous* really is must know *psyche* and the divine part of *psyche* … what remains of soul (after separation from body) is that which we said was an image of *Nous* presenting something of its light like the light of the sun. (Enn 5.3.9)

---

[5] As is common in so many neo-Platonic and other contemporary Gnostic texts, for example, Numenius' second god and Albinus' 'celestial mind'. Sadly space doesn't allow a detailed exposition of all the variants of neo-Platonic and Gnostic cosmology here and I am concentrating on Plotinus as an important representative of that thought-world whilst emphasizing that Plotinus is just one of many variants of the 'world soul emanation' theme that was criss-crossing across Southern Europe, Africa and Asia Minor during Augustine's intellectual development. For more on the various schools and their interpretation see Louth (2007), McGinn (1991) and Tripolitis (1978).

And this divine light of creation and *Nous* is exactly what is intimated in the individual soul when it engages in contemplation/*theoria* (an activity not confined to humanity but found in all manifestations of the cosmos – rocks, planets, birds, trees and so on):

> * All goes on noiselessly, for there is no need of any obvious external contemplation or action; it is *psyche* which contemplates … Contemplation and vision have no limits … the same vision is in every soul for it is not spatially limited. (Enn 3.8.5)

Thus, in summary, for Plotinus the One emanates *Nous* which in turn emanates *psyche* and thus from our *psyche* we can return to the One via contemplation in *Nous*. Contemplation will play a key role in Plotinus' scheme for it is by this means we return to our source.[6] Drawing on the Platonic legacy of the *Phaedrus,* Plotinus associates this contemplative capacity of *theoria* with the *logismos* of the self which can then bring the lower *epithumia* and *thumos* back towards the *Nous* and ultimately the One (Enn 3.8.5). We shall return to the implications of this shortly.

The Plotinian soul

Unlike the Gnostics however (see Plotinus's *Against the Gnostics*) Plotinus does not believe that *psyche* has fallen and that matter is necessarily bad (supported by his notion of the light of *theoria* that permeates all being, including *psyche*):

> If the *psyche* has not actually come down but has illuminated the darkness, how can it truly be said to have declined? The outflow from it of something in the nature of light does not justify the assertion of its decline; unless the darkness lay somewhere below it and it moved spatially towards it and illumined it when it came close to it. (Enn 2.9.11)[7]

---

[6] As Armstrong puts it: 'He shows contemplation as the source and goal of all action and production at every level: all life for him is essentially contemplation' (*Enneads* Vol 3: 358).

[7] In the second *Ennead*, Plotinus references the Gnostic notion of a descent from *Nous* of *Sophia* from whom the evil Demiurge of the Hebrew scriptures derives. This account is substantially supported in the *Nag Hammadi* texts – see, for example, *The Exegesis on the Soul* (Codex II) where the soul is depicted as a virgin 'defiled by many robbers' as she falls to earth. Again, as with the various Platonic schools, there is clearly a rich and varied Gnostic tradition of the origin of the *psyche* and its descent into the world of matter and error.

Thus, unlike the Gnostic vision, Plotinus' view of the *psyche* and its cosmic origins are essentially benign.[8] We are on a continuum with the World Soul and can thus re-engage with it through contemplation. One of the consequences of this, suggests Plotinus in the fourth *Ennead*, is that all our *psyches* are connected in a sort of 'world-wide-web' of soulfulness:

> Now if my soul and your soul come from the soul of the All, and this soul is one, these souls also must be one. But if the soul of the All and my soul come from one soul, again all souls are one. (Enn 4.9.1)[9]

As with the Gnostics, however, there is in Plotinus' cosmology a descent of the soul (*psyche*, literally a 'cooling of the soul') from the realm of the *Nous* to our individual bodies, where we experience 'heaviness and forgetfulness':

> The souls peering forth from the Intellectual Realm descend first to the heavens and when they have put on a body they proceed to bodies progressively more earthy, to the limit to which they extend themselves in length. Some even plunge from heaven to the very lowest of corporeal forms; others pass, stage by stage, too feeble to lift towards the higher the burden they carry, weighed downwards by their heaviness and forgetfulness. (Enn 4.3.15)

Thus each being has a fixed material part of the soul and a higher part connected to the World Soul. Some souls descend further into the realm of matter/the body than is necessary and so get enmeshed too much in its venality: 'Its close association with the body hinders its intellective act and fills it with pleasure, desire and pain' (4.8.2). Therefore the human *psyche* is for Plotinus a somewhat amphibious proposition (4.8.4) – it has its feet firmly in the clay of matter and its head gazing through contemplation at the pure *Nous* and thus, ultimately, the One:

---

[8] Armstrong (*Enneads* 4: 394) points out that Plotinus takes over the tension in Plato that we explored in the previous chapter between the pessimistic view of matter in the earlier *Phaedo* and the later optimistic view of creation found in *Timaeus*. Plotinus' own view in passages such as these is largely positive towards the role of the material aspect of creation. His work in treatises such as Enn 4.8 points forward, suggests Armstrong, 'to the abandonment of the doctrine of matter as the principle of evil and its positive valuation as an expression of the infinity immediately derived from the Good by the later Neoplatonists' (Enn 4: 394).
[9] See also Enn 5.1.2: 'All *psyche* is present everywhere, made like to the father who begat it in its unity and universality.'

So it is with the individual souls; the appetite for the divine Intellect urges them to return to their source, but they have, too, a power apt to administration in this lower sphere; they may be compared to the light attached upwards to the sun, but not grudging its presidency to what lies beneath it. (Enn 4.8.4)

We are fallen and if the *psyche* stays in this state too long it eventually becomes enmeshed in the material. Then it will only be concerned for itself and it has 'lost its way' (4.8.4). As Plotinus freely admits and as commentators such as Armstrong stress (see previous footnote), Plotinus and his later followers (Christian and non-Christian alike) retain the Platonic pessimism regarding the nature of matter and the body (Enn 4.8.3) despite their move towards more positive evaluations of the nature of matter. In the following chapter when we trace the remnants of these neo-Platonic lines of thought in emergent Christian systems we shall continue to encounter this Plotinian/Platonic notion of the *psyche* as the trapped feather or plume in the coarse matter of the body.

Therefore the individual Plotinian psyche has three components (2.9.2, 5.3.3):

1. A higher part directed to the *Nous*.

2. A middle part which will determine the destiny of the person.

3. A lower part directed to the material world.

Unlike the Stoics and Epicureans he argues in the fourth *Ennead* that *psyche*, by its nature, cannot be composed of any non-psychic material such as fire, breath or *pneuma* because 'of necessity life is inherent to soul: this material entity, then, which we call soul must have life ingrained within it' (Enn 4.7.2). The soul (Enn 4.7.11-17) is divine and immortal and consequently:

a) it possesses life and being in itself (it is not the product of dead matter);

b) its knowledge comes from reminiscence of past life, and;

c) it cannot be destroyed.

The immortal soul descends at birth and gets cloaked with matter. It ascends on death and sheds this excrescence. As in Plato's theory of attunement ('*harmonia*' in *Phaedo* 85) the soul is described as being by necessity in harmony or accord with all around it rather like the lyre when tuned. This tuning occurs for Plotinus through inward withdrawal of the self in contemplation (especially through contemplation of truth, beauty and goodness) in a truly Platonic fashion:

> So we must ascend again to the good, which every soul desires. Anyone who has seen it knows what I mean when I say that it is beautiful. It is desired as good, and the desire for it is directed to good, and the attainment of it is for those who go up to the higher world and are converted and strip off what we put on in our descent (just as for those who go up to the celebrations of sacred rites there are purifications and strippings off of the clothes they wore before and going up naked). (Enn 1.6.7)

Purpose of life

The individual *psyche*, then, has 'forgotten' its homeland. It longs and yearns for it but doesn't really know how to return – this will be taught to the individual by the philosophers (Enn 5.1.1). We lie 'in gloom and mud' (Enn 1.8.13), dwellers 'in the Place of Unlikeness' (1.8.13, taken from Plato's *Statesman* 273D). Therefore *katharsis* and purification, just as with Plato, will lead the soul back to its home. This is primarily achieved, as in Plato's texts, through the pursuit of moral virtues and intellectual training. By exercising the four cardinal virtues we are thus (through *ascesis*) able to increase the light of the *psyche* by courage/*andreia*, wisdom/*sophia*, self-control/*sophrosyne* and justice/*dikaiosyne*. Or, of course, we can choose to live according to the needs of the body and get trapped by it (see Enn 1.6.8, 4.3.7 or 6.4.16). By following these desires we shall be born again in plant or animal form (in this respect not eating meat, drinking wine, celibacy and not engaging in animal sacrifices all help the chances of good reincarnation). We are outsiders and refugees here in the world of sense and should make every effort to get back to the non-material intelligible world (Enn 1.6.8). This requires life-long intellectual and moral training. We have the potential to do this ourselves through the divine spirit within us. Here Plotinus differs from both the Christians and Gnostics alike by lessening the importance of public liturgies in attaining this goal (Enn 6.9.4) and in this respect he sounds distinctly twenty-first century.

Of course, as we would expect of a disciple of Plato, for Plotinus there are only three types of person who are likely to return to the *Nous*: the philosopher, the musician/music-lover and the lover (*erotikos*) (Enn 1. 3.1-3).[10] The latter two, being 'quick in beauty' and susceptible to being enraptured, are both therefore likely candidates for return (needing however always the solicitude and guidance of the philosopher). Both possess a dim memory of previous existence and have a natural aptitude for return. Through the ministrations of the philosophers they must be 'led, under a system of mental discipline, to beauty everywhere and made to discern the One Principle underlying all, a Principle apart from the material forms, springing from another source, and elsewhere more truly present' (Enn 3.1.2). As we saw with Plato, and as we shall return to later, the practice and appreciation of *eros* is important for all such seekers (as well as the practice of the four Platonic virtues, appreciation of mathematics and pure forms and the practice of dialectic as demonstrated by Plato).

Having followed these paths the seeker may, at some point, have a sudden vision of the *Nous*: 'our awareness of that One is not by way of reasoned knowledge nor of intellectual perception, as with other intelligible things, but by way of a presence superior to knowledge' (Enn 6.9.4) – and will be plunged back into the *Nous* from whence it came. Subject and Object are removed, the two become one:

> Just so Intellect, veiling itself from other things and drawing itself inward, when it is not looking at anything will see a light, not a distinct light in something different from itself, but suddenly appearing, alone by itself in independent purity, so that Intellect is at a loss to know whence it has appeared, whether it has come from outside or within and after it has gone away will say 'it was within,' and yet it was not within.' (Enn 5.5.7)

The seeker is then completely fulfilled – in 'not seeing he sees', all outer pleasures will fall away as, in Plotinus' famous phrase, we engage in 'a flight of the alone to the Alone' (6.9.11).

---

[10] Cf. *Phaedrus* 248d/e where Plato gives four types that may return to the source: the philosopher, the musician, the lover and the lover of beauty (*philokalos*). 'Some scholars have suggested that the remaining three characters are not separate persons but aspects of the philosopher. This also corresponds with the Byzantine notion of *philokalia*, which describes the longing for spiritual beauty in the monastic tradition', Dr Eugenia Russell, personal communication.

The Plotinian schema for the deliverance of the soul

So then, in summary, we can characterize the Plotinian vision of the soul and its ascent to the divine as having the following key characteristics:

1. It is primarily based **on the teachings of Plato and the Greek philosophers.** Plotinus sees himself as offering a system that derives from and exemplifies the teachings of the great master Plato. Although he clearly sweeps up the earlier neo-Platonic schools and interpretations he sees himself as directly encountering Plato and his text, making it accessible to his contemporaries. Later neo-Platonism under Iamblicus will emphasize once again the role of the gods in achieving unity with the One, however Plotinus tends to downplay the role of theurgy and liturgy in the life of the seeker and re-emphasizes the truth that is found in the 'sacred writings' of the Greek masters, especially Plato.

2. **We are from a source beyond this world.** We contain that source within ourselves and long for a return to it through expression of our *eros*. Kenney (2013: 23) calls the higher part of the Plotinian soul 'the unitive or erotic soul', emphasizing the role of *eros* in returning the higher part of psyche to the World Soul. *Eros*, and the practice and pursuit of *eros* through art, culture, beauty and love, are thus essential parts of the return 'of the alone to the Alone'. The whole cosmos for Plotinus, says Kenney (2005: 21), 'crackles with synaptic life as these intelligible minds contemplate their inter-relationships'. It is alive for Plotinus with *Nous* and its interactions, of which we are an erotic part. The typical neo-Platonic cosmology thus suggests that the Good causes movement by its effects on the cosmos around it by not moving itself (it is the object of desire but cannot exist in space and time). In our realm and that of the planetary spheres there exist demiurges, *daimones* and lesser gods. They order the world and are also in charge of oracles and dreams. For neo-Platonists such as Albinus these lesser gods created our bodies but the soul/*Nous* was formed by God. The neo-Platonic cosmos is therefore a very crowded one full of *daimones*, lesser gods and demiurges. We shall return to them when we head into the desert with the early desert Christians.

3. **Contemplation is the means by which we return to this source.** Because of our amphibious natures (living between matter and spirit) our *psyches/* souls are essentially unstable: 'our focus shifts up and down, now highly

temporal and fractured, now informed by the intelligible, the stable and the authentic' (Kenney 2005: 23; cf. Enn 4.8.8). It is through contemplation/ *theoria* that the soul discovers its 'more ancient nature' (Enn 6.9.8). This *theoria* seeks to stabilize the soul so that it can be present to its true origins in the One. Porphyry tells us in his *Life of Plotinus* that it seems as though the master achieved this state of unity with the One at least four times in his life (*Vita Plotini* 23) following, says Porphyry, the road to contemplation set out by Plato in *The Symposium*. In such a state, says Porphyry, Plotinus was able to perceive 'that God who has neither shape nor any conceptual form but is seated above intellect and everything intelligible'. Such contemplation, so Porphyry and Plotinus tell us, will so lift the soul from its involvement with gross matter that it will never again want to be reincarnated into material form again.

4. **The source of our selves is non-material**. We have 'fallen' into the world of matter. The soul has 'cooled' (Greek term, *psyche*) from its origins in a higher realm but still retains the imprint of its origin to which it is deter-mined to return. We are 'weighed down' (Enn 6.9.7) in our present body but the process of contemplation will enable us to be 'born aloft' again. As Philo of Alexandria, one of Plotinus' important antecedents, states 'the soul in the body is like a foreigner, a sojourner in a strange, hostile land' (Conf 17.77) for the body is the prison or tomb of the *psyche* and the soul carries the body around like a corpse: 'Therefore man must not settle down into the body as if it were his own native land' (All III: 22.69).

Again, as we have seen, this is a common neo-Platonic and Gnostic theme – i.e. that we have fallen from a pure state into a corrupt world. Albinus, for example, states that the material passions bind the *Nous* and anchor it here 'and it is these passions which are the cause of the soul's subsequent evils' and not the divine element (see Tripolitis 1978: 33); 'it is therefore the responsibility of each soul to master these passions and thus upon death of the body, to return to its allotted star'.[11] As in Plato, the

---

[11] The ascent and the descent of the soul on death and birth through the seven planetary spheres is of course a mainstay of Gnostic and neo-Platonic thought. Much later writing will involve the transmission of secret passwords to induct the soul through these spheres in order to reach the One after death. Each sphere, says for example Poimandres, has a particular attribution or quality that needs to be overcome: from Saturn deceitfulness, Jupiter evil under-takings for wealth, Mars impious audacity and rashness of impulsive deed, the Sun overbearing arrogance, Venus passions, Mercury contrivance of evil and the Moon power to wax and wane (see Tripolitis 1978: 20).

rational part of the soul pre-exists the body and in learning we simply recall what was previously known. All of these themes we shall see re-emerging in the Christian desert tradition in the following chapter.

5. Certain actions and ways of living, for example **moral purification and intellectual training**, will help the process of the return of the soul to its true origin. Contemplation in itself is insufficient for Plotinus; we must also engage in ethical action and right conduct to form our souls. This is coupled with moderate ascetical practices (nothing too extreme – Plato's constant injunction to *sophrosyne* is taken seriously) and the importance of philosophical dialogue. In this respect philosophical dialogue becomes part of a wider religious and spiritual practice, what Pierre Hadot famously called 'a way of life' (Hadot 1995). As mentioned above, the practice of what will come to be known as the four cardinal virtues is especially important in this respect. This, of course, is a common notion amongst the neo-Platonists generally who adapted the idea from the Platonic corpus. Thus Albinus, for example, stresses that the practice of the differing Platonic virtues will perfect different parts of the *psyche*: prudence perfects *logismos*, *sophrosyne* perfects *epithumia*, courage perfects *thumos* and justice will help harmonize all three components and bring them under *Nous* (see Tripolitis 1978: 151).

6. **'Inner' contemplation will lead to the 'ascent' of the soul:** As Plotinus states in Enn 6.9.7: 'We must withdraw from all the external, pointed wholly inwards, not leaning to the outer; the total of things ignored, first in their relation to us and later in the very idea.' The One lies not outside but within. Such an introspection will inevitably, Plotinus assures us, lead to the in-breaking of the Divine *Nous* such that 'the soul taking that outflow from the divine is stirred; seized with a Bacchic passion, goaded by these goods, it becomes love' (Enn. 6.7.22). This internal turn will of course also be reflected in Augustine's writing where the 'inward' search will lead eventually to the truths he is seeking.

7. **The Ascent can be experienced in sudden 'ecstasies':** In this respect Plotinus was once again reflecting the great neo-Platonic tradition to which he was heir. As Philo of Alexandria, an important influence on Plotinus, stated: 'the psyche becomes possessed by sober intoxication, like a Corybantic frenzy, and is inspired with a still stronger longing which carries it up to the highest summit of the intelligible world and it seems to approach the Great King himself. As the mind strives eagerly to see Him, pure and

unmingled rays of concentrated light shine forth like a torrent, so that by their brilliance they dazzle the eye of the intellect' (Opif 23.7). Similarly, in Enn 6.9.8, Plotinus describes the choreography of the contemplative life as being rather like a 'choral dance'. The natural movement of the soul 'is in circle around something, something not outside but a centre, and the ·centre is that from which the circle derives'. At times we see the One and are caught up in its ecstasy; at other times we move around the circle and the vision is obscured: 'We are always around it but do not always look at it; it is a like a choral dance: in the order of the singing the choir keeps round its conductor but may sometimes turn away, so that he is out of sight, but let it but face aright and it will sing with beauty … when we do but turn to him then our term is attained; this is rest, this is the end of discordance, we truly dance our god-inspired dance around him.'[12] Both authors here reflect Plato's experience of 'phrenzy' we explored in the previous chapter.

8. **The Plotinian search for the soul is essentially an *erotic* process.** As the soul yearns for its origin through *eros*, *eros* must play a significant role in its return to the source. As we have seen the lover, the musician and inevitably the philosopher are deeply imbedded in the search for truth and as he tells us at the end of the *Enneads*, the soul 'loves God and longs to be at one with Him in the noble love of a daughter for a noble father' (Enn 9.9.9).

9. **The goal of the process is deification.** By following the practices of contemplation, the exercise of moral virtue and engaging in the dialectic of the philosophers we shall reach the Plotinian goal of identification with the *Nous* and ultimately the One: 'You must become first of all godlike and beautiful if you intend to see God and beauty' (Enn 1.6.9) and thus the soul will end up becoming love itself (Enn 6.7.22 and 6.9.9). Discovery of self becomes discovery of the Divine (Enn 5.1.1).[13] As he states at the end of the *Enneads* (6.9.9), 'The soul then in her natural state is in love with God and wants to be united; it is like the noble love of a girl for her noble father … There one can see both him and oneself as it is right to see: the self glorified, full of intelligible light – but rather itself pure light – weightless, floating free, having become – but rather, being – a god; set on fire then, but the fire seems to go out if one is weighed down again.' In this life the vision will be

---

[12] For a beautiful description of the influence of this and similar passages on the future development of the Christian liturgy see White 2015.
[13] In this Plotinus follows Plato's *Theaetetus* (176b).

fleeting, as suggested above, but once cast away from the material burdens of this realm we shall achieve true deification with the Divine (Enn 6.9.10-11): 'the man is changed, no longer himself nor self-belonging; he is merged with the Supreme, sunken into it, one with it: centre coincides with centre.'

The last and striking aspect of the process of contemplation and deification described by Plotinus (and common to all the Platonic schools; see for example Dionysius the Areopagite) is that the processes and techniques described must be 'hidden from the vulgar gaze'. Plotinus' scheme is essentially an elitist one, not for the vulgar herd: 'The Supreme is not to be made a common story, the holy things may not be uncovered to the stranger, to any that has not attained to see' (Enn 6.9.11).

We can therefore summarize a list of characteristics of a picture of the soul and its redemption that we can call 'Plotinian' thus:

1. It is primarily based on the teachings of Plato and the Greek philosophers.
2. It suggests that we are from a source beyond this world.
3. Contemplation is the best means by which we can return to this source.
4. The source of our selves is non-material.
5. Intellectual and moral training can lead us back to that source.
6. 'Inner' contemplation will lead to the 'ascent' of the soul.
7. This ascent can be experienced in sudden 'ecstasies'.
8. The Plotinian ascent is primarily an erotic process.
9. The goal of the process is deification.

In mapping these characteristics what I wish to convey is a shorthand picture of the soul, derived primarily from Platonic sources, that will persist within Western and Eastern models of self (within and without Christian, Jewish and Muslim cultures) for at least another thousand years, and as we shall see in later chapters, well into the modern era. It is not intended as a definitive account of the Plotinian schema, nor does it aim to imply that Plotinus, and Plotinus alone, was of importance for subsequent neo-Platonic pictures of the soul in Western cultures. What it does intend to convey is a cipher or map of certain Platonizing traditions that remained, I shall suggest, well within post-classical Christian notions of the soul.

We shall now return to Augustine and see how his system differs from and agrees with that of the Plotinian schema.

St Augustine: *Finis Africae*

As stated already, St Augustine was no stranger to the writings of Plotinus and the neo-Platonists. As outlined in his *Confessions* he encountered practitioners of neo-Platonism and the neo-Platonic writings whilst as a young man seeking God in Rome and Milan. Born in 354, his *Confessions* describe the fields of influence operating on a young man growing up in the twilight world of the late Roman Empire. Raised by pagan and Christian parents Augustine embodies the struggles of one world ending (late paganism) and a new one emerging (medieval Christianity) and his struggle to find expression of his picture of the soul is no less convoluted.[14] The Plotinian schema described above was clearly attractive to the young Augustine and one he sought to pursue as a young man in Italy. However, the mature Augustine of *On the Trinity* sought a synthesis between the neo-Platonic and the Christian before arriving at what is effectively a new distinctly Christian way of talking of the soul. In this respect Augustine, unlike Plotinus, sought to amalgamate elements in his schema from the Christian scriptures with which we began this chapter and which he became increasingly familiar with after his conversion to Christianity. For Augustine the Greek and Hebrew scriptures increasingly became the essential starting point for all reflection on the nature of the self which will reach its apotheosis in his late work *On the Trinity*. In his readings of the Christian scriptures Augustine would no doubt have acquainted himself with the contrasting New Testament uses of the term ψυχή which we outlined earlier (to say nothing of the different emphases within the Jewish scriptures) and especially the relationship between *psyche* and *pneuma*. There, as we saw, he would have discerned the new uses to which *psyche* was being put by the followers of Christ. Philosophically, Augustine would

---

[14] Born in 354 in Thagaste, North Africa, the young Augustine travelled to Italy in 383 at the age of twenty-nine. During this time he experimented with neo-Platonism as well as continuing his connections with the Manichees. In the *Confessions* he describes experiences of 'ascent' around the year 386/87 whilst he is in North Italy where he comes under the influence of St Ambrose and his Platonic Christian circle based at Milan. This culminated with baptism by Ambrose at Milan in 387 at the age of thirty-three. In 388 he returned to Africa where he was ordained priest at the age of thirty-seven in 391. Five years later he was made Bishop of Hippo Regius. Shortly after this he began work on the *Confessions* between 397 and 401. Three years later he began work on *On the Trinity* in around 404 which was finally completed sixteen years later in 420. He died in 430 at the age of seventy-six. Regarding the secondary commentary on Augustine, McGinn nicely summarizes it in the sentence: 'Concerning Augustine there are few new debates and perhaps even fewer cases of scholarly consensus in disputed areas' (McGinn 1991: 232).

have been faced with the varying perspectives of the differing neo-Platonic schools described above. His synthesizing intellect was such that he was able to finally present a picture of the soul that amalgamated elements from both whilst being sufficiently unique for it to be called a new Christian perspective on the *psyche*. We shall turn to this now.

Augustine's picture of the soul

According to Trapè, 'the essential task of Augustinian spirituality is the restoration of the image of God to man' (1986: 454), or as Augustine himself puts it in the *Literal Commentary on Genesis*: 'It was in the very factor in which he surpasses non-rational animate beings that man was made in God's image. That, of course, is reason (*ratio*) itself, or *mens* (mind) or *intelligentia* (intelligence) or whatever we wish to call it.' (Comm Gen 3.20.30; see also Trin 14: 25). As we have already seen, the chief aim of the Platonic ascent to the divine was to develop the individual *psyche* such that it could contemplate the World *Nous* and thus ultimately the One. Whilst clearly influenced by the Platonic model, Augustine presents us with a significantly modified picture. In the first place, as we have seen, Augustine places the Greek and Hebrew scriptures at the origin of his search and thus when he comes to write the later *On the Trinity* in his fiftieth year he will begin in the first eight books by presenting an exposition of those same scriptures in support of his triune view of the divine. This he will then relate in the second edition of the book, written between 413 and 420, to the 'image' of the divine in the human soul – in particular with reference to memory, will and understanding (books 9–15 of *On the Trinity*).[15] For Plotinus the *theoria* of the intellect will lead us to the *Nous*. Augustine, on the other hand, preferences memory as the attribute of the *psyche* most likely to bring us to the divine. It should also be noted that as discussion of the personality moves from Greek to Latin the Platonic tripartite soul begins to dissolve in favour of the more monic Augustinian self which although reflecting the triune God in its component parts seems more integrated than the somewhat wayward parts of the Platonic triadic *psyche*.[16] As well as reflecting the triune life in its constituent parts Augustine, in contrast to the

---

[15] Bernard McGinn, in a number of articles, has drawn attention to the difference between 'likeness' (*similitudo*) and 'image' (*imago*) of the soul to God in Augustine's writings. For more see McGinn 1991: 243/44 and McGinn 2010.

[16] However in the next chapter we shall return to Evagrius and Origen and how they interpret the Platonic tripartite soul through their respective Christian lenses.

Platonists, places Christ as the key mediator and educator of the soul. Christ for Augustine is 'the way, the truth and the life' (Jn 14.6) and as he says in his *Homily on the Psalms* 84.1: 'The Lord himself heals the eyes of our hearts to enable us to see what he shows us' (see also Conf 7.18.24).

Intimacy with the *persona Christi* will thus lead to the divinization of the soul, not through our own efforts or through merits of our own, but simply through the love and grace of God freely given (in contrast to the Platonic way where our own effort, contemplation/*theoria*, will inevitably lead to union with the Divine): 'The Son of God was made a sharer in our mortal nature so that mortals might become sharers in his Godhead' (Hom Ps 52.6)[17] and 'It is quite obvious that God called human beings "gods" in the sense that they were deified by his grace, not because they were born of his own substance ... he alone deifies who is God of himself, not by participation in any other' (Hom Ps 49.1.2).[18] Thus God deifies us only by adoption, through no quality inherent in our own natures (unlike in the Plotinian schema). Possibly from his Manichean past, Augustine had a lifelong suspicion of matter and the flesh and saw human nature as essentially corrupt. He was suspicious of our ability to achieve deification from this corrupted flesh by our own means and so championed the power of God's grace over any 'Pelagian' notions of what we would nowadays refer to as 'original blessing'. In this respect the body of Christ on earth, the church, remained the *sine qua non* for reaching the state of bliss denied us by our nature. Although glimpses of this could be afforded in this life the true union would not be possible for Augustine in this world. As he states at the outset of the *Confessions*: 'the house of my soul is too small for you to enter, make it more spacious by your coming. It lies in ruins: rebuild it' (Conf 1.6).

The Augustinian schema for the deliverance of the soul

Thus, although there is clearly an overlap and dependence upon the Plotinian schema in Augustine's picture of the soul there is sufficient difference for us to contrast the Plotinian schema we outlined earlier with the Augustinian schema. As I noted with the Plotinian schema, Augustine's will have an equally significant impact on humanity's understanding of its self (particularly in the West) for at least a thousand years, and well into

[17] 'Filius enim Dei particeps mortalitatis effectus est, ut mortalis homo fiat particeps diuinitatis.'
[18] 'Manifestum est ergo, quia hominess dixit deos, ex gratia sua deificatos, no de substantia sua natos ... et ille deificat qui per seipsum non alterius participation Deus est.'

our own times. As with Plotinus, I will characterize Augustine's schema as having nine basic characteristics:[19]

1. As Plotinus bases his schema on the books of Plato and the Greek philosophers, so Augustine's primary sources are the **Hebrew and Greek scriptures**. For example, the first books of *On The Trinity* concentrate on what God reveals concerning God's self in the Scriptures.

2. The impetus for the creation and transformation of the soul lies with God. Unlike Plotinus' One that is to be sought by us, **Augustine's God seeks us out**: the Divine is proactive in pursuing our salvation. Augustine's God is a very personal affair. As the dynamo for Plotinus' schema was primarily *eros,* for Augustine it is primarily *grace/gratia* – see, for example, Conf 7.21.27 where he reiterates a common theme in his writing: 'So totally is it a matter of grace that the searcher is not only invited to see you, who are ever the same.' As he tells us in Trin 14.17 God will rescue us from the shipwreck of the world through grace – we cannot do this by ourselves so are dependent upon God in this respect: 'You called, shouted, broke through my deafness; you flared, blazed, banished my blindness … you touched me and I burned for your peace' (Conf 10.27). For Augustine grace is gratuitous; his schema for salvation is in no way elitist, unlike that of Plotinus. As described in the *Confessions,* even the wine-bibbing and decidedly non-intellectual Monica can receive the equal grace of ecstatic vision of the One that is entrusted to Augustine himself (see Kenney 2005: 118).[20] The other consequence of this for Augustine's schema is that he explicitly rules out the transmigration of souls and the ability of souls to be reborn over and over again as was common in the neo-Platonic schemes. As he writes to St Jerome in Letter 166: 27:

> I do not know a more revolting opinion than that these souls should make some indefinite number of trips through an indefinite number

---

[19] As will be clear by now, the complexity and range of Augustine's thought makes it difficult to summarize simply. In this schema I am drawing primarily on the descriptions of the self given in the *Confessions* and *On the Trinity.*

[20] As Kenney puts it: 'When Monica's soul ascends to Wisdom at Ostia a failure is being redressed. This ascension is not part of a larger metaphysical process nor does the soul exercise a natural function … This is because the soul is fallen and the higher world is not its own. It seeks what it does not possess; it is shown what it cannot be in its present state' (Kenney 2005: 118).

of cycles of ages, only to return again to that burden of corrupt flesh to pay the penalty of torment.

Augustine suggests that his benevolent personal God will not allow such a perpetual torment of the soul.

3. **Creation is broken/flawed.** Unlike the Plotinian scheme where a beautiful soul is held imprisoned in corrupting matter, the soul itself is corrupted in some way that Augustine finds difficult to pin down (see Trin 8.2.3). But he has no doubt that sexuality and concupiscence has a large part to play in this corruption. We can contrast this with the Plotinian schema where, as we saw, beauty and *eros* are both vital engines in the mechanism by which we return to the *Nous*. As Augustine puts it in the *Homilies on John* 2.2: 'For no-one can cross the sea of this world unless he is carried by the cross of Christ.'[21]

4. Although Augustine's schema is not primarily driven by *eros,* as in Plotinus' schema **we have a longing for the source implanted in us** and this desire will be the drive of our earthly search for the Divine. This impels Augustine's stress on the interior search (so tellingly described in the *Confessions*) which will, he assures us, ultimately lead us to knowledge and experience of God. As in Plotinus' schema this search is primarily directed within. As McGinn puts it: 'Augustine taught that "to go within is to go above", that is, the movement into the soul's ground would lead to a discovery of God within who is infinitely more than the soul' (McGinn 1991: 242). Or as Augustine puts it in the *Homily on the Psalms* 130.12:

> God is within, spiritually within, but also spiritually on high, though not in a spiritual sense, as high places are distant from us ... God who is within us is most high, spiritually exulted, and the soul cannot reach him unless it transcends itself.[22]

5. **Sudden ecstasies are possible** on our journey to the Divine. In the sudden ecstasy in Milan recorded in the *Confessions* (Conf 7.17.23) Augustine talks of the *ictus cordis* – the sudden 'blow on the heart' of the ecstasy. As he writes

---

21 'Nemo enim potest transpire mare huius saeculi, nisi cruce Christi portatus.'
22 'Sed intus est Deus eius, et spiritaliter intus est, et spiritaliter excelsus est; non quasi interuallis locurum, quomodo per interualla loca altiora sunt ... Ergo intus Deus altus est, et spiritaliter altus; nec peruenit anima ut contingat eum, nisi transierit se.'

in Comm Gen 12.12.25: 'When however the attention of the mind is totally turned aside and snatched away from the senses of the body, then you have what is more usually called ecstasy.'[23] And in the *Confessions* 10.40.65: 'From time to time you lead me into an inward experience quite unlike any other, a sweetness beyond understanding. If ever it is brought to fullness in me my life will not be what it is now, though what it will be I cannot tell you.' The ecstasy is a *foretaste* of the bliss to come – this bliss cannot be attained in full in this realm. Book 12 of the *Literal Commentary on Genesis* is given over to a lengthy exposition of the topic. Here he details 'three kinds of vision' possible with or without the involvement of the body: the 'bodily' (*corporale*) because it is perceived through the body and present to 'the senses of the body', the 'spiritual' (*spiritale*) which is 'not of the body' and the 'intellectual' (*intellectual ab intellectu*) which is 'of the intellect'. In this passage he is clear in distinguishing *psyche/mens* from spirit/*pneuma* in his exposition of the texts from St Paul we cited at the beginning of this chapter. In this respect Augustine is clearly influenced by the Pauline sense of *psyche*. As he concludes 'bodily vision reports back to spiritual and spiritual in its turn reports back to intellectual' (Comm Gen 12.24) for 'such ecstasies are strange and wonderful indeed' (Comm Gen 12.26), a fact he expounds by numerous strange and curious examples verging on the paranormal.

6. **Augustine's path is a way of ascent** from the material to the spiritual, as famously described in the Ostia Vision in *Confessions* 9.10.23/24: 'Step by step (Monica and Augustine) traversed all bodily creatures and heaven itself, whence sun and moon and stars shed their light upon earth. Higher still we mounted by inward thought and wondering discourse on your works, and we arrived at the summit of our minds; and this too we transcended to touch that land of never failing plenty.' Withdrawal from the world is necessary to find God. In this respect Augustine lies close to his Platonic influences as described in book 7 of the *Confessions* where an early attempt at spiritual ascent is attempted using the 'books of the Platonists'. Although Augustine 'attains to That Which Is' (Conf 7.17.23) during this attempt he also realizes that without Christ as mediator (see above) the ascent cannot be sustained.

7. For the Platonists, the development of the *theoria* was essential to 'enter

---

[23] '*Quando autem penitus auerititur atque abripitur animi intention a sensibus corporis, tunc magis dici extasis solet.*'

into the mind of the Divine'. **For Augustine the equivalent role is played by *memoria*** (see Conf 10). Augustine's famous art of '*confessio*' is in itself a play of memory and much of the book is concerned with the art of memory and how its cultivation brings us closer to the divine: 'confession is Augustine's way of understanding – a special divinely authorized speech that establishes authentic identity for the speaker and is the true and proper end of mortal life' (O'Donnell in *Augustines Confessions* Vol. 1: xlii). Or as Louth puts it, *memoria* 'means for (Augustine) more than just a faculty of recollection: it really means the whole mind, both conscious and unconscious, in contrast to mind – *mens* which refers only to the conscious mind' (Louth 2007: 142). Of course one of Augustine's chief contributions to the Western understanding of self is his division of the soul into memory, understanding and will in *On the Trinity* and its consequent reflection of the triune God (to which we will return in a moment). This, I would contend, reflects his move away from the Platonic focus on *Nous/mens* to a structure of the soul that is more triune in nature, for:

8. **The human soul reflects the triune nature of the divine**. The human soul is the image of God for Augustine. As God is Triune (as demonstrated in the first six books of *On the Trinity*) therefore the soul must be triune. These are its attributes of memory, will and understanding as discussed in the later books 8–10 of the work (for example in Trin 10.11.18 or 9.5.8 where the soul is divided up into *mens, notitia* and *amor*/mind, knowledge and love). As Louth puts it, for the later Augustine: 'The image of God is man, or to be precise, man's rational soul. And since God is the Trinity, the image of God in man's soul is trinitarian' (Louth 2007: 147). This, Augustine famously elaborates in books 8 and 9 of *On the Trinity* as the relationship in the soul between lover, loved and love:

> But with these three, when mind knows and loves itself the trinity remains of mind, love and knowledge. Nor are they jumbled together in any kind of mixture, though they are each one in itself and each whole in total … Thus mind is of course in itself, since it is called mind with reference to itself, though it is called knowing or known or knowable relative to its knowledge; also as loving and loved or lovable it is referred to the love it loves itself with. (Trin 9.1.8)

Mind, love and knowledge, as he states in Trin 9.5.8, reveal a trinity which is 'confused by no mingling; although each is singly in itself, and all are wholly in one another, whether one in both or both in one, and so all in all'. Thus, by attention to memory, understanding and will through contemplation the soul attains *sapientia* and moves from *scientia* (Trin 14.12.15) for when the mind truly knows and loves itself it will possess genuine knowledge of the soul. Accordingly, the interior journey of knowledge of self will lead inevitably to knowledge of God. Louth again: 'The trinity of memory, understanding and will manifested in the mind's remembering itself, understanding itself and loving itself, is something that is as eternal as the soul. The trinity has been in the mind since even before the mind came to participate in God' (Louth 2007: 156). And as Augustine puts it in his Letter to Consentius (120): 'We must rise from what we know of the human soul to some understanding of the Trinitarian Godhead.'[24]

9. **Christ is the divine mediator to the soul.** Thus, when we have the humility to accept Christ's presence in the soul we can have the true contemplation of the Trinity:

> The Son of God came (in the form of) a man and became humble; you are therefore instructed to be humble, it does not teach you to become a brute animal instead of a man ... He who comes to me, is incorporated in me, he who comes to me is made humble. (Hom John 25.16)

The moment of baptism is the beginning of this process of renewal in Christ, however the full extent of our identification with Christ will be a slow one that will be achieved through a life-long commitment to, and identification with, Christ:

> So then the man who is being renewed in the recognition of God and in justice and holiness of truth by making progress day by day, is transferring his love from temporal things to eternal, from visible

---

[24] But note that in the *Literal Commentary on Genesis* Augustine is rather coy as to the actual nature of *animus*/soul and what it is made from. As he states there: 'I will affirm nothing as certain about the soul, which God breathed into man by blowing into his face, except that it comes from God in such a way as not to be the substance of God and yet it is incorporeal, that is, not a body but a spirit, not begotten of the substance of God nor proceeding from the substance of God, but made by God (*ut non sit substantia dei et sit incorporeal, id est not sit corpus, sed spiritus, no de substantia dei genitus nec da substantia dei procedens sed factus a deo*) and not made in such a way that the nature of any kind of body or of non-rational soul can be turned into its nature; and consequently made from nothing.' (Comm Gen 7.43). Again this is a clear distinction from Plotinus and the neo-Platonic notion of soul.

to intelligible, from carnal to spiritual things; he is industriously applying himself to checking and lessening his greed for the one sort and binding himself with charity to the other. And his success in this depends upon divine assistance. (Trin 14.23)

Central to this process is the role of the Church and its sacraments which is Christ's presence on earth (see, for example, Conf 7.10.16; 7.18-19, 24-25). For ultimately 'we will be like God, but only like the Son, who alone in the triad took a body in which he died and rose again' (Trin 14.24).

As with Plotinus, we can therefore summarize these characteristics of the Augustinian picture of the soul as follows:

1. It is primarily based on the Christian scriptures.

2. Augustine's God actively seeks us out.

3. We live in a flawed and broken cosmos.

4. We have a longing to reunite with our divine maker.

5. The union can occasionally be experienced in sudden 'ecstasies'.

6. 'Inner' contemplation will lead to the 'ascent' of the soul.

7. Memory and confession will play an important role in this journey.

8. The human soul reflects the triune nature of the divine.

9. Christ is the divine mediator to the soul.

Now when we compare Augustine's schema with that of Plotinus there are of course several overlaps (for example in points 5 and 6) but generally, as we saw in the New Testament use of *psyche,* we encounter in Augustine's writing a new way of understanding the soul, its relationship to the divine and how we can pursue the divine in this human life. As stated earlier, it is this picture which will prove so important in defining Christian Western notions of selfhood for the next millennium following his death.

Conclusion

We have seen in this chapter how in the early Christian centuries the Platonic understanding of the soul developed as writers such as Augustine, using scriptural sources as their starting point, embraced new Christian understandings of the soul. I have taken Augustine's work as a paradigm of soul-making in the late classical/early Christian period. As we shall see in the following chapter, his use of soul-language was by no means the only possible alternative to Christians in this twilight period at the beginning of the medieval period. However in the discussions that follow I shall use the two paradigms plotted in this chapter – the Plotinian and Augustinian – to stand for two opposing visions of the self that will persist, as we shall see in the latter part of this book, up to contemporary times. Although in one respect Augustine's vision will triumph over the Plotinian, his voice will not, by any means, remain the last word on the subject. Thus, early Christianity (and one could argue all later Christianity) is presented with two opposing 'soul-ologies': a Platonic/Plotinian one where the soul, as part of the 'great chain of being', naturally ascends through multiple rebirths; and the Augustinian picture of disruption/irruption and corruption where the salvation of the individual is only assured by the gentle (and unpredictable) action of God's grace. We shall therefore conclude Part I of this book by exploring in the following chapter the subsequent fate of these two 'soul pictures' and how the Church applied itself to presenting a coherent soul-language for its followers.

CHAPTER 4
PLATO IN THE DESERT: ORIGEN AND EVAGRIUS

Creeds, councils and controversies

In the previous chapter I presented two models, or pictures, of the soul that I suggested emerged from late classical/early medieval sources – what I termed 'the Augustinian' and the 'Plotinian'. As we saw there they offered two soteriologies drawing on two primary sources: in the case of Augustine, the Christian scriptures, and in the case of Plotinus, the Platonic corpus. I would like to end Part I of this book by mapping out two interrelated pictures of the soul that sought once again to reconcile the Platonic view of the self with the scriptural view of the self in the work of Evagrius of Pontus and Origen. In doing this I shall take the two models of the soul from the last chapter – the Plotinian and Augustinian – and use them as touchstones to investigate the work of the two 'desert fathers'. In doing so I may be accused of retrospective thinking but, as argued in the last chapter, I would like to suggest that the two pictures of Augustine and Plotinus give us convenient shorthand for two clear developments in the late classical world – the development of neo-Platonic systems of the self on one hand, and the emergent (and shortly triumphant) 'orthodox' Christian view of the self. Origen and Evagrius, I contend, occupy a third twilight zone between the two where the pagan sun hasn't quite set while the full moon of medieval Christianity is beginning to rise. From our own twenty-first century perspective the 'third way' of Evagrius and Origen, so roundly condemned by the early councils, has found appeal to many commentators seemingly presenting a steer through the pitfalls and traps of modernity.

As mentioned earlier, when we look at official church teaching on the soul over the past 2,000 years what is most surprising is how few pronouncements there are as to its nature. Where the church speaks out it is usually in condemnation of a movement or trend that it feels is leading the conception of the self awry. Two such figures who received the attention of the early church councils were Origen and Evagrius.

The first disquiet with Origen's teaching is expressed by Gregory of Nyssa in 393 in an anti-Origenistic tract (see O'Connell 1987: 76). This was taken up six years later in an Eastern synod in 399 held at Nitria (see Kelly 1998: 203). Tanner, following Diekamp, Murphy and Sherwood, does not attribute the official condemnation of Origen's teaching to the Second Council of Constantinople in 553 (Tanner 1990: 119).[1] The editors of the Cerf edition of Origen's *De Principiis,* Crouzel and Simonetti (SC 252, 1978: 200), agree that the anathemas of 553 which are not in the official acts of the Second Council of Constantinople were discovered in 1672 by Lambeck, arguing that the 553 anathemas don't explicitly mention Origen but the sixth century Origenist monks of Palestine. As Tanner points out, however, the Byzantine emperor Justinian was unhappy with various elements of doctrinal excess he perceived in the contemporary church which he attributed to Gnosticism, Kabbalism and Origen's writings and so pushed forward the condemnations.[2] These early condemnations are later repeated in the 680 Council of Constantinople where Origen is explicitly condemned with Evagrius of Pontus, whilst the Second Council of Nicaea in 787 condemns the '*fabulas*' and 'mythic speculations' (*mýtheimata*) of Origen and Evagrius. As we shall see in a later chapter, the Fourth Constantinople Council held in 869–870 (begun in Hagia Sophia on 5 October 869 and ended on 28 February 870) and designated as the Eighth Ecumenical Council by the West (but not recognized as such by the Byzantines; see Tanner 1990: 157) made a point of condemning 'the irrational doctrine of two souls – *duas animas*/ δυο ψυχάς' and declared that faith in '*unam animan rationabilem et intellectualem*' was essential to all Christians and stated that 'it is necessary to declare anathema everyone who irreligiously and senselessly holds that a human being has two souls'. Within this clear unhappiness about Gnostic and Platonic views of the soul it also upheld the condemnations of earlier Councils of 'Origen and his useless knowledge' and Evagrius and his '*vana sapuit*', a condemnation that was last (and finally) repeated at the Councils of Basel-Ferrara-Florence-Rome (1431–45) which likewise condemned Origen and his doctrine of the 'penitence of demons and condemned beings'.

The views of both Origen and Evagrius, then, excited a lot of (negative) attention from the early councils. One of the consequences of this is that

---

[1] Many commentators rather point to the local council of 543 as one of the key sources of condemnation. Whether this condemnation was officially carried at the General Council of 553 is a moot point.

[2] For a full list and excellent discussion of the condemnations see Konstantinovsky 2009: 20–2.

on a scholarly level it is often difficult to recreate with some accuracy the actual original teachings of the two as so much has been destroyed and distorted.[3] Crouzel and Simonetti stress that we can thank Origen's editor and champion Rufinus for saving *De Principiis* but, they add, 'we cannot trust him', for 'there are not only long additions and omissions, but mistranslations, some deliberate, some perhaps unconscious, paraphrases in which the point and force of the original are lost, and countless minor alterations' (Cerf Edition of *De Principiis*: xlvii).

Of course into such vacuums, empty speculation and conjecture will often fly. However, in this chapter I shall try and piece together some of the teaching of Origen and Evagrius on the soul, not least as it shines not a little light on those early ambiguous Christian centuries when Christian thinkers (such as Augustine) were attempting to forge a Christian conception of self and soul as they felt themselves emerging from the long shadow of Plato. In the previous chapter we saw how Augustine wrestled with his neo-Platonic inheritance to forge his own picture of the soul. My contention in this chapter will be that although Origen and Evagrius will ultimately be condemned by the institutional church their teachings and influence lived on to have perhaps a greater influence on the subsequent Christian conception of the soul than either of them could have dared possible. In so doing they preserved that same Platonic tradition and allowed it to retain its foothold in the Christian imagination.

The Christian Platonists – Origen and Clement

Origen himself was greatly indebted to the teachings of Clement of Alexandria and to the neo-Platonic Ammonius Saccas, who also acted as a tutor to Plotinus and whom many commentators have seen as the logical antecedent for both of their systems of thought (see Porphyry, *Life of Plotinos*: 3 and Eusebius *Ecclesiastical History*: VI.19.5). Through these two sources he was able to incorporate a great deal of the Platonic conception of the soul into his writings. Thus, Clement in the *Stromata*: III.10.68 described the *psyche* as being comprised, in traditional Platonic terms, of *epithumia, thumos* and *logismos*. In Origen's own writings, as with the Platonists, God is wholly one,

---

[3] As with so much in intellectual endeavour, politics and factions have too often got in the way of rational speculation – a fact no less evident, as we shall see in the next chapter, in the psychological realm as the theological one.

monad and pure *Nous* and source of all intellect (Princ 1.1.6) and the human rational soul is also immortal and immaterial. God is incomprehensible, greater than all creatures yet seen in all his works by analogy, especially in beauty, so important, as we have seen, to the Platonic tradition. Unlike the unmoved prime mover of the Platonists, however, Origen's God is acting, personal, intelligent and possesses will (see Comm John 32: 28) and, rather like Augustine's God, is moved by the *pathos* of love. The *Logos* or Son of God is the Creator and is the perfect image of God (Princ 1.2.2.6). He is eternally generated from the essence of the Father through the outpouring of God's splendour (Comm John XIII.25; Princ 1.2.5). In distinction to the Alexandrian Arians, for Origen 'there is not when *logos* was not' (Princ 1.2.9). The *Logos* is still lesser than God the father ('The father is greater than me', Princ 1.2) and from the Son proceeds the Holy Spirit (Princ 1.3). God the father also creates *logika* – pure intelligences and minds – directly (Princ 1.2.2) which are subject to change and movement. At this point the Platonic/Plotinian system begins to take over, which presumably drew the ire of the early Council Fathers. For after the creation of minds, says Origen (and in this respect following very closely the Plotinian schema we outlined in the previous chapter), these minds neglected the contemplation of God and drew nearer to matter in a Plotinian version of the fall. Like Plotinus, Origen plays on the word *psychesthai,* 'those that grew cold', to stress that in this fall they cooled, became nearer matter and were estranged from their origins in God (Princ 2.8.3).[4]

Thus, as with the neo-Platonists, in Origen we end up with a hierarchy of created matter divided into stars, planets, angels, humans and *daimones* (Princ 1.6.1-2). In Tripolitis' words:

> Thus according to Origen, the sensible universe is not as the Gnostics believed, an accidental result of fallen spirits, but was created by God through His goodness and love as a penitential dwelling for fallen beings. (Tripolitis 1978: 97)

Therefore Origen's universe is not an evil place, as it was to be for the Gnostics, but simply God's 'second best' creation – a position essayed by

---

[4] On the falling away see Princ 8.3: 'We have to inquire whether perhaps the name soul, which in Greek is termed *psyche*, be so termed from growing cold (*psychesthai*) out of a better and more divine condition, and be thence derived, because it seems to have cooled from that natural and divine warmth, and therefore has been placed in its present position, and called by its present name.' See also Plato *Cratylus* 399d-e, Aristotle *De Anima* 1.2.405b and Tertullian *De Anima* 25, 27 for similar interpretations on the origins of *psyche*.

neither Augustine nor Plotinus and testimony to the originality of Origen's thought.

As regards the nature of the soul, Origen, like Augustine, finds in the scriptures various interpretations as to the nature of the human self (Princ 3.4.5). He does not give a definitive answer but stresses that the rational part of the soul is immortal, incorruptible and incorporeal (Princ 4.4.9) and it can never cease to exist: 'the soul not only survives the earthly body but by the power of the God also remembers its former existence' (Princ 2.10.4; cf. Plotinus Enn 4.3.26-27). Therefore each possesses in themselves a mixture of *Nous* and *sarx*. If *Nous* predominates then one inclines to God, if *sarx* then towards the passions (Princ 3.4). In Princ 3.2.1-4 he goes further to suggest that each person has a good angel and bad angel that guide them accordingly. Presumably, these are the remains of our old Platonic friends, the *daimones* – not entirely bad at this point but still able to assist in either fashion.

After death, we descend below earth for 're-education' (Princ 2.6) followed by ascent into the air and ascent (as with the neo-Platonists) through the planets. At each planetary stage, as we find in many of the neo-Platonic and Gnostic schemas, the soul is purified and discovers lost secrets. Evil souls cannot ascend and remain beneath the earth due to being too bound up with matter, for in this life the baser parts of the soul come from too much contemplation of devils and material things. However Origen's schema remains essentially optimistic so that eventually all souls will be purified and return to God (including, notoriously, Lucifer himself).

Comparing Origen's schema with the Plotinian and Augustinian, Origen is clearly closer to Plotinus than Augustine. His is essentially an optimistic view of creation and matter where all souls, through the natural action of goodness, will ultimately be reconciled to God. As Tripolitis puts it:

> In a manner similar to Plotinus and other contemporary Platonists, Origen maintained that man's goal in life should be to realize his true nature, which is divine, and to strive to regain his original pure state and likeness to God. (Tripolitis 1978: 122)

Thus, in interpreting Genesis 1: 26–27 Origen maintains that we are created in the image of God but have not yet acquired the likeness of God (Princ 3.6.1). The *Logos* became incarnate to hasten this trend so that the journey back to the father is possible by believing in Christ and constantly imitating him. As emphasized in the Plotinian view (and to a certain extent in the

Augustinian), the goal of humanity is to be refashioned into the likeness of God, as he puts it in Princ 3.6.1:

> Moses, before all other philosophers, describes the first creation of man in these words: 'And God said, Let Us make man in Our own image, and after Our likeness;' and then he adds the words: 'So God created man in His own image: in the image of God created He him; male and female created He them, and He blessed them.' Now the expression, 'In the image of God created He him,' without any mention of the word 'likeness,' conveys no other meaning than this, that man received the dignity of God's image at his first creation; but that the perfection of his likeness has been reserved for the consummation, – namely, that he might acquire it for himself by the exercise of his own diligence in the imitation of God, the possibility of attaining to perfection being granted him at the beginning through the dignity of the divine image, and the perfect realization of the divine likeness being reached in the end by the fulfilment of the (necessary) works *(quod imaginis quidem dignitatem in prima conditione percepit ... ipse similitudinem consummaret)*.

> The highest good, then, after the attainment of which the whole of rational nature is seeking, which is also called the end of all blessings, is defined by many philosophers as follows: The highest good, they say, is to become as like to God as possible *(Igitur summum bonum ad quod natura rationalis universa festinate, qui etiam finis omnium dicitur, a quam plurimis etiam finis omnium diritur, a quam plurimis etiam philosophorum hoc modo terminator, quia summum bonum sit, prout possible est, **simile fieri deo**)*.

Our bodies, therefore, will become 'spiritual bodies' at this consummation:

> So also, with respect to the state of the body, we are to hold that this very body which now, on account of its service to the soul, is styled an animal body, will, by means of a certain progress, when the soul, united to God, shall have been made one spirit with Him. (Princ 3.6.6)[5]

---

[5] Origen is at pains to stress that unlike Aristotle, he does not suggest there is a fifth element in the (re-)composition of the self as apparently suggested in his lost book 'on philosophy': 'for the faith of the Church does not admit the view of certain Grecian philosophers, that there is besides the body, composed of four elements, another fifth body, which is different in all its

Following this line of thought, in the twenty-seventh treatise of the *Homily on the Book of Numbers*, Origen accordingly sets out the stages of the soul's ascent to God as an allegorical interpretation of Israel's exodus from Egypt.[6] However, complete union cannot be attained in this life while clothed with the mortal body (Princ 3.6.3). Therefore, unlike Plotinus' schema this cannot happen in this life for it is a gradual process taking many aeons (Princ 3.6.6). So we have a process that begins with moral purification, then leads to knowledge that enables us to discern the real from the unreal and ends with the *Logos* united with the spirit.

Origen, Plotinus and Augustine

Drawing upon Origen's account of the soul above we immediately see that it occupies a halfway position between the two postulates of Augustine and Plotinus we explored in the previous chapter. We can summarize the main tendencies of his schema thus:

1. As well as basing his exposition on the Christian scriptures, we can see in Origen's exposition much more of a Platonizing tendency than is visible in that of mature Augustine.

2. Like Plotinus (and unlike Augustine) he suggests that we are from a (non-material) source from beyond this world. There has been a 'fall' and a 'cooling' of the *psyche* to this earth. Origen (like Plotinus and unlike Augustine) is happy to talk of the pre-existence of souls before their fall (see Princ 3.3.5).[7]

---

parts, and diverse from this our present body; since neither out of sacred Scripture can any produce the slightest suspicion of evidence for such an opinion, nor can any rational inference from things allow the reception of it, especially when the holy apostle manifestly declares, that it is not new bodies which are given to those who rise from the dead, but that they receive those identical ones which they had possessed when living, transformed from an inferior into a better condition' (Princ 3.6.6).

[6] 1st step: self knowledge and understanding – 'know thyself'; 2nd step: take up the struggle against sin and passions (27.6); 3rd step: reach *apatheia* – 'moral freedom and sovereignty' (27.6); 4th step: detachment from marriage – recommends celibacy and asceticism; 5th step: the 'watchtower' – the 'soul has a distant view of the splendours in store' (27.9; cf. *Enneads* 4.4.5); 6th step: the rational and irrational struggle for control – gift of visions and discernment of spirits (27.11 and Princ 3.2.1-7); 7th step: arrival at state of blessedness – *gnosis*; 8th step: becomes a minister to help others (27.12); 9th step, the last stage: *ekstasis* – the seeker is completely possessed by the *Logos* and has intuitive contemplative knowledge of God (27.12; cf. *Enneads* Book 9).

[7] Where he discusses the Pythian *daimones* possessing souls from birth: 'there were certain causes of prior existence, in consequence of which the souls, before their birth in the body,

3. Although contemplation is important to acquire our road back to the source (as it was for Plotinus), unlike Plotinus, the incarnate *Logos* is our best guide to restoration of our primary state.

4. Origen's God is not an unmoved Platonic mover, but rather the God of the Christian scriptures who actively seeks us out in love. Like Augustine, Origen stresses that the love of Christ lies at the heart of Christian salvation.

5. The material world is not as flawed as Augustine suggests and by intellectual and moral training we can return to our source. We are split beings, partly spiritual, partly material, so we must work on the spiritual element accordingly.[8] 'Humans', he writes in Princ 1.1.6, 'are formed from a union of body and soul/*ex corporis animaeque concurs.*' Following Plato, Origen retains the tripartite division of the soul into *logismos, thumos* and *epithumia,* a pattern that Augustine has moved away from.

6. Like Augustine and Plotinus, Origen suggests sudden ecstatic realizations of the union are possible in this life. However full union must wait until after death, and then only after many rebirths and much 're-education'.

7. Although Origen does not emphasize the erotic to the extent that Plotinus does, he does emphasize the Platonic role of beauty in the ascent. See, for example, Comm Songs: Prol (cf. Plotinus Enn 6.7.34).

8. Like Plotinus, the goal of the process is deification – to come to the likeness of God. Unlike Plotinus (and like Augustine), all will be saved, not just the intellectually capable. As we saw above in Princ 3.6.1, 'the highest good, they say, is to become as like to God as possible' (*quia summum bonum sit, prout possible est, simile fieri deo*).

---

contracted a certain amount of guilt in their sensitive nature, or in their movements, on account of which they have been judged worthy by Divine Providence of being placed in this condition'.

[8] See, for example, Princ 3.4.1 where he states: 'two souls are said to co-exist within us, the one is more divine and heavenly and the other inferior from the very fact that we inhere in bodily structures which according to their own proper nature are dead, and altogether devoid of life (seeing it is from us, i.e., from our souls, that the material body derives its life, it being contrary and hostile to the spirit), we are drawn on and enticed to the practice of those evils which are agreeable to the body'.

9. Unlike Augustine, there is in Origen a 'planetary ascent' through the seven spheres after death. The *daimones* are important helpers in this journey occupying an ambiguous place, either able to act for good or ill. In this respect Origen seems to recall a transitory stage where these beings still retain some of their Platonic positive quality but are already morphing into the later 'demons' of the Christian imagination.

In summary, then, Origen's system is a fascinating 'halfway house' between Platonic and Christian thinking on the nature of the soul. From the last chapter we see after Augustine a bifurcation of Western European thought on the soul. Augustine, brought up a Platonist, turns his back on the Platonic tendency (represented here by Plotinus) in order to develop a Christian notion of the self that will dominate the early Middle Ages. We can thus see Origen's system as a tantalizing vision of a lost Christian-Platonic way that was posited but not followed by the emerging church. From the reaction of the Church Fathers essayed at the beginning of the chapter it was clearly seen as too Platonic, yet at this stage in the evolution of Christian self-understanding it was still possible to use a fundamentally Platonic schema to articulate Christian self-understanding. In Origen's writings, therefore, we get the distinct impression that we are at war with ourselves (much as Plato had suggested). For example, in Princ 1.1.7 he argues for a separation of soul and body that reads very much like the Platonic view: 'Whence comes it that the power of memory, the contemplation of invisible things, yes, and the perception of incorporeal things reside in the body?'

In many respects, as we shall see shortly, Origen will become 'Plato's spokesperson in the desert' for the notion of a self divided against itself will become a familiar trope in the desert tradition in, for example, the writings of Cassian and Evagrius (which will subsequently be of such importance to the Western monastic tradition). Key Origenistic images such as the falling away of the soul from God in the 'cooling', the need for purification of the 'higher part of the soul' and the possibility of vision of the *Nous* in this life will all become part of the terminology of the desert dwellers and Origen's neo-Platonic thoughts appeared to find a more receptive audience away from the centres of church authority in the cities. Origen's preferred term for the Church was the '*schola animarum*' – the 'school of souls' – and his notion of the Christian life as a slow progress of the soul from 'cooling to warming' will become one enshrined in the desert tradition:

I think, therefore, that all the saints who depart from this life will remain in some place situated on the earth, which holy Scripture calls paradise, as in some place of instruction, and, so to speak, class-room or school of souls, in which they are to be instructed regarding all the things which they had seen on earth, and are to receive also some information respecting things that are to follow in the future, as even when in this life they had obtained in some degree indications of future events, although 'through a glass darkly,' all of which are revealed more clearly and distinctly to the saints in their proper time and place. (Princ 11.6)[9]

In this respect, one of the key attributes to be acquired by Christians in this life is purity of heart which he derives from the Beatitudes:

Here, if any one lay before us the passage where it is said, 'Blessed are the pure in heart, for they shall see God,' from that very passage, in my opinion, will our position derive additional strength; for what else is seeing God in heart, but, according to our exposition as above, understanding and knowing Him with the mind? (Princ 1.1.9)[10]

What he calls *theoria et intellectus* – the development of the *Nous* through *theoria* and contemplation – will ultimately vouchsafe us the vision of God in union that we desire:

And in all things this food is to be understood as the contemplation and understanding of God (*in omnibus autem cibus hic intelligendus est theoria et intellectus dia*), which is of a measure appropriate and suitable to this nature, which was made and created; and this measure it is proper should be observed by every one of those who are beginning to see God, i.e., to understand Him through purity of heart (*videre deum, id est intelligere per puritatem cordis*). (Princ 11.7)

Origen, however, is always at pains to 'let the reader choose for himself' and remains ultimately as much a philosopher as a theologian:

---

[9] '*Paradisum dicit scriptura divina, velet in auditorio eruditionis loco et, ut ita dixerim, auditorio vel schola animarum.*'

[10] '*Beati mundo corde, quoniam ipsi deum videbunt … nam quid aliud est corde.videre nisi secundum id, quod supra exposuimus, mente eum intelligere atque cognoscere.*'

And now we have brought forward to the best of our ability, in the person of each of the parties, what might be advanced by way of argument regarding the several views, and let the reader choose out of them for himself that which he thinks ought to be preferred. (Princ 3.4.5)

His subsequent condemnation reveals the perils of allowing one's readers to think for themselves!

Plato in the desert: Evagrius of Pontus (344–399)

A survey of the surviving work of Evagrius of Pontus enables us to trace the afterlife of Origen's (Christian-Platonist) ideas of the soul and its consequent effects on Western self-understanding. An ardent Origenist (Bamberger 1970: xxv), like Origen he speculated on the pre-existence of souls and the return of souls. Also like those of his master, Evagrius' works were destroyed and tampered with after the condemnation of the councils. However one of his most important works, the *Kephalaia Gnostica,* destroyed after the condemnations of the councils, survived in Syriac and Armenian translation and to this day he is still venerated by the Syrian church where his feast day is 16 January. Using these sources we have been able to recover (as with Origen's works) much of the original as condemned (Bamberger: xxvi).[11]

Looking at the *Kephalaia Gnostica* (KG), we find a pre-existing cosmology that is both reflective of Origen and Plotinus allying Evagrius' work closer to the Platonic tradition than that which will later be associated

---

[11] The history of the redaction of the Evagrian manuscripts is complicated. As Dysinger points out in his excellent summary of the status of these manuscripts, apart from Syriac and Armenian translations only about one sixth of the text survives in Greek. Frankenberg's 1912 translation from the Syriac into Greek (designated as S[1] by Guillaumont) is notable in containing none of the Platonist/Origenist doctrines condemned by the Church Councils in 543 and 553 (it also includes a commentary by the sixth century anti-Origenist, Babai the Great). In 1958, as part of his critical edition, Guillaumont reproduced a translation of an extant Syriac version (designated as S[2]) which contained the expurgated Origenist statements. It is from this version that we draw here. As Dysinger puts it: 'The existence of both expurgated and unexpurgated versions of Evagrius's works during the sixth century reflects an uneasy attitude of reverence for his writings combined with anxiety concerning their orthodoxy which is well-attested elsewhere in the monastic literature of the period.' See Dysinger: http://www.ldysinger.com/Evagrius/07_Antirrhet/00a_start.htm. In the following I shall draw upon these translations. See also Konstantinovsky 2009 for a comprehensive treatment of the redactions.

with Augustine. Thus, at the beginning of creation there is a single Henad, 'a single undivided integral whole whose nature was pure intelligence' (Bamberger: lxxv). As with Origen, we then see a falling away from this original purity as a second creation takes place as spirits fall from original innocence to a muddied existence darkened by matter. The fate of each spirit is determined by their guilt and decides into which bodies they fall: 'they pass into bodies that are more or less material, more or less dark, more or less thick'. Angels, as bodies of fire (much as in Origen's schema), are not affected by matter, whereas human beings, formed of earth, are mired in sensuality. Devils have the darkest bodies, being most immersed in matter 'most thickened by hatred, anger and resentment and most devoid of light. They consist of air, which being devoid of light, is ice-cold' (KG 3.50).

Therefore the soul or *psyche* of the individual person is a piece of the original *Nous* of the cosmos; it is also the source of affectivity and the passions. In angels *Nous* predominates whilst in humans the *psyche* comprises this *Nous* mixed primarily with *epithumia*. In devils it is *Nous* mixed with *thumos* that predominates.[12] Angels possess the *theoria* of God (Bamberger: lxxviii) to which man can strive by purification.

Therefore, each person in their soul reproduces the conditions of this primal fall and conflict. The internal struggle of the ascetic, so beloved by the desert fathers and mothers, therefore becomes a battleground in miniature of these grand battles raging throughout the cosmos and the individual ascetic has a duty to battle their internal 'soul-forces' as part of this wider cosmic battle. Developing the Platonic system, Evagrius shows his originality by suggesting how it must be adapted by the ascetic. Thus, *thumos* and *epithumia* become for the ascetic 'their helpmates', 'so that with the first he may drive away the wolf-like concepts, while with desire he may lovingly tend the sheep, assailed as he often is by the rain and winds' (*Commentary on Ecclesiastes* 3: 11). The *logismos* becomes the 'shepherd' of the soul that has *epithumia* and *thumos* as its sheepdogs to bring the *psyche* into order (a neat reinvention of Plato's charioteer and entirely suitable for its Christian reinvention, as with Origen, Evagrius is very happy to baptize Plato).[13] In contrast to Augustine, Evagrius presents us with a basically optimistic view of the destiny of the soul (like Origen) where *epithumia* and *thumos* will be our guides in spiritual ascent. As with many of the desert

---

[12] KG 3.34: 'The "demon" is the reasoning nature which, because of an abundance of *thumos*, has fallen from the service of God.'

[13] However excess of *thumos*, says Evagrius in KG 3.34, is what creates the *daimones* and elicits their fall.

fathers and mothers, Evagrius does not see the passions as intrinsically disordered or bad.

Classification of the movements of the soul

From this schema, ultimately derived from its Platonic/Origenistic sources and fertilized in the fourth century deserts, Evagrius is able to develop what is probably his most important and original contribution to the development of monastic thought: the discernment and classification of the *logismoi* or movements of the soul. As I have argued elsewhere (Tyler 2014) this classification is not only important for the Christian tradition but extends to contemporary psychology where recent years have seen a renewed interest in this tradition and its contemporary psychological application. In the *Praktikos* (chapter 6), he gives us his 'general categories of logismoi (λογισμοὶ)'. However it is noteworthy how he chooses carefully the language to designate each movement of the soul. Thus, gluttony when first introduced (γαστριμαργίας, Prak 7) is described as a *logismos*. Lust, on the other hand (πορνείας, Prak 8), is introduced as a *daimon* (δαίμων): 'Contaminating the soul, it bends it down towards these sorts of deeds.' In future appearances (Prak 51, 58; *On Prayer* 90; *On the Thoughts* 16) it is consistently referred to as a *daimon*.

With regard to the next movement of the soul, love of money (φιλαργυρίας in Prak 9), Evagrius is unspecific whether it is a *logismos, daimon* or passion. Sadness, likewise (λύπης, Prak 10), is distinctly ambiguous, introduced as a *logismos* in *Praktikos* 9; when he refers to it again (in chapters 19 and 25) it is described as a *daimon*. Anger (ὀργῆς, Prak 11) is described as a 'most fierce *pathos*/ πάθος' which 'causes the soul to be savage all day long, but especially in prayers it seizes the *nous*, reflecting back the face of the distressing person'. As we would expect it is connected with the *thumos* (and as we saw earlier is connected in Evagrius' mind with the fall of the *daimones*) which may be why in *Praktikos* chapter 23 he refers to it not as a *pathos* but as a *logismos*. The famous monkish 'noon-day demon' of acedia (ἀκηδίας, Prak 12), for whose description of which Evagrius is rightly celebrated, is consistently referred to as a *daimon* (Prak 12, 23, 27, 28) and even at times being described as the 'most oppressive *daimon* of all'. Like sadness, vainglory (κενοδοξίας, Prak 13) is introduced as a *logismos*, to which it is referred to in *Praktikos* chapters 13, 30 and *On the Thoughts*, chapter 14, but in *Praktikos* 58 it is referred to as a *daimon*. Finally, pride (ὑπερηφανίς, Prak 14) is consistently a *daimon* throughout (see for example Prak 33).

Evagrius thus classifies the movements of the soul as follows: pride, *acedia* and lust are unambiguously *daimones*. Gluttony is likewise consistently a *logismos*. Vainglory and sadness are ambiguously described as *daimones* or *logismoi*, whilst anger is either a *pathos* or *logismos*. Finally, the character of love of money is not specified. Again, the neutrality of some of these terms is instructive. The *thumotic* demons, he tells us in *On the Thoughts* (chapter 1), can bend 'the appetites of gluttony, love of money and vainglory' to their ends. Further on he suggests that the order at which they appear to us is dictated by the sequence with which Jesus received them in the desert, thus gluttony is always first: 'gluttony is the first of the passions as Amalek is the prince of the nations' (*On the Thoughts* 1; PG 1145A) and the subsequent order goes:

Gluttony – Lust – Avarice – Sadness – Anger – Accidie – Vainglory
(see also *Skemmata* 42)

What may appear as a random sequence on initial acquaintance begins to make sense when we view it from the neo-Platonic/Origenist perspective of Evagrius' world view. For these *thumotic* leftovers from the creation, the *daimones*, are able to use the passions and *logismoi* to evoke misleading pictures of the *nous* in the mind of the recipient:

All the thoughts of demonic origin introduce into the soul concepts of sensory concerns: because of this the *nous*, stamped with the imprint of these concerns, carries them about within itself; and (so) from the concern itself it (can) henceforth recognize the approaching demon. (*On the Thoughts* 2)

For:

All thoughts producing *thumos* or *epithumia* in a way that is contrary to nature (are caused by demons). For through disturbance of these two powers the *nous* mentally commits adultery and becomes incensed, and is no longer able to welcome in itself the representation (*fantasia*) of its (divine) lawgiver.

In *On Prayer* chapter 51 he tells us that the *daimones* want to activate these desires in us 'in order to coarsen the *nous* through them, so that it is incapable of praying as it ought. When the passions reign through (our) irrational part, they do not allow (the *nous*) to move rationally and to seek the Word of God.' Which, for Evagrius, is the natural movement of the soul; what Cassian will later call the natural movement of a feather, floating free unencumbered by the moisture of passion (*Conferences* 9). Not only that, but the *daimones* can assist each other in their action on the soul. In *Praktikos* chapter 13 he tells us how the *daimon* who works with vainglory begins with a *logismos* and then is able to invite into the *psyche* three more *daimones*: lust, pride and sadness:

> The spirit of vainglory is most subtle and it readily grows up in the souls of those who practice virtue. It leads them to desire to make their struggles known publicly, to hunt after the praise of men. This in turn leads to their illusory healing of women, or to their hearing fancied sounds as the cries of demons ... It has men knocking at the door, seeking audiences with them. If the monk does not willingly yield to their request, he is bound and led away. When in this way he is carried aloft by vain hope, the demon vanishes and the monk is left to be tempted by the demon of pride or of sadness. (Prak 13)

To counteract these vagaries in the *psyche* he tells us in *Praktikos* 15 that the 'wandering *nous*' is stabilized by reading, vigils and prayer, whilst 'burning *epithumia*' is stabilized by hunger, toil and solitude and 'churning *thumos*' by the singing of psalms, patient endurance and mercy. He therefore advises how the monk may work with each part of the Platonic soul. When there are disturbances in the *thumos* (Prak 22), the demons will advise a withdrawal into greater solitude whilst what is wanted is more engagement with those around the seeker. Likewise, when the *epithumia* is disturbed by these outside forces the demons will suggest more social intercourse whereas more withdrawal may be the remedy. This theme is taken up again in the *Kephalaia Gnostica* where each part of the soul will have the attention of a different *daimon*:

> Knowledge and ignorance are united in the *nous*, while *epithumia* is receptive of self-control and luxury, and love and hate normally occur to *thumos*. (KG: 1.84)

Yet, as is constantly stressed by Evagrius, and flows from his metaphysics of the soul, the shepherd of the *logismos* can use the various parts of the soul to restore harmony by playing one part off against the other. In *Praktikos* 24, *On the Thoughts* 16 and *Skemmata* 8 he tells us that *thumos* can be used against *epithumia* and vice versa. Although see *On the Thoughts* 5 where *thumos* is singled out for particular caution as a tool of the demons:

> Day and night, therefore, they are always trying to provoke it. And when they see it tethered by gentleness, they at once try to set it free on some seemingly just pretext; in this way, when it is violently aroused, they can use it for their shameful purposes. So it must not be aroused either for just or for unjust reasons; and we must not hand a dangerous sword to those too readily incensed to wrath, for it often happens that people become excessively worked up for quite trivial reasons.

For:

> He who has mastery over his incensive power has mastery also over the demons. But anyone who is a slave to it is a stranger to the monastic life and to the ways of our Saviour. (OTT: 13)

Therefore we use the natural powers of the psyche, *thumos, epithumia and logismos* (33; see also KG 3.59), to fortify ourselves against the *daimones*, by which means we avoid the stirring of passions and achieve the goal of this ascetical striving – the *apatheia*, or overcoming of the passions:

> If all evil is created by the three parts of the soul, that is by the *logistikon*, by *epithumia*, or by *thumos*, and if it is possible to use these either well or badly, it is clear that evil is created by their use contrary to nature. And if this is the case, there is nothing that has been created by God that is evil. (KG 3.59; Gaullimont source S[1])

For:

> The *nous* is healed by knowledge; the *thumos*, by love; and the *epithumia*, by chastity. And the cause of the first is the second, and that of the second is the third. (KG 3.35; Gaullimont Source S[1])[14]

---

[14] In Prak 35, Evagrius tells us that the passions of the soul derive from men and the passions of the body from the body, so that 'The passions of the body are cut back by self-control; those

What we see from these accounts of the soul in Evagrius is the ambiguous position which the *daimones* hold in this post-Platonic cosmos. Still recognizably Platonic, Evagrius struggles to place the texture of the Christian fabric within the Platonic self. Unlike Augustine who will ultimately reject the Platonic framework, Evagrius (like his mentor Origen) develops it as a means of expressing his new Christian vision of the soul and its relationship to the cosmos. As with Plato the *daimones* must of course play a significant part albeit in a darker fashion than their Platonic cousins.

Apatheia

The overcoming of the passions, the *apatheia* of the psyche (ψυχῆς ἀπάθειαν), so connected with the vision of the 'purity of the soul' in contemplation, is thus at the heart of Evagrius's schema, and given a new emphasis in his development of Origen's ideas. Bamberger (1981: lxxxii) goes further to argue that because of its use in the *Gospel of Thomas* it 'is not unlikely that this theme formed an element of the primitive catechesis and derived from the teaching of our Lord himself' therefore '*apatheia*, far from being a mere transposition of the Stoic experience, is rather akin to the fear of the Lord. Still more significantly, it is parent to love, *agape*.' In the Evagrian scheme it is clearly the means by which we shall be reunited with the *Nous* of the Creator:

> *Apatheia* is what we shall call the soul's health, and the soul's food is knowledge, which is the only means by which we shall ordinarily be united with the holy powers. (Prak 56)

As with Augustine, and unlike Plotinus, grace is essential in Evagrius' conception of the pursuit of *apatheia* (Prak 100) as it is not an entirely man-made state, but requires the ministration of priests and the reception of the sacraments: 'Conceived by obedience *apatheia* is preserved by fear of the Lord. It is nourished and grows through the practice of humility and the cultivation of sorrow for sin' (Bamberger 1981: lxxxv; see also Prak 60, 77, 81). For it is never stable, always relying upon the grace of God and always

---

of the soul are cut back by spiritual love.' Guillaumont suggests a strong Aristotelian influence here (SC 170: 581). For example, compare with *Nicomachean Ethics* X: 2.1173b.7-9: 'The passions of the body are derived from the body – gluttony, fornication etc … The passions of the soul, eg anger, arise from interaction with others.' *Acedia* is the only passion (Prak 36) that embraces the whole soul (*psyche* and *Nous*) and so is the 'most dangerous'.

open to demonic assault. As he states in *Praktikos* 33: 'Recall your former way of life and your old faults, and how, when you were subject to passions, you crossed over to *apatheia* by the mercy of Christ' (see also *Praktikos* 53).

So Evagrius' *apatheia* is more about love/*agape* than indifference and is the goal of Christian life: 'The Kingdom of Heaven is *apatheia* of the soul along with true knowledge of existing things' (Prak 2). This will work its way into Cassian's *Conferences* as '*puritas cordis*' (Conferences 1.4),[15] and thence into the Western monastic tradition via St Benedict of Nursia. Yet *apatheia* is not an end in itself. In the *Chapters on Prayer* 57, he talks about a higher state of *theoria* of the blessed Trinity which leads to *gnosis* which he describes as an experiential knowledge of God given directly by the Almighty. So we have presented before us a movement from *apatheia* to *physike theoria* to *theoria* of the Blessed Trinity and finally *gnosis* of the experience of God. As Bamberger states he gives no precise description of these final states (1981: xc) but rather associates them with the phenomena of light that we shall find again in the later Eastern hesychast tradition exemplified in the writings of Gregory Palamas:

When the spirit has put off the old man to replace him with the new man, created by charity, then he will see that his own state at the time of prayer resembles that of a sapphire; it is as clear and bright as the very sky. The Scriptures refer to this experience as the place of God which was seen by our ancestors, the elders, at Mount Sinai. (Evagrius PG 40: 1244A;[16] see also DS 2: 1781)

What develops is a sense of peace, harmony and tranquillity as we recognize once again our rightful place in the created order of things:

The proof of *apatheia* is that the *nous* begins to behold its (own) proper gentle radiance; that it remains tranquil in the presence of visions during sleep; and that it looks at matters calmly. (Prak 64)

For we are effectively returning to the primordial *Nous* as inherited by Evagrius from Origen and ultimately derived, as we have seen, from Plato. In this respect Evagrius mirrors Plotinus.

---

[15] At other times he uses the words *tranquilitas* and *stabilitas*.
[16] Or as he puts it in KG 5.39: 'In pure thoughts (there) is imprinted a splendid sky to see and a spacious region where it appears how the *logoi* of beings and of the holy angels approach those who are worthy.'

In summary, it is possible to suggest that Evagrius' schema, which will be so influential on consequent Christian spiritual anthropology especially through its influence on John Cassian and ultimately St Benedict of Nursia, can be seen as the conduit whereby Plato's schema of the soul is baptized and channelled into subsequent Christian self-understanding. Further, as I have argued here, we can only really make sense of that anthropology if we grasp the wider metaphysical Origenist speculations as to the origins of the world and the *psyche* that lie as the hinterland to Evagrius' schema. Halfway between what we have characterized as the Plotinian and the Augustinian sense of self, Evagrius' schema, inhabiting the twilight world of late antiquity, retains the last remnants of the old Platonic sense of self whilst adapting to the emerging vision of a Christ-centred world founded on grace and mediated by the Church. In many ways Evagrius' speculations raise more questions than they answer and we shall come back to these in Parts II and III later.

Conclusion

Deriving from the Platonic/Origenist tradition, Evagrius, I suggest, can be classified as an original psychologist in his own right. Taking the metaphysical apparatus of Origen and combining it with the precise psychological observations of the desert fathers on the movements of the soul he is able to develop a Christian theory of soul which is a natural successor to the Platonic tradition we have explored in Part I of this book. Condemned, as we have seen, by successive church councils Evagrius' brilliant synthesis was nevertheless able to survive on the fringes of Christianity in the monastic tradition, East and West, to flower once again in our own, postmodern, times marked, as we shall see in Part II of the book, by its renewed interest in the Platonic conception of the soul. The heart of this vision of humanity is that we are made for contemplation and it is contemplation that defines the essential nature of what it is for us to be human beings. As Abbot Bamberger puts it:

> For Evagrius, the very definition of man must be established in terms of his contemplation. It is contemplative union with God which is man's ultimate end, and which establishes man in his full self-realization as the image of God. In this outlook man is not defined as a rational animal (Aristotle) but rather as a being created to be united with God in loving knowledge. (Bamberger 1981: xcii)

This essentially metaphysical view of the soul as the place where we meet the transcendent in contemplation is one that we shall return to at the end of this book. However before we reach this point we need to return to the origins of psychology in the West and the psychoanalytic 'return of the soul'.

PART II
THE RETURN OF THE SOUL

Prelude

We have surveyed in Part I how several early Christian thinkers struggled to make sense of the question of personal identity in light of the Christ event. Their solutions, I have argued, reflected the Platonic matrix within which they worked – each of them incorporating or rejecting it (or elements of it) as they thought fit. We have seen that one key aspect of this project was the extent to which each constructed a 'soul-language' of the *psyche* to take into account varying cosmological, metaphysical and soteriological views of human destiny in the light of the new metaphysics presented by the Christian Gospels. We have begun to see the extent to which the Orthodox view of the Church has interpreted these positions by various conciliar rulings. One of the key arguments of the book is that despite the substantial work conducted throughout the medieval period in refining the Christian discourse of the soul, some of these elements were left unresolved or unrecognized until the early modern period.[1]

Consequently in Part II we shall re-engage with the soul-discourse in our own era through the lens of the twentieth century discourse of the founding fathers of psychoanalysis as they sought to resolve the 'soul-question' through their own self-analysis. In doing so I shall make parallels to the early Christian period – with its heretics, orthodoxy and apostasy – before turning in Part III to some final words on the possible nature of a future soul-discourse for our own times.

---

[1] Lovers of scholastic theology will, of course, be disappointed by this account as I have chosen not to investigate its contribution here. There are two reasons for this. The first is that editorially I felt it would render an already substantial book unwieldy. Secondly, I have worked on many of these areas in my earlier *The Return to the Mystical* (Tyler 2011) and I refer the interested reader to that work. Of course this leaves the contribution of Thomas Aquinas untouched which I hope to return to at a later date.

CHAPTER 5
OTTO RANK AND THE BATTLE FOR FREUD'S SOUL

Rank's heresy

In May 1930 the founders of the modern practices of psychology, psycho-analysis and psychiatry gathered in Washington DC to participate in what was called the 'First International Congress on Mental Hygiene'. Four thousand people from over fifty-three countries, including Australia and the USSR, gathered, largely to baptize the new discipline of psychoanalysis and introduce it as a respectable and viable form of clinical intervention. Included in the purpose statement for the convention was the idea that it was necessary to determine 'how best to care for and treat the mentally sick, to prevent mental illness, and to conserve mental health' (*Proceedings of the First International Congress on Mental Hygiene*). As with most such gatherings, scientific and intellectual seeking was clouded by the internal politics of a nascent movement that was still vulnerable and trying to assert its respectability in the face of a sceptical world. Accordingly, when Dr Otto Rank, one of Freud's first disciples and advocates, rose to speak there was excited anticipation regarding how he viewed the direction in which analysis was moving, especially at this the moment of its first public 'coming out' in America. The paper was not to disappoint expectations. In a short ten minute extract, Rank deftly condensed his views on analysis, psychology and the forces that were at that moment shaping the future of analysis, the effects of which we still live with today. In his speech Rank contrasted 'the scientific' approach to 'human behavior and personality' (Sp: 221)[1] with what he called the 'human side': that 'characteristic which ... can't be measured and checked and controlled'. This latter, he argued, 'was the only vital factor in all kinds of therapy, mental health'. That which is 'human and cannot be schematized' had to be distinguished, he suggested, from 'intellectual knowledge' of the human *psyche*, for the scientific attitude does not so much neglect the personal as lead to a denial of it in order to 'maintain the scientific attitude'.

---

[1] See Bibliography for abbreviations used for Rank's writings.

From the perspective of nearly a century later, what is most striking reading Rank's words at the congress is how strongly he identifies the nascent analytic movement with the 'scientific' rather than the 'human' approach. Following several recent decades of Freud-bashing,[2] it is a commonplace today to see Freudian analysis (and Freud himself) as falling short of the 'scientific' methodologies with which contemporary psychology tends to wrap itself. Rank saw this right at the birth of the analytic movement and was able to encapsulate in his speech and writings this trend within analysis in particular, and psychology in general. Rank's paper was essentially one that went to the fundamental heart of *what we think psychology (or psychoanalysis/psychotherapy) is*. Once again, an enquiry was being made into the mysterious nature of *psyche* – this time not in the language of the ancients but in our own well-used twentieth and twenty-first century phrases. It is this debate, and especially Rank's understanding of the soul (*die Seele*), that we shall explore in this chapter.

Psychology as interpretation

One of the key themes of Rank's speech to the Mental Health Congress, and much of his writing after his break with Freud in the 1930s, was that psychology is not so much a 'science of facts' as an 'art of interpretation'. As he put it in his *Mental Hygiene Speech*:

> Psychology does not deal primarily with facts as science does but only with the individual's attitude toward facts. In other words, the objects of psychology are *interpretations* – and there are as many of them as there are individuals. (Sp: 222)

By situating the truths of psychology in the hermeneutical turn rather than

---

[2] See Gomez 2005 for a good survey of the recent 'Freud Wars'. She sums up the 'wars' thus: 'It will come as no surprise to hear that "The Freud Wars" were neither won nor lost. Inside and outside the psychoanalytic world, psychoanalysis continues to be viewed in line with the different verdicts reached, with little discussion and scarcely a hint of resolution. Essential psychoanalytic concepts from the "unconscious" to the "ego" have entered into ordinary language, suggesting an informed endorsement, but adjacent disciplines such as psychiatry and psychology typically treat it as little more than an old-fashioned conjecture. Even within psychoanalysis itself ... there is no consensus on where its authority lies: practitioners and theorists are divided as to whether its ideas are scientific or interpretative by nature.' (2005: 8). This chapter will patrol Gomez's 'scientific/interpretative' frontier.

the aimless seeking for quasi-empirical 'facts' Rank had essentially anatomized the nature of analysis as a clinical discipline. In this he was not alone. For it is an interesting historical coincidence that at precisely the time Rank was working on his notion of self in America his fellow Austrian, the philosopher Ludwig Wittgenstein (1889–1951), was having similar thoughts about the nature of psychology. Like Rank, Wittgenstein was beginning to develop a theory of psychology that emphasized its hermeneutic above any quasi-empiricial status. This work would flower towards the end of his life in the writings that followed that published as Part I of the *Philosophical Investigations* and would occupy him, as we shall see in Chapter 7, for the last few years of his life spent in Ireland and Cambridge.

As Wittgenstein wrote in the *Philosophical Investigations*:

What is your aim in philosophy? – To show the fly the way out of the fly-bottle. (PI: 309)

For Wittgenstein, as much as for Rank, the aim of the philosopher or psychologist was to effect change in the student or client. For Wittgenstein, therefore, the aim of the psychologist/philosopher was not to propound certain theories or explanations but to observe the 'foundations of possible buildings', achieved by a certain 'clarity of vision':

Clarity, perspicuity (*Durchsichtigkeit*) are an end in themselves. I am not interested in constructing a building, so much as having a clear view (*durchsichtig*) before me of the foundations of possible buildings. My goal, then, is different from the scientist and so my think-way is to be distinguished. (VB: 459)[3]

This was also how Wittgenstein saw the value of Freud's contribution to our understanding of the mind. For Wittgenstein, Freud's observations were not those of a pseudo-scientist but of someone who 'changes the perspective' of their interlocutor:

When a dream is interpreted we might say that it is fitted into a context in which it ceases to be puzzling. In a sense the dreamer re-dreams his dream in surroundings such that *its aspect changes* …

[3] Written as a draft foreword to *Philosophische Bemerkungen* in 1930. See also *Zettel* 464: 'The pedigree of psychological phenomena: I strive not for exactitude but *Übersichtlichkeit*.' We shall return to Wittgenstein's 'perspicuous view' in Chapter 7.

In considering what a dream is, it is important to consider what happens to it, the way its aspect changes when it is brought into relation with other things remembered, for instance. (LC: 45–46)

Thus both Wittgenstein and Rank present us with a bifurcation in the twentieth century's attitude to the self: we can either chase after quasi-scientific explanations of psychic phenomena or see the exploration of the *psyche*, especially from a clinical perspective, as a seeking after *interpretation and meaning*. Thus in Rank's *Mental Hygiene* lecture, he speaks not of presenting a new psychological theory, but rather of a new 'world view'/'*Weltanschauung*'. Rank's characterization of the shift as one of *Weltanschauung* is instructive. Whilst reflecting on his own need for the *Übersichtliche Darstellung/clear overview*, Wittgenstein also puzzled as to whether it was a *Weltanschauung* after all:

A main source of our misunderstandings is that we do not *übersehen* (oversee) the use of our words. – Our Grammar is lacking an *Übersichtlichkeit* (overview). – The *Übersichtliche Darstellung* produces the understanding which allows us to 'see connections'. Hence the importance of finding and inventing *Zwischengliedern*.

The concept of the *Übersichtliche Darstellung* is of fundamental significance for us. It designates our *Darstellungsform* (viewpoint), the way we see things. (Is this a *Weltanschauung*?) (PI: 122)

Wittgenstein was concerned that his approach to philosophical or psychological problems, his *Übersichtliche Darstellung*, should not just be another competing view/*Weltanschauung* with others in the post-scientific marketplace of contemporary culture (hence the phrase 'Is this a *Weltanschauung*?'). In his last writing *On Certainty*, written as he lay dying in Cambridge, he clarifies the concept by contrasting a *Weltanschauung* with a *Weltbild*. In contrast to the *Weltanschauung*, which sees itself as *the* way of seeing, the *Weltbild* is *a* way of seeing:

It (the *Weltanschauung*) takes itself too seriously, as the ultimate explanation and foundation of our convictions. In contrast, the concept of a *Weltbild* completely avoids the knowledge game. (Genova 1995: 50)

In formulating and developing his notion of the *Weltbild* Wittgenstein was influenced by his reading of Oswald Spengler's work of 1923, *Der Untergang des Abendlandes/The Downfall of the West* (Spengler 1923). In a note amongst the *Vermischte Bemerkungen* he remarks, *inter alia*, that Spengler (as well as Russell, Hertz, Schopenhauer, Boltzmann, Frege, Kraus, Loos, Weininger and Straffa) has influenced him (VB: 1931) and Drury notes that in the early 1930s Wittgenstein was recommending that he read the work.[4] Although rather sprawling and baroque, Spengler's classification, based upon Goethe, does contain germs that will later develop into Wittgenstein's *Weltanschauung/Weltbild* distinction. Amongst other things Spengler points out a difference between theorizing that 'atomizes' our perspective on the world and theorizing that takes a broader picture:

> The tendency of human thought (which is always causally disposed) to reduce the image of Nature to the simplest possible quantitative form-units that can be got by causal reasoning, measuring and counting – in a word, mechanical differentiation – leads necessarily in Classical, Western and every other possible physics, to an atomic theory. (Spengler 1926: 384)

This 'atomizing', scientistic tendency is contrasted with the '*Formgefühl und Weltgefühl des Erkennenden*' – 'The Form-feel and World-feel of the knower' (Spengler 1923: I.494):

> The thinker, in imagining that he can cut out the factor of Life, forgets that knowing is related to the known as direction is to extension and that it is only through the living quality of direction that what is felt extends into distance and depth and becomes space. (Spengler 1926: I.387)

From Spengler, then, Wittgenstein clearly takes the notion of 'seeing a whole' and 'forming connections' to make that whole. This is brought out in a passage from *Logik, Sprache, Philosophie*, the work on which Wittgenstein collaborated with Waismann:

> Our thought here matches with certain views of Goethe's which he expressed in the *Metamorphosis of Plants*. We are in the habit,

---

[4]See R. Rhees *Recollections of Wittgenstein* (Oxford: Oxford Paperback 1987), 128. However Wittgenstein also adds in his conversation: 'I don't trust Spengler about details. He is too often inaccurate. I once wrote that if Spengler had had the courage to write a very short book, it could have been a great one.'

whenever we perceive similarities, of seeking some common origin for them. The urge to follow such phenomena back to their origin in the past expresses itself in a certain style of thinking …

We are collating one form of language with its environment, or transforming it in imagination so as to gain a view of the whole of space in which the structure of our language has its being. (Waismann 1965: 80)

The *Übersichtliche Darstellung*, then, as Wittgenstein comes to formulate it in his later philosophy, is influenced by a Spenglerian/Goetherian 'taking an overview', that allows us to 'see the world aright'. Consequently Wittgenstein's philosophy 'leaves everything as it is'. Its aim, in his words, is 'to present everything before us' so that we can have a grasp of the *Weltbild* rather than the *Weltanschauung*.

Wittgenstein's distinction between *Weltbild* and *Weltanschauung* helps to clarify the point that Rank was trying to put across in his *Mental Hygiene Lecture* – that the psychological, or more specifically the psychotherapeutic, position is not another competing *Weltanschauung* in the competitive post-scientific marketplace but that it is essentially a fundamentally different *Weltbild* that makes us 'see the world aright'. These two perceptions Rank classifies as a 'battle' between two world views which, adds Rank, 'have been in conflict with one another since the dawn of science with the early Greeks and even long before' (Sp: 222). The scientific error, suggested Rank, was the 'glorification of consciousness, of intellectual knowledge', which even analysis 'worships as its highest god – although it calls itself a psychology of the *unconscious*' (Sp: 222). Again, Rank's insight here is instructive. From the beginnings of analysis Freud had sought to develop various meta-theories to account for the phenomena he had observed in the clinical setting. To account for the strange psychological phenomena that Freud was observing in his work he speculated that there was an 'unknown area' that lay beneath ordinary cognition: 'The Unknown Thing' or *Das Unbewusste* (usually translated into English as 'the unconscious'). As his career went on he changed and reconfigured his understanding of its contents, but essentially he saw this 'unknown area' as consisting of desires, wishes and impulses (*Trieben*), primordial and often destructive, arising from biological bases, especially of a sexual nature, and needing to disrupt the ordinary everyday function of self (Freud's *Ich*, normally translated as 'ego') in order for their wishes to prevail. The precise nature of these impulses remained vague, as did their origins. By definition, said Freud, we couldn't know what they were, but rather they were made manifest by strange quirks of everyday behaviour – the slip of the tongue, the dream, unexpected behaviour – all these revealed the true contents of the 'unknown area'.

From this it becomes clear that Freud's view of the mind is quite a dark one: we are in perpetual conflict. Or as he once said 'the I is not master in its own house' (*A Difficulty in the Path of Psycho-Analysis*, 1917). For over 200 years Western culture had promoted the idea of the mind being controlled by a 'rational self' from which all action and behaviour flowed. Freud's ideas turned this notion on its head. No longer the rational self, but an irrational, self-seeking, potentially murderous 'other' was constantly seeking to destroy the serenity of the known cognitive 'I'. Freud described this conflict as that between the rational conscious 'I' (*Ich*) and the darkly disturbing 'It' (*Es*) seeking its own satisfaction. From the 1920s onwards he added another layer – the 'Over-I' (*Über-Ich*) which we derive from the parental voice of early childhood – this voice seeks to help the 'I' in suppressing the 'It', but can make excessive demands of its own on the 'I' leading to another source of disturbance in the psyche. The aim of psychoanalysis becomes, then, the attempt to strengthen the 'I' in its struggle with the 'It' and 'Over-I' to allow for more strength to the self. As Freud famously put it in one of his last works: '*Wo Es war lass Ich werde*'/ 'Where "It" was, let "I" become' (*New Introductory Lectures*, 1933). In these lectures he compares the process of psychoanalysis to that of land reclamation of the Zyder Zee in his beloved Holland which he visited on holiday every year. That is, a breach is made into the sea of the unknown self, by dream analysis, word association, work with transference etc. and then, slowly, this breach is filled in as with rubble into the sea. Slowly the sea of unknowness is reclaimed for the solid ground of consciousness. This, as Rank saw it, was the essence of the model of analysis presented by Freud – one where an ethical 'I' or 'Over-I' would reclaim the self from the dark seething mass of the unconscious.[5]

Rank thus saw the Freudian project as one of subjection of the mass of the unconscious to the power of reasoned consciousness so that the unconscious is 'rationalized' and 'intellectualized scientifically'. For Rank the intellectualization of the person is one that can never achieve the goals that analysis, for example, seeks. This more ambiguous view of analysis was the

---

[5] In a recent excellent analysis of Freud, *Freud: The Reluctant Philosopher* (Princeton: Princeton University Press, 2010), Alfred Tauber makes a similar point as to the essentially moral and rational nature of Freud's programme: 'In an instrumental sense, reason becomes the tool by which humans become moral in each context – Kantian and Freudian … despite the deterministic character of the Freudian universe, he, like Spinoza before him, understood that personal insight and understanding constituted the basic freedom humans possess'. (p. 133).

one that Rank advocated and could be said to have triumphed after the fall of Freud's theories from grace in the 1980s and 1990s. In contrast to Freud's view of analysis, which in Rank's words seeks 'to control and predict human behaviour', Rank saw his own interpretation differently:

> Experience has taught me that understanding and explaining do not get you anywhere – unless it comes as a result of personal experience through suffering, which scientific ideology tries to spare the individual from childhood on. (Sp: 223)

Such a challenge to the hegemony that was developing in the nascent analytic community in the 1930s was swiftly dealt with, as we shall see shortly.

Thus, Rank's masterstroke was to take the arena of analysis (and indeed psychology) from that of the search for 'facts' about the *psyche* (or mind) to the world of interpretation. To use the Wittgensteinian language, the analyst lives in the realm of the *Weltbild* not *Weltanschauung*. Interpretation is all:

> (The patient's) whole adjustment or maladjustment, his whole attitude toward the world, depends upon his interpretation of himself, rather than upon himself – in other words, not so much on what he is but upon what he thinks he is, or what he wants to be, or what he would like to be, or what other people want him to be, and so forth. (YL: 245)

Following this line of argument, and referring back to the models of *psyche* with which we began, the therapist, counsellor or spiritual director is therefore not a second-rate scientist or empiricist but is working from a different 'world view' (or better, *Weltbild*). One, as Wittgenstein states, where 'all possible world views' are held in balance. The therapist is allowed an insight into all world views and then presents them to the listener. For both Wittgenstein and Rank the practice of counselling and therapy is unlike other modes of healing, in particular, scientific based modes. After Rank's split with the powers of psychoanalysis in the 1930s he will increasingly use the terminology of 'the soul' to identify this healing mode. As he put it in *Psychology and the Soul*:

> Psychology can be seen as a mutual reflexive phenomenon, a mirage of our true self that we glimpse only in the mirroring reflection of another soul. (PS: 7)

The soul had indeed returned to the modern world …

The interpretation of Freud

Rank's conflict with the nascent powers of psychoanalysis at the Mental Hygiene Congress in 1930 was not untypical of the twists and turns of interpretation that Freud's work was subject to, even while he was alive. Bettleheim, in his *Freud and Man's Soul* (1982/2001), famously explored how the English translation of Freud's work had created a certain Anglo-Saxon tone somewhat alien to the thrust of the German original. As he stated 'the English translations of Freud's writings distort much of the essential humanism that permeates the originals' (Bettleheim 1982: 4). He stressed that Freud himself wrote clearly and elegantly on his themes, and one of the sources of the later success of his work undoubtedly lay in his finely wrought German prose style. By the 1920s his fame had spread across Europe, as well as his notoriety, and in Britain there was the desire to have English versions of his writings available. The task of translating this work fell to a member of the Bloomsbury group – James Strachey (1887–1967) – brother of the famous Bloomsbury aesthete Lytton Strachey, who had sought analysis himself with Freud in Vienna. Because of Freud's scandalous reputation (his writings on sexuality had earned him a certain notoriety in Vienna), Strachey felt it necessary to medicalize and imperson-alize Freud's prose as much as possible to make it more acceptable to the scientific and medical communities in Britain.[6] Thus, whenever Strachey was faced with Freud's terms for the mind and the apparatus of psycho-analysis – and Freud, like Wittgenstein, would usually resort at this point to commonplace terms in ordinary language use – Strachey preferred to invent Greek or Latin equivalents that sounded a little more medical or specialized. Thus, as we have seen, whenever Freud refers to the components of the self: *Ich, Es* and *Über-Ich* (literally 'I', 'It' and 'Over-I' as I have rendered them above), Strachey uses the terms 'ego', 'id' and 'superego'. That this went against Freud's own mind on the matter can be seen in his defence of the use of simple pronouns in his *The Question of Lay Analysis*:

> You will probably protest at our having chosen simple pronouns to describe our two agencies or provinces (of the soul) instead of giving

---

[6] Strachey's 24 Volume *Standard Edition of the Complete Psychological Works of Sigmund Freud* appeared between 1953 and 1974 published by the Hogarth Press and now published by Penguin. Most of Strachey's editorial choices were taken up by later editors and created the climate by which Freud's works were, and still are, discussed in the English-speaking world.

them sonorous Greek names.[7] In psycho-analysis, however, we like to keep in contact with the popular mode of thinking and prefer to make its concepts scientifically serviceable rather than to reject them. There is no merit in this; we are obliged to take this line; for our theories must be understood by our patients, who are often very intelligent, but not always learned. The impersonal 'it' is immediately connected with certain forms of expression used by normal people. One is apt to say, for example, 'It came to me in a flash; there was something in me which, at that moment, was stronger than me.' (GW: 14.219)

Strachey's tendency to invent Greek or Latin equivalents for Freud's terms created a whole new raft of technical language whilst at the same time introducing a new level of complexity to the simplicity of Freud's approach. The 'slip of the tongue' (*Fehlleistung*) becomes 'the parapraxis' and the 'unknown thing' itself becomes the more familiar 'unconscious'.

Nowhere is this shift more apparent, argues Bettleheim, than in the translations of Freud's terms for the self as a whole. For here (as Rank understood) Freud's preferred terms are *die Seele, seelische* and *Seelenleben*, literally, 'the soul', 'soulish' and 'soul-life', all of which Strachey replaces with 'the mind', 'mental' and 'mental life'. The effect of this, argues Bettleheim, is to replace Freud's 'direct and always deeply personal appeals to our common humanity' with 'abstract, highly theoretical, erudite and mechanized – in short, "scientific" – statements about the strange and very complex workings of our mind' (Bettleheim 1982: 5). This was again the critique brought by Otto Rank against the Mental Hygiene Congress in 1930. Psychoanalysis, argues Bettleheim, thus becomes 'a purely intellectual system – a clever, exciting game' rather than the invitation to explore the richness and darkness of the individual soul-life.[8] Freud's own vision for the future of the modality he had initiated was neither a profession in hock to the scientific-medical establishment (hence his defence of non-medically trained analysts in *The Question of Lay Analysis*, 1926) nor a form of life

---

[7] In Strachey's translation for the *Standard Edition* 'of the soul' (*seelische*) is omitted: '*Sie werden es wahrscheinlich beanständen, daß wir zur Bezeichnung unserer beiden seelischen Instanzen oder Provinzen einfache Fürwörter gewählt haben, anstatt vollautende griechische Namen für sie einzuführen*' (GW: 14.219).

[8] Perhaps this may no longer be the case with psychoanalytic training but it is sadly all too apparent still amongst university graduates wanting to apply post-Freudian concepts to academic arguments, often without recourse to personal analysis or experience of the terms explored by Freud ...

dominated by the clergy and religious ways of thinking (hence the genesis of his *The Future of an Illusion*, 1927). As he wrote to Oskar Pfister in 1928:

> I do not know whether you have guessed the hidden link between 'Lay Analysis' and 'Illusion'. In the former I want to protect analysis from the doctors, and in the latter from the priests. I want to hand it over to a profession that does not yet exist, a profession of secular ministers of souls (*weltlichen Seelsorgern*), who don't have to be doctors and must not be priests. (Letter to Oskar Pfister 25.11.1928)[9]

Thus, the battle for Freud's soul – or more specifically his translation of *Seele* – can be seen in the wider context of the battle for the soul of analysis: whether it was to become a medically or clerically dominated profession or neither. As he wrote to Pfister in 1909: 'In itself psychoanalysis is neither religious nor non-religious, but an impartial tool which both the spiritual and layman (*der Geistliche wie der Laie*) can use in the service of the sufferer' (Letter to Pfister 9.2.1909). Freud was particularly aware in this context of the American tendency to 'turn psychoanalysis into a mere housemaid of psychiatry' (Bettleheim 1982: 36), the exact process that Rank observed in 1930. Rank, like Bettleheim, will emphasize the 'descent to the dark realm of the mothers' (see Tyler 2014) that they perceived as lying at the heart of the Freudian project rather than the intellectual (or 'cultural') work of the reclamation of the Zyder Zee of the Id by the nobly battling Ego. Rather, as I have already suggested, Rank and Bettleheim's Freudianism is one that leads us to the dark realms within where the unambiguous triumph of reason and Enlightenment Values is not a foregone conclusion. Oskar Pfister, the Swiss Protestant pastor with whom Freud corresponded most of his life, put it succinctly in one of his letters:

> Your substitute for religion is basically the idea of the 18th Century Enlightenment met in a proud modern guise. I must confess that, with all my pleasure in the advance of science and technology, I do not believe in the adequacy and sufficiency of this solution of the problem of life. (Pfister to Freud, 24.11.1927)

The truth, as is usually the case with any interpretation of Freud, Freudianism and psychoanalysis, no doubt lies somewhere between the two. Yet the

---

[9] '*Einem Stand von weltlichen Seelsorgern, die Ärzte nicht zu sein brauche und Priesten nicht sein dürfen.*'

ambiguity in Freud's own terminology allowed two opposing interpretations to arise which, for Bettleheim and Rank at least, became enshrined in their fervent wish to retain the 'soulish' element in Freud's work. For these two followers of Freud the retention of the word 'soul' was not an irrelevance but went to the heart of their respective interpretations of his work and the damage done, as they perceived it, to his legacy by an unhealthy over-emphasis on the medico-scientific gloss on his work.[10] For Bettleheim, there is no reason for the (mis-)translation of Freud's *Seele* by 'mind' apart from 'a wish to interpret psychoanalysis as a medical speciality' (1982: 76). And his retention of the word 'soul' in his interpretation of Freud preserves for him two facets of Freud's project lost by the over-emphasis on 'mind': the need to emphasize the spiritual and emotional aspects of the analytic journey. As we saw with Rank, Bettleheim's main bone of contention with the mistranslations was the tendency to over-emphasize the rational, conscious Freud at the expense of the unconscious, irrational (and frankly spiritual) Freud:

> Freud uses *Seele* and *seelisch* rather than *geistig* because *geistig* refers mainly to the rational aspects of the mind, to that of which we are conscious. The idea of the soul, by contrast, definitely includes much of which we are not consciously aware. (1982: 77)

By not providing us with a precise definition of 'soul', argues Bettleheim, Freud is deliberately reflecting the ambiguous nature of the *psyche* itself. Thus Bettleheim's 'soul' is a cipher for all that is ambiguous and indecipherable in the *psyche*. It is, as I have stated elsewhere, a call to the 'unknowing' that lies at the heart of the *psyche* and psychological life. Yet Bettleheim's definition or rendering of 'soul' remains somewhat crude. Decrying any Platonic notion of immortality his 'soul' is still very much an 'it'; though 'intangible', 'it is deeply hidden, hardly accessible even to careful

---

[10] Darius Gray Ornston in a perceptive essay (Ornston 1992) skilfully deconstructs some of Bettleheim's harsher criticisms of Strachey, and latterly Anna Freud. If, as I suggest here, Rank and Bettleheim lay bare differing interpretations that reflect the ambiguity in Freud's own text then Ornston and Bettleheim would of course both be 'correct'. As with much of my text I want to observe how various authors have used the term 'soul', often to their own ends, and will suggest at the end of my text the usage which I probably find most useful at the present time. This however will no doubt prove as ephemeral and ultimately distracting as most of the other definitions explored during this book. Such a judgement is for posterity.

investigation ... but it nevertheless exercises a powerful influence on our lives' (1982: 77/8); what this 'it' is, Bettleheim demurs from explaining.

Rank's soul

'Soul' and 'soulish', *Seele* and *seelische*, were therefore terms of utmost importance for Rank's exposition of the nature of the *psyche* and the life of the individual.[11] As he wrote at the beginning of *Seelenglaube und Psychologie* (literally, 'Soul-belief and Psychology', published in 1930, the year of his fateful lecture to the Mental Health Congress): 'To write a history of psychology is to write a history of the soul' (SP: 1). For him psychology is nothing less than *Seelekunde* – a difficult phrase to translate – a 'service of/ witness to the soul'. In choosing to base his analysis (and much, as we have seen, of his later work) around the term *soul*, Rank was deliberately pointing out the fact that we have explored already in this chapter – that psychology cannot simply be considered an empirical science, rather the philosophical, or indeed we might say, the metaphysical, is as important in considering the *psyche* as the empirical. Thus the term 'soul' becomes for Rank a cipher to widen the ambit of psychology to take in artistic, creative and philosophical reflection on the self as well as the straightforwardly empirical.

Rank had first begun to enunciate his views on *das seelische* a few years before the Mental Health lecture in works such as *Beyond Psychoanalysis* (1928).[12] Here he suggests that the chief discovery of analysis has been the rediscovery of the 'soul-life' (*das seelische Leben*) of the patient.[13] This, Rank argues, analysis has tried to understand 'scientifically from a materialistic point of view' (BePs: 228), which he argues can never succeed, as the problems besetting patients cannot be resolved entirely on the biological level. Equally, the attempt by analysis to reduce the patient's soul-life to 'their past' will not succeed. Whereas Rank accepts the importance of biological explanations of the patient's life, he wants to suggest that biology

---

[11] Kramer in his translation of Rank's American lectures is a little more positivistic: 'the word *seelischer* has no English equivalent. By *seelischer*, usually translated as "psychical", Rank means four interrelated psychical, or, what we now call psychological phenomena: consciousness, emotional experience, feeling and willing' (Kramer 1996: 104 n.1). I hope the present chapter will restore 'the soulish' as understood by Rank to its rightful place in the psychological lexicon.

[12] Presented to the Boston Society of Psychiatry and Neurology in April 1928.

[13] Once again we encounter problems with the translation here. Kramer renders it 'the emotional life' or 'the psychical' in his translation of the lecture.

on its own is *insufficient*; the therapist rather needs to approach the problem of the patient as much *philosophically* as *biologically* (BePs: 228). Having reduced the biological to its secondary role in explanation, Rank goes on to disagree with Freud's choice of the sex-drive as 'supposed to explain everything entirely':

> Thus Freud has dethroned medical materialism with regard to the so-called neuroses, but what we really want to thank him for is that he failed in the attempt to set up in its place the purely biological – and so, involuntarily, has brought the real *seelische* into its own again. (BePs: 229)

In this respect Rank again applauds Freud for reintroducing the *mythic* element into our comprehension of the *seelische* – for, as Rank suggests, Plato also knew – the mythic is the proper discourse for the soul (BePs: 229). As I have already argued above, psychology does not deal with facts, but with the *interpretation* of facts; this is no better shown than in the dream interpretation:

> In the dream we ourselves interpret physical and psychical states (facts), but this 'interpretation' is as little 'analysis' of 'facts' as is our analytic 'interpretation', which represents only another kind of symbolization and rationalization. (BePs: 230)

Hence the analytical situation (what Rank calls 'the analysis of analysis') becomes an arena for the love emotion and the ethical gaze of the therapist to the client and vice versa – this is for him *das seelische*:

> While the mechanism of being in love can be studied in the patient's I, the ethical element cannot be developed without analysis and the *other* person – which in the analytical situation is the analyst. (BePs: 231)

From this 'I-psychology' and 'You-psychology' (as he designates the love and ethical phases) arises the truth not just of analysis, but existence itself:

> The only 'trueness' in terms of actual *seelische* reality is found in emotion, not in thinking, which at best denies or rationalizes truth, and not necessarily in action unless it follows from feeling and is in harmony with it. (TR: 40)

The 'love life' (see *The Significance of the Love Life* 1927), for example, is a particularly acute example of the *seelische*, and is a particular arena that the analysis is peculiarly equipped to work with. For analysis, ultimately for Rank, is 'at bottom a love therapy' (WT: 20). The therapist re-enacts the parental relationship, but with more love and less fear than the child/patient experienced.

The analysis of analysis

The discovery of this *seelische* reality is complicated by the fact that in their varying interpretations the analysts themselves shape the discourse of the patient. A Freudian patient, suggests Rank, will become acquainted with the mechanics of libido theory, castration complex, Oedipal complex and so on and so start to use this terminology in their responses to their analyst so that 'the analyst will praise or blame him according to whether he correctly handled the theoretical grammar or used correctly the necessary vocabulary' (BePs: 233). Similarly, the Jungian patient will understand their therapeutic interpretation in terms of Jungian typology, the Adlerian by the social element and so on. For 'the cultured patient of today already knows a little about analysis before he comes for analysis' (BePs: 233). Such analytical interpretation can thus lead the patient *away* from the *seelische*, especially with the unconscious cognitive connivance of the analyst. Thus, in contrast to Freud and the early fathers of analysis, Rank was one of the first psychologists to recognize the ready ease with which patients could slip into the 'psychologese' of their analysts (or indeed from the general media). Now if this was true in 1930 how much more true must it be today! Indeed, suggests Rank, some clients 'suffer from too much introspection' (YL: 244) and more analysis may indeed by detrimental: 'they need something else. They need a *seelische* experience' (YL: 244) – indeed he suggests that too much consciousness may therefore be a bad thing! Only the emotional experience (*Gefühlserlebnis*) of the *seelische* can correct this unhealthy introspection (see WT: 55) – this *Gefühlserlebnis* will also by necessity lie close to the roots of creativity.

The *seelische Leben* is thus 'the real driving force' of the personality 'reaching with its roots into the depth of the unconscious' (PG: 60) and is really a corrective to over-dependence on the logical, empirical and conscious. Therefore, the relationship with the client is more important than any interpretation (PG: 64, PS: 2). Rank therefore considered 'psychology to be a science of relations and inter-relations ... a science of relativity' (YL: 245), thus the need in Rank's view of analysis for there to be an 'active' and dynamic relationship with the patient (as opposed to Freud's 'indifference'/'*Indifferenz*').[14] For, as also acknowledged by Ferenczi, the analytic situation is one that is mutually creative between patient and analyst and by moving beyond the focus on the biological Rank thus creates a space in therapy for a true creative relationship between the participants. It is no coincidence that the first book Rank wrote having met Freud was *The Artist* in which he emphasized the importance of the development of the creative personality (see YL: 242).

The creative life-force of the soul

Thus we see in Rank's *seelische* – the soul-life – a creed of spontaneity and desire to return to contact with the source (libidinal?) root of existence. Similar views were expressed by Freud and Jung in the early years of their collaboration before their split before the First World War. Both founding fathers of analysis realized that psychology went beyond the mere empirical to such an extent that it touched the hem of religious and spiritual yearnings. As Jung wrote to Freud in 1910:

> Religion can be replaced only by religion. Is there perchance a new saviour in the International Fraternity – we need the eternal truth of myth. (Jung to Freud 11.11.1910)

Despite Rank's later suspicion of Jung's agenda, Rank's *seelische* can thus be seen as a sort of distant cousin of the young Freud and Jung's libidinal – it is really a form of Nietzsche's life-force.[15]

As well as libidinal, it is non-cognitive, going, as it were, *under* the cognitive radar to present the patient with the unmediated or raw taste of the reality they are living. Thus, Rank's approach to psychology 'having overcome materialistic, ethical and social ideologies' (BePs: 234) would construct a 'metapsychoanalytical psychology' which would open up the possibility of the *seelische*, which from this perspective will shine back a

---

[14] 'The doctor should be opaque to his patients and, like a mirror, should show them nothing but what is shown to him' (SE: 12.115).

[15] We shall return to this in the following chapter.

mirror on the 'biological, ethical and social aspects of psychology' – essentially then a 'philosophic theory of cognition' (BePs: 234). The analyst thus becomes an artist who participates in and prompts the creative life of the patient by allowing a space for the *seelische* to emerge (YL: 244). In works such as *Will Therapy* (1936) he emphasized the *technique* of the analyst rather than any particular *theory* they might hold so that by concentrating on the personal interaction in the here and now a direct route is thus made to the libidinal sources of the unconscious:

> The therapist should learn, therefore, not definite rules and prescriptions, tricks and catches, general theories and typical interpretations, no definite theory and technique of psychoanalysis but to analyze, which means, in my opinion, the understanding and handling of the therapeutic situation. (WT: 5)[16]

Yet what Rank had done was simply to spot what Wittgenstein had also contemporaneously tried to articulate in his own philosophical psychology and is being explored throughout this book – the unique nature of the human *psyche* and how it resists the clean lines and delineations of any pseudo-scientific investigation.

Condemnation of Rank

Rank's genius was to perceive the essentially ascientific nature of Freud's work.[17] As we have seen his exegesis of Freud takes Freud's *seelische* and brings it to a position not so distant from that of the early Christian and Platonic writers we discussed in the earlier chapters. As he put it:

> The scientific approach – with its artificial emphasis on *one* truth and its aim to control and to predict – strives ultimately only for security, but it is a false security that does not do away with the cosmic fear of the individual and hence does not make us any more happy. (Sp: 223)

His tragedy was to enunciate this interpretation to a nascent Freudian world that saw itself as pursuing an essentially scientific approach. Beginning

---

[16] In this and other passages Rank still often makes a strong dichotomy between the inner 'soulful' and the outer world (p. 235), a division, which we shall see later, that distinguishes his work very clearly from that of Wittgenstein (see PS: 3).

[17] 'The basic problem of all psychology: is it physics or metaphysics?' (SP: 6).

with the publication of his *The Trauma of Birth* (1924), the problem would come to a head after he had delivered his 1930 speech at the Congress of Mental Hygiene in Washington. Despite a stirring speech of support from his follower, Jessie Taft, the majority of the convention was unsettled and unhappy with Rank's speech. Mary Chadwick, a Fellow of the British College of Nurses who spoke next, expressed incredulity at hearing Rank's words and made a plea to the convention (referring to Aladdin) not to discard the lamp of Freudianism for the false light of Rank's approach (see Liebermann 1985: 291). She was followed by A. A. Brill, President of the American Psychoanalytic Association, who in his general denigration of Rank's talk added:

> I was particularly impressed by one remark of Dr Rank's – namely that he is no longer a psychoanalyst. I have known that for some time, but I have never heard him say it before … I feel all the stuff to which Dr Rank treated us this morning is but an indication of his own present maladjustment. … My feeling about Dr Rank is that it is this emotional upheaval that is responsible for his present confusion.
> (Liebermann 1985: 291)

Later that day Brill would put forward a motion to the Congress (seconded by Harry Stack Sullivan) that Otto Rank be removed from the roll of honorary members of the American Psychoanalytic Association. Not only was Rank removed from recognition by the association, but anyone who had been analysed by him had to go through a second new analysis if they were to be readmitted to the association. In Liebermann's words: 'the Rankian Heresy would be expunged at any cost' (1985: 293). The mirror that Rank held up to Freud and the Freudians cast too strong a light. Rank really had shone a light on Freudianism (Aladdinesque or not), but unfortunately Freudianism was too young and vulnerable to accept the vision of Freud that he presented them with.

Conclusion: The return of the soul to psychology

I have argued in this chapter that Rank's work essentially reflects the ambiguity that lies in Freud's writings (and indeed in 'Freudianism'). On the one hand Freud throws open the 'royal road to the unconscious' with all its darkness and ambiguity. But, on the other hand, Freud, the nineteenth century ethical master, decries the control of the 'It' over the conscious rational 'I' and sees the need to continue the 'cultural work' of the reclamation of the Zyder Zee. As Rank put it in *Psychology and the Soul*:

> Recognizing the unconscious, Freud acknowledged the soul; but by explaining the soul materialistically, he denied it … The soul is neither brain function, as modern neurology believes, nor sublimated biological drives, as Freud conceived it. (PS: 3)

It is on precisely this watershed between ethical confrontation and unconscious descent that Rank's work hovers and caused him so much trouble in his lifetime. Knowing that there is a dark 'realm' in the unconscious is one thing, but wanting to plunge into it and explore it is another.[18] If, as Rank saw, this is a problem in early Freudianism, how much more of a problem will it become to us the sons and daughters (and grandsons and granddaughters) of Freud? How far might we simply 'blame the unconscious' and how far must we take ethical decisions to counter the effects of the darker realms? In many respects it is the old debate between free-will and determinism given a new postmodern, twenty-first century twist.

Thus the 'soulish' for Rank emphasizes the art of interpretation through relationship: 'psychology is no science in the sense of physics or biology, but a science of relationship (*Beziehungswissenschaft*). It is not an interpretation of facts (like physics or biology) but an interpretation of attitudes to oneself (*sonder Interpretation von Einstellungen des eigenen Selbst*) which in so-called objective psychology we project onto others. Psychology is self-interpretation through others, just as physics is self-interpretation through nature' (SP: 193).

As psychology expands, suggests Rank (SP: 7), so does the realm of the *soulish* diminish. For 'the true object of psychology was originally something supernatural and beyond the human (*Aussermenschliche*): *die Seele*' (SP: 7, my translation) and 'the person became the object of psychological interest and investigation only when the original soul-concept faded from consciousness'. No great friend of religion, Rank concludes that 'religion was and is as much psychology as our modern scientific

---

[18] 'Deep down, we don't want to observe ourselves and increase self-knowledge. First of all, the search for self-knowledge is not an original part of our nature; second, it is painful; and finally, it doesn't always help but often is disturbing' (PS: 5). Perhaps, as he suggests in his last work *Beyond Psychology*, the rational desire to control the unconscious (to reclaim the Zyder Zee) is a 'fear of the life-force itself' (BP: 277).

psychology is, unavoidably, soul study (*eine Seelenlehre*)'. Thus psychology is for Rank a gradual evolution or loss of soul that was first and foremost expressed in religious terms: 'psychology gradually evolved by denying and rejecting its first object, the soul' (SP: 8). Psychology, suggests Rank, will inevitably ignore the soul and all its 'contradictions and irrationalities' (PS: 9) for 'man, being a theological rather than a biological being, never lives on a purely natural plane' (BP: 196).

In summary, Rank seemed perturbed by the outlines in the mud of the unconscious left by the receding tide of religious consciousness. This is what he termed 'the soul'/'the soulish'. Even if he had been a great advocate of religion (which he wasn't), there seems no great desire in Rank's writing to restore religion to its former importance in the intellectual and psychological life of his contemporaries.[19] Rather, it was as though we could follow the demands of the soul by descending further into the unconscious. Unlike Jung in the letter quoted earlier, Rank was always alert to psychology's pretensions towards overcoming religion and realized ultimately this goal would be unachievable:

> Psychology, which gradually displaced religious and moral ideologies, cannot fully replace them, for it is a negative, destructive ideology – an ideology of resentment in Nietzsche's sense. (PS: 126)

Not surprisingly, considering what he had experienced between the psychological schools and the Nazis, Rank concluded in 1939, on the eve of World War Two, that human behaviour was essentially irrational despite all the best attempts of psychology to provide it with a rational basis (BP: 11). Human nature 'lies beyond any psychology, individual or collective' (BP: 12). Such irrationality, by definition, cannot be caught in the rational net of language thus leading Rank to return to the need for the creative artist to express that which is beyond the rational. Six months after writing this final credo in *Beyond Psychology*, Rank was dead:

> Man is born beyond psychology and he dies beyond it but he can live beyond it only though vital experience of his own – in religious terms, through revelation, conversion or re-birth. (BP: 16)

---

[19] 'For the Church and liberalism are incompatible, and the Hierarchy of the Catholic Church, with the doctrine of the Infallibility of the Pope (re-stated in 1870), is more akin to the Hierarchy of Dictatorship' (BP: 194).

For Rank, the whole edifice of Freudian psychology was based on a flight from the 'life-force' as, through rationalization, the Zyder Zee of the unconscious is corralled. This itself was based on *interpretation*, even though Freud claimed to be dealing with *facts*. Such a misunderstanding leads to the building up of the whole edifice of psychology which he effectively at the end characterized as the 'flight from the soul'.[20] Thus, the 'return of the soul' was not just an intellectual exercise for Rank but one that lay at the necessary heart of the healing of Western culture. Freud's real achievement for Rank was the establishment of the analytical situation itself 'in which we can find epitomized the paradoxical workings of all the irrational forces in human nature' (BP: 278), which, in itself, is sufficient, providing we do not get lured into the rationalized, pseudo-scientific theories that Freud projects onto his material.[21] Freud's mistake, for Rank, was to not realize that the patient was already conscious of the material but had not chosen to verbalize it.[22] Therefore consciousness and unconsciousness are not static states of mind (with a supposed causality) but rather a *function* of the constantly changing and fluid dynamic *psyche* ('In *seelische* life, there is no one stable viewpoint, as such', WT: 30). Rank's view of analysis is one that must explore the irrational arena of the *psyche* without the moralizing rationality of Freud's ethical construct. This will be for Rank the therapy of the future: a 'soulish' therapy that will not just admit 'our basic primitivity' (BP: 289) but allow dynamic expression of it in the practice of analysis. This dynamic balancing of the rational and irrational elements in the human psyche will be the ultimate goal of 'soul-therapy'. Such a therapy will mean we shall ultimately be able to live in the present with all its contradictory and confusing emotional pulls:

---

[20] 'For (Freud's) psychology is born of the spirit of inhibited and inhibiting negation of life and as such does not lead to life' (BP: 278). In Freud's defence, the founder of analysis in works such as *The Question of Lay Analysis* does intimate at the provisional and occasional nature of all psychoanalytic findings: '*In der Psychologie können wir nur mit Hilfe von Vergleichungen beschreiben*' – 'In psychology we can only describe things by the help of analogies' (GW: 14.219, SE: 20.193).

[21] And as such Rank here prefigures the work of late twentieth century practitioners such as R. D. Laing who argued that the labelling of 'neurotic' or 'psychotic' was as much social (and perhaps arbitrary) as social norms demanded: 'There really is no psychology of the neurotic as opposed to normal psychology, but only a psychology of difference, that is to say, the neurotic's psychology is only pathological from the rational point of view prevalent in a given civilization' (BP: 280).

[22] 'It is astonishing how much the patient knows and how relatively little is unconscious if one does not give this convenient excuse for refusing responsibility' (WT: 24). 'The verbalizing itself, not the explanation or interpretation, is the specifically therapeutic agent in the sphere of consciousness' (WT: 23).

What the individual does not know and will not know, is never the past but the present, the momentary emotional matrix which is perceived by the will as weakness and is denied accordingly ...

(My therapy) allows the patient to understand himself in an immediate situation which, as I strive for it in therapeutic process, permits living and understanding to become one. As far as I know, this is the first time in the history of mankind, where we find a striving for an immediate understanding of experience, consciously, in the very act of experiencing. (WT: 26/27)

With this concentration on the present, the dynamic active nature of the patient and the development of will held together in the development of *creativity,* we have the essence of Rank's approach to therapy (see MP: 268).

Although non-theological in nature, Rank's 'return of the soul' suggested an alternative future for nascent twentieth century psychology. Just as we saw in Part I, early psychology had to make similar decisions. Like Origen and Evagrius, Rank too would ultimately be declared heretical in these formative years.

Although he rarely quotes Rank, we find a similar solution to a perceived impasse in the course of psychology in another psychological heretic – this time of the Jungian school. And it is to James Hillman and the Jungian soul that we turn in the next chapter.

CHAPTER 6
THE SOUL-MAKING OF JAMES HILLMAN: THE RETURN OF THE REPRESSED?

The heretic trickster

Variously accused of 'intellectual brilliance, subtlety and elusiveness, tricksterism, self-contradiction and moments of silliness' and being a 'dedicated subversive' (see Tacey 1998: 215 and Kidel 2011), James Hillman (1926–2011) was one of the most colourful and controversial followers of Carl Jung. From an 'orthodox' Jungian background (he was the Director of Studies at the C. G. Jung Institute in Zurich after the founder's death), like Rank he slowly moved away from psychoanalytic orthodoxy, conceiving new ways of conceptualizing human selfhood whilst at the same time facing the limitations of analysis and psychology itself. The titles of some of his last books, including *We've Had a Hundred Years of Psychotherapy and the World's Getting Worse* (Hillman 1992), reveal Hillman's increasing disillusionment with the psychological establishment and his need to articulate fresh ways of describing the search for the self. At the end of the second millennium, for Hillman, psychology had become obsessed with materialist, reductive and individualist solutions that were destabilizing not only to individuals but to society in general. He was particularly fond of targeting the medical paradigm for treating mental problems and challenged this approach at every opportunity. From the point of view of our study here what is interesting is that Hillman, like Rank, returned to the language of 'soul-making' to clothe his critiques. Unlike Rank, however, who left very little in the way of a 'school' or impact on wider culture Hillman's notion of soul has had a large, and very diverse, impact on a variety of cultural and psychological approaches (see, *inter alia*, Davis 2003; Zoja 2005). At the time of writing, within five years of Hillman's death, there seems to be no let-up of interest in his work and legacy which seems set to continue well into the future. Accordingly, in this chapter I will examine some of the uses to which Hillman puts the term 'soul', in particular examining his somewhat pointed critique of its use in the Christian tradition, before considering how useful, if at all, his analysis will be for the future discussion of 'soul' – particularly in Christian circles.

As with most of the analysts we have discussed in this book, it is difficult to take one 'moment', 'theory' or 'glimpse' that encapsulates the whole of Hillman's thought and work. Like Freud, Jung, Wittgenstein and Rank (to say nothing of Origen, Plato and Augustine) Hillman changed his aim throughout his life as he sought a moving target. Tacey in his perceptive analysis of Hillman's work (Tacey 1998) isolates four epochs in Hillman's work: from the 1950s to the late 1960s he was a conventional Jungian analyst (leading, as stated, the C. G. Jung Institute's study programme in Zurich). Leaving Zurich in the late 1960s he began a career as a 'post-Jungian' developing his own new theory of 'archetypal psychology' primarily within the academic setting. Unhappy with the academic world he launched out in the early 1980s into 'ecopsychology' that sought to widen his insights in psychology to the whole world, especially through the neo-Platonic notion of the 'World Soul'. Tacey suggests that from the early 1990s he moves beyond psychology to become a popular writer with 'little concern for scholarly impact' (1998: 215). This, we can assume, encapsulates the late period of Hillman taking in the popular success of his *The Soul's Code: In Search of Character and Calling* (1996), appearances on the Oprah Winfrey show and the embrace of the new medium of the internet.[1]

For the purposes of this chapter I shall concentrate on his work from the late first period and second period of his career in my analysis of his writing on 'soul' and 'soul-making'. Here Hillman develops his notion of 'soul-language' whilst still being comfortable to elaborate his views in an academically rounded fashion. Unlike Tacey, who concludes his survey by suggesting that Hillman effectively re-invented himself every decade, I would rather argue that the groundwork of his theories (with all their strengths and inconsistencies) was largely constructed by the late 1970s and a lot of the subsequent course of his career and its influences are logical consequences of the positions essayed during that formative period. Accordingly, I shall draw in particular on the works of that decade in presenting Hillman's vision of the soul.

From the late 1960s onwards Hillman's avowed aim was to restore *psyche* to psychology. It will probably not surprise us then, following the discussion

---

[1] The posthumous publication of Hillman's commentary on Jung's *Red Book* and its scholarly interview with Sonu Shamdasani suggests a return to serious academic concerns towards the end of his life, albeit still in the mischievous iconoclastic style for which he was famous (Hillman 2013).

in Part I of this book, that his *fons et origo* for this pursuit lay in early Greek philosophy and, of course, Plato. As he stated in the 1992 Preface to the revised edition of *Revisioning Psychology*, his aim would be:

> To restore the mythical perspective to depth psychology by recog-nising the soul's intrinsic affinity with, nay love for, the Gods … Or, as the Greeks may have said, to reaffirm the tragic connection between the mortal and the immortal, that natural plight of the soul that lies at the base of any psychology claiming to speak of psyche. (RVP: xi)

This 'return to the Gods' he characterizes as 'soul-making' which, for him, must lie at the heart of psychology. Not only psychology but academia too, he argued, have stolen the 'soul' from 'psychology':

> When psychology becomes a specialism and the psyche is set forth in an academic textbook, the soul disappears. When the soul is taken over by the university in the secular spirit of enlightenment, it loses all actuality, all substance, and all relevance for life. Thus academic psychology has been a psychology without soul from the beginning. (MA: 130)

Indeed, he suggests, the true history of the soul cannot take place in univer-sities and college-centred psychology courses. Only on the wild frontier of analysis can soul-making really happen. Thus as the scientific secular investigation of the psyche advanced so the true nature of soul became more hidden, for 'the Age of Reason had reached its last borders: the borders of reason itself, the mind and its own darkness' (MA: 137). That which reason could not comprehend, suggests Hillman, would be classified as the 'unconsious', the 'insane', the 'irrational' ('One might have called Uranus or Neptune "non-Saturn" or Australia "un-Asia"', MA: 138). The symbolic, imaginative and mythic had, for Hillman, been consigned by the early fathers of psychology (such as W. Griesinger, E. Kraepelin and H. Maudsley) to the negative or shadow side of the rational conscious with the concom-itant 'un-' and 'in-' prefixes. Thus, Hillman's psychology will re-divinize the unconscious. By 'en-souling' it, by bringing the pagan deities back within their rightful realm, he will allow the true nature of the soul to reveal itself:

> The term 'unconscious' is suitable for describing states where consciousness is not present – coma, for instance; but to use the word

for the imaginal region, for morally inferior or culturally ignorant behaviour, for instinctual release reactions, and for a causal agent who 'sends' dreams and to which one can turn to ask an opinion, is an erosion of categories. To personify it and regard it as one's inhibitory daimonic voice, or totem animal, or *familiaris* is not merely superstitious. Such habits are sacrilegious, because they deprive the Gods of their due. (MA: 174)

So Hillman will replace the Freudian and Jungian reification of 'the unconscious' with 'the Gods' (primarily of Ancient Greece) that he sees as the fount of psychic activity (in *Re-Visioning Psychology* he calls this the 'return to Greece'). Drawing on Yates' 1966 *The Art of Memory*, Hillman connects his programme to the Renaissance development of memory by creating 'an inner temple of fantasy' in which stood 'statues of mythical figures' (MA: 178) where 'the principles of the imagination used as universals for this system were mainly the Gods and heroes and themes of classical mythology, the pagan pantheon, sometimes expressed as zodiacal constellations'.

Already it will be clear from these quotations that we are dealing with no ordinary clinical psychologist. As well as soul/*psyche*, Hillman drew on a whole panoply of early Greek terms to colour his increasingly popular books, internet interviews and celebrity chats, most of which we have already encountered in Part I of this book. Thus the *daimones*, tragedy, katharsis, the World Soul and indeed the Greek gods themselves (all with a clear neo-Platonic provenance) all make an appearance in his writing in all their polytheistic glory. As stated above, Hillman is in many ways representative of a whole 'soul-movement' that has arisen in psychology over the past two decades. Bearing in mind Tacey's critique of Hillman ('Although there is intellectual energy and vigour to be gained from swinging from one extreme to another, Hillman's reversals and contradictions do not inspire confidence in his work', Tacey 1998: 230), I do not intend here to steer a path through the whole conflicted world of Hillman, rather, as stated above, I want to concentrate on what Hillman's pantheon can contribute to our understanding of the return of soul-language to contemporary discourse, especially as it relates to the early Christian disputes as explored in the first part of this book.

Hillman's soul

As we have seen, early on in his career Hillman insists that 'soul-language' is *the* discourse that contemporary psychology must adopt. In view of the argument of the whole of the present book, this is both exhilarating and challenging. Here we have an avowedly secular (and often anti-Christian) humanist taking the traditional theistic language of divinity and repackaging it for a contemporary, secular and perhaps slightly jaded audience. As he stated in one of his first books, *Suicide and the Soul*:

> The terms 'psyche' and 'soul' can be used interchangeably, although there is a tendency to escape the ambiguity of the word 'soul' by recourse to the more biological, more modern 'psyche'. 'Psyche' is used more as a natural concomitant to physical life, perhaps reducible to it. 'Soul' on the other hand, has metaphysical and romantic overtones. It shares frontiers with religion. (SS: 43)

Thus, early on, Hillman recognizes that 'soul-language' has an ambiguity that, in particular, can present a challenge to the scientific/rational way of approaching psychology whilst also having a 'religious character'. As he put it a few years later in *Insearch*: 'Soul makes meaning possible, turns events into experiences, is communicated in love and *has a religious concern*' (I: 42). To those of a religious bent this can all initially sound encouraging – and in fact *Insearch* is the result of one of the few instances where Hillman explicitly addressed a group of Christian ministers. However, as with his mentor Jung, such an open heart towards 'religion' can sometimes be a two-edged sword.[2]

Hillman begins his fullest account of what he means by 'soul' in *Re-Visioning Psychology* (1975) by suggesting that he understands the pitfalls of essentialism when it comes to soul/psyche-talk. For he states that:

> By soul I mean, first of all, a perspective rather than a substance, a viewpoint toward things rather than a thing in itself. This perspective is reflective; it mediates events and makes differences between ourselves and everything that happens. Between us and events, between the doer and the deed, there is a reflective moment – and soul-making means differentiating this middle-ground. (RVP: xvi)

[2] For an analysis of Jung's ambiguous attitude to Christianity see Tyler 2015.

I state that he 'suggests the pitfalls of essentialism' because although he uses quasi-Wittgensteinian language of perspective,[3] this quote does reveal the inherent problem within Hillman's soul-position. For despite his avowed revolutionary hermeneutic, or rather non-dualism, his very first construct of 'soul-making' introduces dualism between 'us' and 'events', 'the doer' and 'the deed'. Hillman may want to advocate an undifferentiated hermeneutic or 'reflective moment' but rather his construct has unintentionally imported a dualistic perspective from the very beginning. Tacey too recognizes this problem in Hillman; critiquing him from a Jungian perspective rather than a Wittgensteinian one, he states:

> While Hillman criticises Jung for being a dualist, it is James Hillman who, in the last analysis, is the ultimate dualist, because he can never reconcile inner and outer, psyche and society, ego and underworld, therapy and activism … Hillman's inability to grasp paradox leads to the disastrous outbreak of overt contradiction. (Tacey 1998: 230)

Tacey criticizes Hillman for not 'holding the contradiction of opposites'. Using a Wittgensteinian perspective (which I will develop in the next chapter) I would rather criticize Hillman for holding a somewhat illusory and probably indefensible notion of 'inner' and 'outer', 'us' and 'them' (whether the 'they' are *daimones*, Gods or other people) that cannot be reconciled within the system that he is proposing.

This error is borne out by the rest of the passage above from *Re-Visioning Psychology* where Hillman returns to the traditional understanding of soul as an 'inner place or deeper person or ongoing presence – that is simply there even when all our subjectivity, ego and consciousness go into eclipse' (RVP: xvi). What is, we may ask, this 'inner place'? A super-self? A deeper-self? An over-self? Hillman describes it later in *Re-Visioning Psychology* as:

> Moving from outside in, it is a process of *interiorizing*; moving from the surface of visibilities to the less visible, it is a process of deepening. (RVP: 140, italics are Hillman's own)

As we have seen throughout this book, this persistent illusion of inwardness is one of the main problems in the history of the 'pursuit of the soul'.

---

[3] Throughout the book Hillman is largely critical of Wittgenstein's approach, without going into much detail of the consequences of Wittgenstein's analysis for psychology.

Indeed, in Wittgensteinian language, it is a persistent fly that will not escape from the fly-bottle of soul-making. For, as commentators such as Tacey note, despite the high-flown postmodern rhetoric, Hillman's soul-language remains resolutely dualist, exporting categories of self into the world whilst maintaining the barrier between them. As we saw when we looked at Plato earlier, this is *an* interpretation of Plato, not necessarily *the only* interpretation of the Greek.

To bridge this gulf between his (super-)self and the world, which opens up with alarming rapidity in his work, Hillman must call on the polytheistic Greek deities to come to his aid: Hermes, Hera, Aphrodite and Zeus are all invoked as necessary components of the polymorphous, polytheistic soul. Some commentators saw this move and questioned: 'But does Hillman *really believe* in these "gods"?' As we saw above, Hillman calls this invocation of 'the Gods' (usually upper-case) as part of his psychotherapeutic call to a return to 'an inner Greece of the mind' (RVP: 29). For 'we discover the Gods in the unconscious psyche – and because of this unconsciousness we are unable to distinguish the Gods from archetypes, or archetypes from heroes and daemons' (RVP: 36). At some times, he suggests, we must speak of 'the Gods' and 'daimones' metaphorically and allegorically (RVP: 36); at other times he seems to take them more literally (see below). Following Tacey, we have to ask – is this a rhetorical device (remember that Hillman began his academic career as a literary scholar in Dublin studying James Joyce), or is he suggesting that we take the 'belief in the Gods and daimones' seriously?

As psychology is based on the soul, psychology is intrinsically religious for Hillman (RVP: 167): not the monotheistic religion of Christianity (or the West) but rather it must be a polytheistic religion – a sort of revival of the ancient Greek pantheon. Psychology is a 'religious' act for Hillman but it is religion not as we know it, for it is religion without the transcendent. Thus we can look at Hillman's use of the terms 'religion' and 'Gods' much as commentators a generation before looked at Jung's pronouncements on the Christian God and asked similarly 'Yes but does he really *believe* in this God?'[4] In Hillman's *The Myth of Analysis* the Gods are presented as mythic archetypes that will form organizing principles in the psyche:

> Classical mythology as it comes down to us gives us one insight that will be essential for grasping the sufferings of the soul. Classical mythology is a collection of highly interrelated families of tales with

[4]I have given my view on this question in Tyler 2015.

much precise detail but without schematic system either in individual tales or among the tales as a group. (MA: 194)

Like psychopathologies, the mythic emanations of the deities blend one into another to produce a miasmic effect on the soul. Unlike modern psycho-therapy, Hillman's mythic analysis will have flexibility to deal with the boundlessness that is the soul's way. For the soul for Hillman is constantly in a state of flux and can never be pinned down into one category – just like, really, Hillman's prose, which also constantly defies categorization (a bit like trying to pin down an eel!):

> Just as psychological diagnoses can change and vary, so too mythology lets things stay in flux or in process. A myth is a description of a process; it is itself a process. It unfolds, moves, and at its different joints leads off into various possibilities … its structure is dramatic. (MA: 195)

Thus, 'the behaviour of the psyche reflects the acts of the Gods', states Hillman, 'because we are created in the Gods' images and can therefore do nothing that they have not already made possible in their behaviour' (MA: 195). 'The Gods' he resolves, 'are the ground of our fantasies'.[5]

So, the answer to the question 'Does Hillman *really* believe in these "Gods"?' becomes largely irrelevant (even though I think the answer must be 'No').[6] For believe in them or not, to maintain the position of soul as 'perspective' without a concomitant resolution of the inner/outer divide (such as Wittgenstein, or indeed Kant attempts) will, I suggest, be doomed to failure without the invention of intervening entities. Such a move is very similar to Hillman's own beloved neo-Platonists whom we saw in Chapter

---

[5] The source of Hillman's notion of 'archetypal psychology': 'the fundamental ideas of the psyche are to be expressions of persons: hero, nymph, mother, senex, child, trickster, amazon, puer etc. They give us our psychic functioning' (RVP: 128).

[6] When, for example, Hillman states that 'psychology reflects theology, but a pagan and polytheistic theology' (MA: 196) I feel he is (as Tacey concurs) taking a polemical position to annoy both atheist psychologists and Christian theists. As to his actual beliefs, I would prefer to leave that to the biographers such as Russell (2013). My task here is simply to observe the phenomenology of his philosophical psychology and see how coherent his system is on psychological, theological and philosophical grounds. As I will conclude, like his mentor Jung, there is much that is bracing and life-enhancing in his work but much that really is inconsistent from psychological, philosophical and theological perspectives. See also RVP: 169, 'the gods are imagined, not taken literally', or RVP: 130, 'A God is a manner of existence, an attitude towards existence, and a set of ideas.'

3 had to create the necessary expository positions of intervening worlds, planetary spheres, demiurges and *daimones* in order to hold together the inner/outer implied (but as I argued earlier not unconditionally) within the Platonic corpus. In response to this problem we saw the metaphysical ambiguity of Origen and Evagrius arising which so disturbed the Church Fathers. As I shall argue in my final chapter, this ambiguity can only finally be resolved by the solution that Augustine had taken (and thence thinkers such as Thomas Aquinas and Teresa of Avila), that is, by rooting the Platonic dynamic of self in the essential movement of the Christian Trinity. Trinitarian thought allows the Wittgensteinian dissolution of the false inner/outer dichotomy, preserving the integrity of the self/*psyche* whilst also allowing it *sub specie aeterni* to keep its window on the transcendent. In this alternative picture of the soul, presented first by Augustine, intervening deities, demiurges and *daimones* are contingent rather than necessary.

The 'window on the transcendent' is probably what most threatens Hillman's position. His *psyche* is indeed active, and very full of the imaginative, but what it lacks is the necessary window on the transcendent that Augustine saw as essential if the inner/outer divide of dualism was to dissolve. Sadly, despite his invocation of the *daimones* and deities, Hillman's system is unable to sustain the weight of the dualism that he seeks to escape.

Unlike Wittgenstein, Hillman is unable to see that he has subsumed the transcendent into the psychological, hence his annoyance, even anger, at the Catholic Church's pronouncements on 'spirit'. For 'spirit' cannot exist in Hillman's system as a separate entity. It must ultimately dissolve in the dualism of 'us' and the 'world event':

> The merging of psychology and religion is less the confluence of two different streams than the result of their single source – the soul. (RVP: 167)

Under the cloak of eradicating Cartesian dualism Hillman sadly preserves it by removing the transcendental apperception. The transcendent function is replaced in Hillman's system by imagination and aesthetic (much as in Rank's system it had been replaced by the creative ethic) and, like Rank's interpretation, it is equally unsatisfactory.

From the Christian point of view (as we shall see in the final chapter), the multiplicity of perspective is held in the unity of apperception which is Christ. Christ is the unity of perception that holds together all the contradictions of the *psyche* (primarily through his transcendent/immanent life in the Trinity). For now it is sufficient to state that by viewing the polyvalent from one position we have already maintained the unity of the soul – Hillman's polyvalent perspective is therefore an illusion.

Soul and spirit

Hillman's desire to subsume spirit into the wider category of 'soul' is coupled in his writings with an equal disdain for, in his eyes, the baleful effects of Christianity on the development of soul-language in particular, and the development of Western civilization in general.[7] The account of this process in the earlier *Re-Visioning Psychology* is expanded in the paper *Peaks and Vales: The Soul/Spirit Distinction as Basis for the Differences between Psychotherapy and Spiritual Discipline* (Hillman 1991, published in *Puer Papers*). Here Hillman begins his account with the decrees of the Fourth Council of Constantinople in 869. Hillman seems here (although he doesn't reference it) to be relying on the work of the twentieth century theosophist, Rudolf Steiner, who in lectures from 1923 onwards stressed the importance of the Council. As Terence Boardman (an advocate of Steiner) puts it:

> At the Christmas Conference for the refounding of the Anthroposophical Society Dec. 24th 1923 – 1st Jan. 1924, Rudolf Steiner restored to western culture something that had been lost for nearly 1100 years, namely, the threefold image of Man – once known as the Trichotomy – the image of Man as consisting of body, soul *and spirit*. This had been missing since the year 869, when it was deviously 'abolished' by fiat of a Church Council. In the years 1916–1924 Steiner laid ever greater emphasis on the historical significance of the 8th Ecumenical Council of Constantinople 869. (Boardman 2008: 1)[8]

---

[7] This from one of his last published conversations with Sonu Shamdasani in LD (2013): JH: 'We're all suffering the two-thousand-year curse that has been laid on us by what you all like so much, the early Church ... Don't forget what the early Church did, a lot of murder, a lot of victimization too ...', SS: 'and destruction of learning and culture', JH: 'I'm afraid I would be with Emperor Julian until he died, and a lot of these other strange Romans who wouldn't give up the old religion' (LD: 218/19).

[8] As Hillman may have got the notion of the baleful Eighth Ecumenical Council from Steiner, so the importance of the 869 Council was drawn to Steiner's attention by Otto Willmann's

Although both Steiner and Hillman are angry with the fathers of the 869 Council they are so for differing reasons. For Hillman the Council dissolved the tripartite self of spirit, soul and matter to a 'dualism of spirit (or mind) and body (or matter)' (PP: 54). A 'third place', 'an intermediate realm of psyche ... the realm of images and the power of imagination' was removed from us by 'theological, spiritual men more than a thousand years ago'. The council, for Hillman, set the seal on 800 years of degeneration within Christianity that had even been evident in the work of St Paul who 'uses *psyche* only four times in his Epistles, favouring, like the Gospel writers, *pneuma* to *psyche*'. The Council fathers have, then, denied us of our soul birthright, suggests Hillman, 'by replacing "psyche" with "spirit"'. We shall say a little more about this shortly but first it is worth noting that from the same paucity of evidence (the canon of the Council dealing with the soul is short and rather ambiguous),[9] Steiner drew exactly the opposite conclusion from Hillman. For Steiner felt that the Council had ultimately *de-spiritualized* the self (a process that would be reversed by his own theosophical movement), as opposed to Hillman's understanding of its *over-spiritualizing* anthropology.

The route back to soul/psyche then, for Hillman, lies in imagination and creativity, much as we saw it did for Rank. Hillman's view of soul differs significantly from that of Rank in two crucial respects. First, as we have seen, Hillman is at pains to cut off the link between the self and the transcendent (or, as he terms it, 'spirit'). Secondly, Hillman, as we have seen, wants to give the imagination far more independence than Rank so that by 'soul-making' he wants to give quasi-independence to the *daimones*

1869 *Geschichte des Idealismus* (see Boardman 2008). The completely opposite conclusions that Hillman draws to Steiner may explain why Hillman does not reference Steiner.

[9] 'Though the old and new Testament teach that a man or woman has one rational and intellectual soul, and all the fathers and doctors of the church, who are spokesmen of God, express the same opinion, some have descended to such a depth of irreligion, through paying attention to the speculations of evil people, that they shamelessly teach as a dogma that a human being has two souls, and keep trying to prove their heresy by irrational means using a wisdom that has been made foolishness. Therefore this holy and universal synod is hastening to uproot this wicked theory now growing like some loathsome form of weed. Carrying in its hand the winnowing fork of truth, with the intention of consigning all the chaff to inextinguishable fire, and making clean the threshing floor of Christ, in ringing tones it declares anathema the inventors and perpetrators of such impiety and all those holding similar views; it also declares and promulgates that nobody at all should hold or preserve in any way the written teaching of the authors of this impiety. If however anyone presumes to act in a way contrary to this holy and great synod, let him be anathema and an outcast from the faith and way of life of Christians' (XI Canon, Fourth Council of Constantinople).

and deities of the imagination: 'if you are in search of soul, go first to your fantasy images … all consciousness depends upon fantasy images' (PP: 57). The two positions are in fact interrelated, for Hillman sees the 'images of the soul' as mediating that which is transcendent, therefore we can dispense with the transcendent and stay with the phenomenological images presented to us (PP: 57). From this simple move (the sublimation of the transcendent into the immanent), as we have seen, most of the rest of Hillman's position derives. He neatly condenses it in *Peaks and Vales* into three points: the need for the 'soul-maker' (he is wary of using the word 'psychologist') to hold on to the *pathology* of the self (PP: 69) – in other words, that one of the defining characteristics of psychology *is* pathology and its concomitant 'link with mortality, limitation and death'. Secondly, the need for the soul-making to connect to the feminine and anima. Despite several bruising encounters with feminist critics, Hillman, largely unquestioningly, adopted Jung's typography of 'the feminine' or 'anima' being connected to 'nymphs, dark witches, lost cinderellas and Persephones of destruction' (PP: 69). And of course the key and third theme in Hillman's soul is the polymorphous nature of the soul to 'discover the many ways of many Gods'. All of this is a lot to derive from one ninth century council!

In fact, the decrees of the unfortunate council that disturbed both psychologists were never accepted by the Eastern Church which very quickly vilified it as a heretical gathering – a fact that both commentators fail to mention. Secondly, rather than any supposed attack on neo-Platonic ideas, the Council was wanting to disabuse some opponents of the Chalcedonian definition of Christ as 'two natures in one person'. Again, the Council was seeking to stress the unity within diversity that is at the heart of the Christian anthropological picture of the soul (as we shall see in the final chapter). The fact that both Hillman and Steiner can draw opposing conclusions from the (disputed) conciliar documents suggests that, like in the work of Jung, a little bit of theology within a psychological domain can be a dangerous thing.

Unfortunately, the mistaken view taken by Hillman is one that has been unthinkingly repeated by many psychological commentators since and, as far as I am aware, has not been challenged. Thus, Donald Capps in his 1995 essay *Enrapt Spirits and the Melancholy Soul* (Capps 1995) repeats Hillman's point uncritically. For both Capps and Hillman, the soulish is that which is dark, unpredictable, 'close to death experiences, dreams and lunacy' (Capps 143):

It moves indirectly in circular reasonings, where retreats are as important as advances, preferring labyrinths and corners, giving a metaphorical sense to life through such words as *close, near, slow* and *deep* ... Soul is vulnerable and suffers; it is passive and remembers. It is water to spirit's fire, like a mermaid who beckons the heroic spirit into the depths of passions to extinguish its certainty. (RVP: 69)

What we can learn from Hillman

Having struggled our way this far through Hillman some readers may be wondering, with the holes that I have picked into his views, whether the struggle has been worth it. I think it is. For one thing, as stated above, Hillman has had a huge influence on contemporary psychological culture and some of his views (such as those on the Council of Constantinople) have been accepted uncritically by others. However, if the current recurrence of 'soul-language' in psychological literature is primarily because of Hillman's influence and if we want to understand that language there is no better place to begin than with Hillman, in all his contradictions and 'twists and turns'. Yet, in addition to this somewhat negative reason for reading Hillman I would like to suggest, before reaching my conclusions to this chapter, that we might find more positive aspects to Hillman's approach, some of which I shall return to at the conclusion of the book. Despite empiricist and scientistic claims that we have witnessed 'the death of the soul' in modern times, Hillman's work reveals that whatever arises in the next 100 years it will almost certainly not be soul-less. In summary, then, I derive the following from Hillman's approach to the soul.

1. 'The third path'
As well as his critique of the 'over-spiritualization' of the self, Hillman, let us not forget, is an equally trenchant critic of the over-scientism and reductionism within contemporary approaches to the *psyche*. The past few decades, since Hillman started his writing, have seen a marked reduction in the significance of the spiritual and religious content of the psychological therapies. The same cannot be said for the empirical and pseudo-scientific approach. Indeed, in many respects, with the rise of quasi-neurological 'explanations' and 'interpretations' of the mind it seems as though this approach may have reached its zenith in recent years. Along with Wittgenstein (whose objections we shall return to in the following chapter), Hillman had a justifiable and deep-seated suspicion

of the over-idolization of psychology as a 'science of the mind' and was every bit as trenchant as Wittgenstein in challenging the unquestioning acceptance of this position. His own approach was to advocate a 'third path' between reductionism and idealism, theology and science, which gave him, he believed, the right to challenge scientific and medical models of psychology, especially psychopathology:

> As connecting link, or traditionally third position, between all opposites (mind and matter, spirit and nature, intellect and emotion), the soul differs from the terms which it connects. (RVP: 174)

For:

> The science fantasy with its reliance upon objectivity, technology, verification, measurement, and progress – in short, its necessary literalism – is less a means for examining the psyche than for examining science. Our interest lies not in applying the methods of science to psychology (to put it on a 'sound scientific footing'), but rather in applying the archetypal method of psychologising to science so as to discover its root metaphors and operational myths. (RVP: 169)

Distrusting too the contemporary language of psychopathology – 'the descriptions of the alienations, sufferings and bizarre life of the soul' (MA: 121) – Hillman felt that such a language 'insults the soul'. Only psychotherapy as imagination (and very much out of the academic context) can 'unleash the soul' (MA: 122). Whether we accept Hillman's critique or not (and many academic psychologists will of course simply dismiss it), as with his critique of organized religion, there is much here to challenge some of the basic, unthinking assumptions upon which contemporary psychology (especially academic psychology) is built, and to which it should be answerable. As we have seen in these last two chapters, Hillman and Rank can both best be described as 'psychological heretics' and it may ultimately be to our advantage to heed their criticisms (or at least take them seriously as I have done here) rather than rushing them immediately to the stake.

Hillman challenges all professionals, no less professional psychologists as well as ministers of religion, to look again at unexamined concepts of self and the psychological life. As he puts it in *Insearch*: 'let the clergy follow the *imitatio Christi* rather than imitate psychotherapy' (I: 46).

2. The symbolic/mythic self

With Rank we saw that creativity must play a decisive role in any future 'soul-psychology'. Likewise, with Hillman we see the importance he attached, as a post-Jungian, to the role of imagination and the symbolic. As he puts it in *Re-Visioning Psychology*:

> Psychological faith begins in the love of images, and it flows mainly through the shapes of persons in reveries, fantasies, reflections and imaginations ... (the ego's) trust is in the imagination as the only uncontrovertible reality, directly presented, immediately felt. (RVP: 50)

For analysis goes on in the soul's imagination and not just in the clinic:

> Essential to soul-making is psychology-making, shaping concepts and images that express the needs of the soul as they emerge in each of us. (RVP: xviii)

We let imagination speak for itself without interpretation. As we saw in the last chapter, from the Wittgensteinian perspective psychology becomes a peculiar art, taking its *Weltbild* to view the 'foundation of possible *Weltanschauungen*':

> Insight would no longer mean translation, no longer mean the reformulation of imaginal speech into psychological language, mainly through understanding our fantasies, interpreting our dreams. We would let the insight contained with the fantasy appear of itself, in its own 'intrinsically intelligible' speech. (MA: 201)

Or as my training analyst, Hymie Wyse, used to put it, in analysis the analyst must pray: 'Lead us not into interpretation!' The soul/psyche for Hillman is at root imaginal and myth is in the natural discourse of the soul. In an earlier work (Tyler 2013a) I stressed the links between the postmodern Jungian view of the symbolic with the premodern medieval understanding of the symbol. As a great medievalist/renaissance man, Hillman, like his mentor Jung, recognizes the symbolic nature of the *psyche* and how the *psyche* really lives in the realm of the symbolic and mythic, for 'the imaginal does not explain, myths are not explanations'. As such the symbolic utterings of the soul 'are bound to ritual happenings; they are stories, as our fantasies are, which project us into participation with the phenomena they tell about so that the need for explanation falls away' (MA: 202). Hillman is here, I believe, pointing out an essential quality of 'soul-language' as we have explored it during this book. As I suggested in an earlier work (Tyler 2011) it is a 'performative' rather than 'informative' language. In the earlier book I suggested, drawing upon the writings of Dionysius the Areopagite, that it was a common element too in the medieval tradition of 'mystical theology'. Just as Hillman's (and Rank's) soul-language invites the reader to reflect back on their own 'soul-status' so the writings of the Areopagite, long enshrined in the Western mystical tradition (and of course drawing on the Platonic/neo-Platonic tradition that we discussed in Part I of this book), throws the reader back upon themselves – decentring the self from the discursive *intellectus* to the symbolic *affectus*. Just as Hillman's soul-language leads us to the 'ritual happenings' of *mythos*, so too the words of the Areopagite are, to paraphrase Hans Urs von Balthasar, 'a moment of celebration', a festival, dance or 'circling movement' (von Balthasar 1984: 157; cf. Dionysius CH: 7.4, Ep: 8):

> The style strides along so consciously loaded, draped with so many sacred garments, that it makes any haste impossible and compels us not only to follow him in his train of thought but also to join with him in his mood of celebration. (von Balthasar 1984: 172)

This, for Dionysius, is the 'indirect initiation' of Hierotheus, reflecting the *myesthai* of the classical initiation into the Dionysian cult (see DN: 1.8, 3.1, 3.2; CH: 2.5 and 1.5, where the whole of Christianity is described as a 'mystery religion'). As von Balthasar points out, even the term *thiasōtēs* – that of the participant in the cult of Dionysius – is used by Dionysius in CH: 2.1, 3.2 and EH: 1.1. Dionysius, following Plato and his neo-Platonic interpreters, makes a contrast between the rational philosophy that persuades by dialectic and the means of *logos* and reason and this latter kind of 'initiation' that is formulated through the *mythos* (Louth 1989: 25); cf. Ep: 9:

> The traditions of the theologians is twofold, on the one hand ineffable and mystical, on the other manifest and more knowable; on the one hand symbolic and presupposing initiation, on the other philo-sophical and capable of proof – and the ineffable is interwoven with what can be uttered. The one persuades and contains within itself the

truth of what it says, the other effects and establishes the soul with God by initiations that do not teach anything. (Ep: 9, D: 1105)[10]

Although Hillman rarely cites the work of Dionysius the Areopagite we can see a clear parallel in his distinction between the logical discourse and the mythic discourse of suffering/*pathein*. As the mystical theologians following Dionysius will see this distinction in that between speculative and mystical theology, so Hillman makes his distinction between psychology as a pseudo-science over-relying on the intellect with the 'suffering/*pathein*' of his own soul-centred psychology:

> Whatever he learned directly from the sacred writers, whatever his own perspicacious and laborious research of the scriptures uncovered for him, or whatever was made known to him through that more mysterious inspiration, not only learning (*mathein*) but also experiencing (*pathein*) the divine things. For he had a 'sympathy' with such matters, if I may express it this way, and he was perfected in a mysterious union with them and in a faith in them which was independent of any teaching. (DN: 2.9)

For Hillman, 'the psyche speaks in metaphors, in analogues, in images, that's its primary language' (LD: 81). We can therefore see Hillman's work as restoring that old neo-Platonic vision of the *psyche* as being at its heart essentially symbolic. It is 'its natural language' for:

> By soul I mean the imaginative possibilities in our natures, the experiencing through reflective speculation, dream, image and fantasy – that mode which recognizes all realities as primarily symbolic or metaphorical. (RVP: xvi)

3. The importance of relationship

Like Rank, Hillman wants to use his soul-language to place relationship once again at the heart of psychology – rather than pathology or intellectualization. Against psychopathologies and all terminology of pathology, Hillman rather calls for psychology to be a 'speech that leads to participation,

---

[10] Louth also draws the parallel with Aristotle's distinction within the Eleusian mysteries – that the initiate does not *learn (mathein)* anything but *experiences or suffers (pathein)* something (Aristotle, *De Philosophia frag* 15).

in the Platonic sense, in and with the thing spoken of, a speech of stories and new insights, the way one poem and one tune ignite another verse and another song' (MA: 206). For:

> Psychological work begins with the human meeting. What we know and have read, our gifts of intelligence and character – all we have gained through training and experience leads to this moment. (I: 16)

It is, as he repeatedly stresses (like Rank before him), a work of love, and the jargon and styles of psychology can often get in the way of the love-relationship that must lie at the heart of all true psychology.

4. The creative and the artistic

Following on from the natural symbolic nature of the soul Hillman, like Rank before him, wants to privilege the creative and artistic at the heart of the psychological process. Hillman's 'third realm' between the scientific and religious approaches creates a space for a certain loosening of our *psyche* where the creative act can be born. The 'third realm' is 'neither object, nor subject nor both' (I: 66). Rather, 'this third reality is a psychic reality, a world of experiences, emotions, fantasies, moods, visions, dreams, dialogues, physical sensations, a large and open space, free and spontaneous, realm mainly of "meaningness"'.

5. Libidinal/bodily/sexual

As well as a creative act, the return to the soul-work is for Hillman a return to the depths, the body and the sexual. This libidinal is used in a Freudian (and Jungian) sense of that which connects and sexualizes all through the libido:

> The real revolution in the soul is not in itself sexual. The human sexual instinct is widely plastic and provides energy for changes in consciousness all through psychological history. If one may read the trend of collective events through the particular experiences of individuals, the deep change now going on (in the 1960s when Hillman wrote this) is merely carried by sexual fantasies as psychic dynamisms, the intention of which is ultimately a revivification and expansion of psychic reality. (I: 117)

This Platonic conception of the universal *eros* drawing all things together in the *psyche* leads us back to where we began this book – in Plato's vision of the union of *eros* and *psyche*. For ultimately Hillman would like to carry on the Platonic tradition which he sees as being rudely (and temporarily) interrupted by the 'curse of Christianity'. (Of course if my arguments in Part I are correct then the Platonic tradition *does* continue within Christianity in a way perhaps Hillman was unaware of.) He thus sees his 'soul-making' as a return to the Platonic in postmodern clothes. The Platonic self allows Hillman to reassert these five aspects of the *psyche* that we found in the early Greeks (and, as we have seen too, in the early Christians): 'the third position', the symbolic, the creative, the relational and the libidinal. We shall return to much of this in the final chapter when we will map a future vision of soul-language. However, as we have argued all along in this chapter, some crucial flaws in Hillman's work, especially the denial of the transcendent and the crude 'inner/outer' hermeneutic, means that his schema possesses deficiencies that must be addressed. We shall return to these deficiencies in our final two chapters when I will suggest ways of viewing the self that will overcome some of Hillman's metaphysical difficulties whilst building on some of his more helpful insights.

Drawing some threads together

It is time then to draw some of the threads of this chapter together, even if Hillman's wild style militates against neat summaries. Hillman positions his own work in that psychological lineage that stresses the 'end of Christianity' and the return of the libidinal and Dionysian. As we have seen, influenced by Nietzsche, Jung had written to Freud in 1910 that psychoanalysis (or as he refers to it, from its Greek fore letters: ψα) will provide a new phenomenon to replace religion, and in particular Christianity. To effect this psychoanalysis will draw on the Dionysian spirit popularized by Nietzsche in works such as *The Birth of Tragedy from the Spirit of Music*:

> I think we must give ψα time to infiltrate into people from many centres, to revivify among intellectuals a feeling for symbol and myth, ever so gently to transform Christ back into the soothsaying god of the vine (*in den weissagenden Gott der Rebe*), which he was, and in this way absorb these ecstatic instinctual forces of Christianity (*jene ekstatischen Triebkräfte des Christentums*), for the one purpose of making the cult and the sacred myth (*den heiligen Mythos*) what they

once were – a drunken feast of joy (*zum trunkenen Freudenfeste*) where mankind regained the ethos and holiness of an animal.

This way the beauty and purpose of classical religion which from God knows what biological need has become a *Jammerinstitut* (literally, 'an Institute of Woe'). Thus Analysis should be a means to help people get in touch with these Dionysian libidinal impulses. (Jung to Freud 11.11.1910)

Thus, as Bishop points out instead of the '*Dionysos gegen den Gekreuzigten*' that we find at the end of Nietzsche's last published work,[11] Jung will 'transform the Crucified back into the God of the grape' (Bishop 1995: 64). This 'Dionysian element' is one to which Jung would constantly return, even after the break with Freud:

> The Dionysian element has to do with emotions and affects which have found no suitable religious outlets in the fundamentally Apollonian cult and ethos of Christianity. (Jung CW: 12.182)

'Intoxication', he writes in the same essay, 'that most direct and dangerous form of possession, turned away from the gods and enveloped the human world with its exuberance.' Thus, for Jung, Christianity was not to be destroyed but rather to be transformed by helping people to return to the springs of the libidinal – the *ekstatischen Triebkräfte des Christentums* – which Jung felt had been abandoned.

So, in Jung, we don't have the destruction of Christianity, but rather the *transformation* of Christianity. Jung is a reformer, in as much as Luther was a reformer. He sees much that is good in Christianity but that it has lost its connection with the *libidinal*. Thus, he will emphasize two main things in his future reform of Christianity: the return to the libidinal and the importance of the symbolic function. Hillman sees himself as picking up where Jung left off. However, rather than Jung's desire to *transform* Christianity, Hillman sees his aim as needing to *transcend* Christianity, 'to escape the 2,000 year-old curse'. In his last dialogue with Sonu Shamdasani, he pours particular scorn on those Christianized Jungians who had hoped (like Jung we presume) to have transformed Christianity by means of analytical psychology:

---

[11] Nietzsche's final written words in *Ecce Homo*: '*Hat man mich verstanden: Dionysos gegen den Gekreuzigten*'/ 'Have you understood me: it is Dionysos or the Crucified One' (in *Warum Ich ein Schicksal Bin*: 9).

Jung grasped the horror, but I don't think the Christian followers have, and there are a hell of a lot of them. They just have the same pattern of redemption, you know, there's light at the end of the tunnel, forever – you really are redeemed ... You're already saved. Christ has already saved you. There's a place waiting for you in heaven. This is unacceptable to a Jewish mind. There's too much trouble, too much horror. You can't get away with it so easily. I'm not saying that the Christians themselves get away with it so easily, or that Jung did ... I am saying that the pseudo-Christianity of Jungianism does, and that's part of my fury. (LD: 217)

He goes further in *Re-Visioning Psychology* in blaming Christianity for the 'return of the repressed' in all the horrors that have beset Western civilization since the nineteenth century 'death of God'. By creating a certain social psyche, suggests Hillman, Christianity prepared a culture within which the shadow could triumph once it was faced with the demise of the old religion. 'The commander's tent flaps in the wind' he poetically suggests, 'while the two-horned bull Dionysus, our Devil, pagan, perverse, psychopathic, all-powerful, once he comes through the mountain wall' (RVP: 224). 'The greatest bulwark of Northern consciousness was its now dead God who commanded battalions of light – moral philosophers, preachers, psychologists' (RVP: 224), but now with the 'death of God', the 'depths rise without our systems of protection'. Hillman struggles again with the dilemma that faced Freud, Rank and ultimately all psychoanalysis: it is all very well to seek the return of the repressed – but once the irrational polyvalent gods of the unconscious have arisen, what the hell do you do with them? Beginning with the repression of *fin de siècle* Vienna, Freud began the slow work of stripping away the layers of repression and denial beginning with the sexual. His followers, as we have seen, continued the work so that by the time Hillman wrote his work in the late 1960s and early 1970s the return of the repressed was in full swing with the sexual and social revolution of those decades. However, the removal of the ego's 'moral restraint' left an inevitable void. Old man Freud recognized, as we saw in the previous chapter, the necessary role of psychology as a *moral* discipline. Hillman's unanchoring of this in his polymathic 'return to Greece' also ushers in some very dark sides of the human psyche. I write this chapter with daily television reports of the gory battles in the Middle East – images of young men from civilized Europe holding up severed heads, engaged in mass acts of rape and torture and countless bloody atrocities suggest that Freud was right and perhaps Hillman was wrong. Perhaps the human *psyche* can only stand so much return of the repressed before moral repugnance kicks in. At least one hopes.

In his commentary on Jung's *Red Book*, Hillman at the end of his life said that the old options of Christianity were 'worn out'. One cannot anymore 'flee to the East' (RVP: 224) as the hippies and transcendental meditators of the 1960s had done. Rather for him the answer lies in the 'fostering of images', in the polymorphously perverse psyche where 'we can place the turmoil of our fantasies within the larger depository of myths' (RVP: 225) which is for him the task of 'recollecting the Gods in all psychological activity' (RVP: 226). Whilst remembering that this 'return to the Gods' is no longer a theological option:

> The difference between psychology and religion boils down to the same as between psychology and science: literalism. Theology takes Gods literally and we do not ... In archetypal psychology Gods are imagined ... They are formulated ambiguously, as metaphors for modes of experience and as numinous borderline persons. (RVP: 169)

This is his 'initiation into the Dionysian consciousness' (MA: 274) without which 'we have only that Dionysus that reaches us through the shadow, through Wotan and the Devil of Christianity' twisted and perverted by 'our misogynist and Apollonic consciousness' (MA: 274). *Psyche* predates Christianity, says Hillman, so the return to the soul is a return to a source that predates Christianity: 'the merging of psychology and religion is less the confluence of two different streams than the result of their single source – the soul' (RVP: 167).

I have tried here to give a systematic account of Hillman's work, but he is very insistent that soul-work must, by its nature, essentially be unsystematic. I think if Hillman were ever to read this chapter on whichever astral plane he now resides, he would take a sharp intake of breath and accuse me of over-rationalization in my approach to the *psyche* (a long-standing criticism!).[12] Consequently, for him, the 'patron saint' of soul-work is the medieval Knight Errant, who in his hermetic wanderings to and fro represents the gentle dance (Dionysius' 'circular movement') which is the soul-work:

---

[12] Although he may appreciate my beginning the book with a dream!

The Knight Errant follows fantasy, riding the vehicle of his emotions; he loiters and pursues the anima with his eros, regarding desire as also holy; and he listens to the deviant discourse of the imagination. (RVP: 161)

For 'the Knight Errant of psychology' is 'partly picaresque rogue, of the underworld, a shadow hero of unknown paternity, who sees through the hierarchies from below. He is a mediator betwixt and between, homeless, of no fixed abode. Or his home, like that of Eros, is in the realm of the daemons, of the metaxy (the middle region), in between, back and forth' (RVP: 161). Perhaps with this picture of the Knight Errant we have the final concluding picture of Hillman, the wandering, infuriating, inspiring, trangressive follower of Hermes, possibly the ultimate incarnation of the lost postmodern soul:

Because of Hermes, psychologizing is always moving between opposing views such as the Apollonic and the Dionysian attitudes, standing at either end of its spectrum, – partly Apollonic Knight, partly Dionysian Rogue, both and neither. (RVP: 163)

Therefore, for Hillman, psychology must always end up annoying all the other disciplines being neither fully Apollonian nor fully Dionysian: 'it is a counter-education, a negative learning, moving all standpoints off balance toward their borders' (RVP: 163) – it is beyond morality and amoral needing to remain true to its essentially amphibious nature. We will search in vain for Freud's moral ego in Hillman's wandering Knight Errant soul:

The notion of human being as centred in the moral person of free will is also a mythical fantasy, an archetypal perspective given by a single Hero or a single God; our freedom to choose, our moral centre and decisiveness, our free will … Here I am attempting to de-moralize the psyche from the moralistic fallacy which reads psychic events in terms of good and bad, right and wrong. (RVP: 178)

Conclusions to Part II

There is no doubt that reading Hillman's *oeuvre* is an exhilarating experience. With a background in literary criticism he is masterful in using provocative and polemic imagery to get his message across. From the perspective of this book his work is informative on two counts.

First, following his example (and the work of other contemporary commentators such as Thomas Moore) many of his successors have employed 'soul-language' as a possible way forward from the dry morass within which much of contemporary psychology is stuck. Whether we agree with his interpretations or not he has done psychology a great service in getting psychologists to critically rethink the roots, bases and aims of the discipline. From some of the secondary literature cited here it will be clear that this is at present an ongoing and lively debate, the terminus of which is by no means assured. By reasserting the 'third position' of the 'soulish' in its symbolic, creative, relational and libidinal aspects Hillman has given voice to an essential ongoing corrective that needs to happen if psychology is to move away from its present positivistic biases.

Secondly, by critically engaging with Hillman we can see what is necessary for a coherent soul-language to work from a philosophical and psychological perspective. Tacey concludes his critical appraisal of Hillman by challenging Hillman's unquestioned 'worship of plurality' (Tacey 1998: 232). For Tacey, Hillman's work shines a light on an entire age 'virtually "allergic" to the idea of wholeness and balance, reading any attempt at unity as an undesirable "imposition" of order' (231). Polyvalency at the expense of unity and balance is, for Tacey, 'a perversity that the psyche will not tolerate' and in support of this he cites the chaos of Hillman's career itself as 'a sort of negative proof for the need for a reconciling vision of coherence and unity' (232). Rather, he argues, we need to find a way of educating ourselves out of this 'post-modern' (or rather 'most-modern') way of living so that we can experience again 'the liberating and healing contribution of wholeness, by experiencing anew the powerful symbols of wholeness which are now almost banned from our postmodern vocabulary' (231). It is therefore perhaps inevitable that such a Knight Errant as Hillman would always have a problem with Christianity. Christianity, as we have seen, for Hillman casts a terrible shadow:

> Religion in our culture derives from spirit rather than from soul, and so our culture does not have a religion that reflects psychology or is mainly concerned with soul-making. Instead we have psychology that reflects religion. Since the religion in our culture has been monotheistic, our psychologies are monotheistic. (RVP: 4)

And 'the prejudices against fragmentation, self-division and animism are religious in their fanatical intensity' (RVP: 168). His psychology is polytheistic, he states, 'less out of religious confession than out of psychological necessity. The many-sidedness of human nature, the variety of viewpoints even within a single individual, requires the broadest possible spectrum of basic structures' (RVP: xx). Again, as we argued above, Hillman's polymania sadly leaves no unity of apperception in his self-conception – the whole cannot be held. His battle against what he terms 'monomania' he characterizes as a 'holy war that had simmered since the age of Constantine: the battle to maintain Christian psychology against that of polytheistic antiquity' (RVP: 4). This battle, he argues, is carried into the modern world sometimes from 'protestantism' and sometimes from the 'Judeo-Protestant tradition' (MA: 265). Accordingly, this covert legacy from Christianity, smuggled into psychology from Freud and Jung, continues to affect psychology by its obsession with 'organising principles in the psyche' such as 'mandalas, crystals, balls, wise men, and other patterns of order' (MA: 265).

Like Rank, Hillman ends up in a position which advocates not just an end to Christianity and 'monomania' but to psychology itself. His final question is: 'Can the soul that stirs again today be served by traditional psychology, whether what we today call psychology meets psyche's needs?' (RVP: 218).

Hillman clearly believed that 'the psyche can no longer be held by its old containers of Christian culture' (RVP: 219) and his whole *oeuvre* represents a challenge to Christianity and its legacy, especially in its reading of the soul. In his final dialogue with Sonu Shamdasani he speculates whether Christian theologians had really taken on board the enormity of Jung and his work (LD: 220). The present work partly arises as a response to Hillman's interpretation of Jung and Freud, and also as a response to the growth of soul-language removed from its Christian context. In the first part of the book I aimed to demonstrate how the early Christian Church worked with its Platonic legacy to construct a soul-work that could present an image of self that held the positive Platonic notion with the birth of the transcendent in Christ. Hillman's work only serves, in my opinion, to justify early Christianity's rejection of straightforward Platonism as being insufficient to explain the psychic reality it was faced with after Christ. Accordingly, to conclude this book I would like to return to Christianity in Part III by means of two great twentieth century 'masters of the soul': Ludwig Wittgenstein and Edith Stein. By dethroning the transcendent Hillman wishes to replace it with the polymorphous. As I have argued in this chapter, in my view this cannot work for two main reasons: first that it mislays the necessary unity of apperception of the *psyche* and secondly by removing the transcendent Hillman must necessarily create (or restore) intermediate entities such as *daimones* or Gods.[13]

If Tacey would like to argue for the coherence and unity of the self, as opposed to Hillman's polyvalent chaos, I would like to go further in the final chapters of this book by arguing for the necessary transcendental perspective if our language of the self is to be coherent. I have already suggested this position in this chapter but in the final two chapters of the book I would like to give the philosophical and theological arguments for this drawing upon the work of Wittgenstein and Stein. In Ludwig Wittgenstein we shall find an analytic philosopher who accepts the modern critique whilst also recognizing the need for the transcendent in our conception of self-hood. In contradistinction to Hillman we shall see how Wittgenstein's work necessarily leaves the transcendental perspective intact in our 'soul-choreography'. Using his writings I shall open up the door which will lead to the final chapter of the book and the end of our journey. For in the subject of our final chapter, Edith Stein, we find a philosopher and psychologist who recognizes that only in the radical notion of the Trinity can the unity and diversity of the soul be held together.

---

[13] See, for example, MA: 265: 'in order to give full value to the differentiated manyness of both the archetypal world of divine figures, daimones, and mythic creatures, as well as to the phenomenal world of our experiences, where psychological actuality is vastly complicated and manifold, we shall focus intensively upon the plurality of self, upon the many Gods and the many existential modes of their effects'.

PART III
WHITHER THE SOUL?

Prelude

In Part II we looked at the 'return of the soul' in the work of the analysts – especially Freud, Jung, Bettleheim, Rank and Hillman. To conclude our journey we shall move into what has been called 'the postmodern turn' as we try to resolve some of the problems that beset the analysts. In doing so I shall draw upon two philosophers who stand on the edge of modernity and look into postmodernity: Ludwig Wittgenstein (1889–1951) and Edith Stein (1891–1942). Both were immersed in the cultural, philosophical and psychological debates of their generation and worked with the leading proponents of key movements of phenomenology, logical atomism, logical positivism and behaviourism. Yet both, ultimately, parted company with these movements to develop a conceptual vision of the human person that goes to the heart of the concerns of this book, i.e. how can coherent human personhood be maintained in the light of the transcendental perspective.

CHAPTER 7
WITTGENSTEIN, TAGORE AND
MERTON: THE POSTMODERN TURN

Wittgenstein's turn

In the summer of 1927 the thirty-eight year old Ludwig Wittgenstein was eventually persuaded by Moritz Schlick, Professor of Philosophy at the University of Vienna, to attend his Thursday evening gatherings of students and professors who shared an interest in investigating the logical and scientific bases of philosophy – what would later evolve into the famous Vienna Circle. Schlick felt that Wittgenstein 'was one of the greatest geniuses on earth' (Mrs Blanche Schlick to F. A. von Hayek in Nedo and Ranchetti 1983: 206) having been one of the first professional philosophers in Vienna to read Wittgenstein's newly published *Tractatus Logico-Philosophicus* and appreciate its enormous significance (see Monk 1990: 241–3). The meetings were tense and Wittgenstein required a certain amount of careful handling to help him engage with the philosophers gathered to appreciate his every word. This is unsurprising. Having worked with Bertrand Russell at the beginning of the twentieth century in Cambridge on the problems of philosophical logic, at first his pupil and later effectively a colleague and rival, the young Ludwig had drawn up the essential framework of the *Tractatus* before enlisting into the Austro-Hungarian *Kaiserlich und Königlich* army at the outbreak of the Great War. The trauma of the conflict was severe in the extreme for the highly-strung son of a sophisticated Viennese *haute-bourgeois* family, not least because of the stress of having to come into contact with the type of people his upbringing and station had conspired to insulate him from (all recorded in his war diaries; see NB and Tyler 2011). After surrender, capture and incarceration at Monte Cassino Abbey in Southern Italy, the thirty year old completed the *Tractatus* with its notoriously gnomic final remarks on *das mystische* before lapsing into one of the most famous philosophical silences of modern times. Turning his back on the academy he first acted as a monastery gardener and then tried, in an ultimately doomed attempt, to teach primary school children in the Lower Austrian backwaters. When Schlick made his approaches Ludwig was effectively doing a form of occupational therapy engaged in the construction of an ultra-modernist (and quite stunning) house for his sister Gretl in the unfashionable Kundmanngasse district of Vienna, hence his reluctance to be drawn once again into professional philosophical discussion.

If he had been somewhat idiosyncratic in his communication techniques in the past from now on he would display an unusual turn of pedagogy that bordered on the eccentric. Consequently, we can imagine the surprise of the great and the good of Vienna when 'one of the greatest (philosophical) geniuses on earth' would during the meeting turn his back on the assembled professors and recite to them the poetry of the Bengali Nobel Laureate, Rabindranath Tagore (1861–1941). Rudolf Carnap in his reminiscences of these meetings suggests that 'I sometimes had the impression that the deliberately rational and unemotional attitude of the scientist, and likewise any ideas which had the flavour of "enlightenment", were repugnant to Wittgenstein' (Monk 1990: 244).

In this chapter I would like to take Wittgenstein's Viennese 'turn' as a starting point to explore why, like his contemporary Rank, Wittgenstein felt the need to turn his back on the scientific/empiricist establishment and forge his own re-evaluation of the philosophical perspective required for an examination of self, a perspective that we are still unpacking half a century after his death. In so doing I will also explore the appeal to Wittgenstein of the works of Tagore that he had read in those meetings. In so doing, like Rank, we shall explore Wittgenstein's response to the neo-empirical, especially with respect to the 'language of the soul' and how a study of his work suggests a way forward for the future of such a language.

Wittgenstein and Tagore: Two sentinels on the borderlands of modernity

In a letter to Paul Engelmann written on 23 October 1921 Wittgenstein expressed his disapproval of another of the Bengali's works – the short play *The King of the Dark Chamber*:

> It seems to me as if all that wisdom has come out of the ice box; I should not be surprised to learn that he got it all second-hand by reading and listening (exactly as so many among us acquire their knowledge of Christian wisdom) rather than from his own genuine

feeling. Perhaps I don't understand his tone; to me it does not ring like the tone of a man possessed by the truth. (LPE: 23.10.1921)

He goes on to suggest in the letter that Tagore may have suffered from a weak translation (something he would correct a decade later by attempting with Yorick Smythies his own translation of the play) or indeed that the fault may lie within Wittgenstein himself. The letter alone goes some way to furnishing an explanation as to why Ludwig was to inflict the Bengali's writings on the bemused members of the Vienna Circle a few years later – it was as though Wittgenstein himself was trying to come to terms with Tagore's writings and make sense of how they should be incorporated (or not) into his own inter-war search for 'the truth' (which would include, *inter alia*, his study of Søren Kierkegaard, Fyodor Dostoyevsky, Count Tolstoy,[1] Oswald Spengler and James Frazer – reflections upon all of whom can be found in the inter-war writings). Accordingly, a few months later we find him writing to Ludwig Hänsel to say that he had revised his opinion as 'there is indeed something grand here' (Monk 1990: 408). Within this re-evaluation of Tagore can be seen Wittgenstein's inter-war (and inter-*Tractatus* and *Philosophical Investigations*) search for the *meaning* of religious truths. Having given (as he thought) final shape to his views on logic and propositional structure in the *Tractatus* it is almost as if he now sought to find similar clarity to these broader religious and aesthetic questions, no doubt spurred, I have suggested, by his encounter in the trenches with, first 'the nearness of death' and secondly the re-working of the Gospels by Leo Tolstoy (see Tyler 2011). From this, what we might broadly term existential approach, arises one of the observations that occurs in his notebooks at the time:

A religious question is either a 'life question' or (empty) chatter. This language game, we could say, only deals with 'life questions'. (Wittgenstein BEE: 183.202)[2]

With this comment in mind it becomes clear which criteria Wittgenstein was applying to Tagore's play – was it indeed a 'life question' or mere 'empty

---

[1] McGuinness (1988) and Monk (1990) both tell the strange story of how shortly after arriving in Galicia during his war service in 1914 he walked into a bookshop which only contained one book – Tolstoy's *Gospels*. At this time he was feeling particularly low and in Monk's words he was quite literally 'saved by the word' (Monk 1990: 115).

[2] My translation: *Eine religiöse Frage ist nur entweder Lebensfrage oder sie ist (leeres) Geschwätz. Dieses Sprachspiel – könnte man sagt – wird nur mit Lebensfragen gespielt.*

chatter'. Initially at first he seemed to think the latter before moving to the former. What was it about Tagore's work that could have elicited this move? Regardless of the writings of both men of letters, the backgrounds and influences on the two men could immediately suggest a bond, if not, to coin Wittgenstein's phrase, a 'family resemblance'. Both were born into grand late nineteenth century families which would be destined to play significant roles in the cultural destinies of their two nations – Wittgenstein's Habsburg Austria and Tagore's Bengal – with both families' wealth arising from the business acumen and wheeling-dealing of a significant patriarch – in the case of Ludwig his father Karl Wittgenstein whose steel empire made the family enormously wealthy after the Austrian economic collapse following the First World War; in Rabindranath's case his grandfather, Dwarakanath Tagore, who amassed a huge fortune from landed estates in the East of Bengal. Both Ludwig and Rabindranath were expected to follow in the family enterprises: Ludwig ended up moving from engineering and aeronautics to falling into the embrace of philosophy under the tutelage of Russell at Cambridge whilst Rabindranath spent the time he should have been tending the family estates composing some of the lyrics and poetry for which he is most famous today.

Faith as a passion

Drury, Wittgenstein's friend and pupil, once told Wittgenstein that he had been reading F. R. Tennant's *Philosophical Theology* to which Wittgenstein replied 'a title like that sounds to me as if it would be something indecent' (Rhees 1987: 90). This response perhaps indicates the direction we should take in applying Wittgenstein's writings to the study of religion and ultimately the soul. From his inter-war study of, *inter alia*, Kierkegaard, Tolstoy, Dostoyevsky and, of course, Tagore,[3] what emerges is Wittgenstein's characterization (following Kierkegaard) of the 'passion of belief' as for example in this quote from his notebooks: '*Weisheit ist leidenschaftlos. Gagegen nennt Kierkegaard den Glauben eine Leidenschaft*: Wisdom is passionless. But faith by contrast is what Kierkegaard calls a passion' (CV: 53e). In this respect one of the key texts for throwing light on Wittgenstein's attitude to religion is the recollections of his pupil Maurice Drury. Drury had originally

---

[3] In later life Wittgenstein would tell Drury (Rhees 1987: 86) that there were only two European writers of recent times who had anything important to say about religion: Tolstoy and Dostoyevsky.

gone up to Cambridge to study for the Anglican priesthood at Westcott House. However, after he had come under the influence of Wittgenstein he abandoned his ordination training and spent two years working with unemployed people in Newcastle and Merthyr Tydfil. With Wittgenstein's encouragement he began to study medicine in 1934 and qualified in 1939. The most important period of his recollections of Wittgenstein dates from the period after the Second World War when Wittgenstein was living in Ireland and Drury working in St Patrick's Hospital in Dublin. After Drury's death in 1976 his recollections were collected and published by Rhees (in Rhees 1987). Commenting on the reason for publishing the remarks Drury stated:

> The number of introductions to and commentaries on Wittgenstein's philosophy is steadily increasing. Yet to one of his former pupils something that was central in his thinking is not being said.
>
> Kierkegaard told a bitter parable about the effects of his writings. He said he felt like the theatre manager who runs on the stage to warn the audience of a fire. But they take his appearance as all part of the farce they are enjoying, and the louder he shouts the more they applaud.
>
> Forty years ago Wittgenstein's teaching came to me as a warning against certain intellectual and spiritual dangers by which I was strongly tempted. These dangers still surround us. It would be a tragedy if well-meaning commentators should make it appear that his writings were now easily assimilable into the very intellectual milieu they were largely warning against. (Rhees 1987: xi)

His philosophy, so Drury suggests, should not leave us cold:

> Christianity says that wisdom is all cold; and that you can no more use it for setting your life to rights than you can forge iron when it is *cold*. (CV: 53e)

As far as Wittgenstein's personal faith was concerned he seemed to possess a firm belief in the passionate nature of belief (hence: 'I am not a religious man but I cannot help seeing every problem from a religious point of view' quoted in Rhees 1987: 94) whilst at the same time remaining sceptical as to religious institutions and behaviour *tout court*. Thus if we are to make sense of Wittgenstein's contribution to the philosophical problems arising from religious faith and to understand his own 'pursuit of the soul' we would do well to look at his conviction of the *passion* of religious faith as much as the 'logical structure' of any supposed religious 'language games'.

A way of seeing

Allied to Wittgenstein's notion of religion as a 'passion' we can add his categorization of philosophy as a 'way of seeing'. As we saw earlier in Chapter 5, Wittgenstein famously characterized the job of the philosopher as presenting an overview or 'way of seeing' – the *Überblick*/perspicuous view or 'overlook' as Wittgenstein himself often called it. In his Cambridge lectures of the 1930s, for example, when he returned to academic philosophy after his time in the 'wilderness', Wittgenstein defines the task of philosophy as one of attempting to 'be rid of a particular kind of puzzlement. This "philosophic" puzzlement is one of the intellect not of instinct' (CLL: 21). From this time onwards he describes his approach to philosophy as one of 'tidying up' our notions of the world, making clear what can be said about the world.[4] Thus in the *Remarks on Frazer's Golden Bough*, written in 1931, he contrasts Frazer's own 'scientistic' approach to certain anthropological events to his own *Übersichtliche Darstellung*. He states his own position as one which has the form: 'Here one can only *describe* and say: this is what human life is like' (RFGB: 121) contrasting it with what he sees as Frazer's approach:

> 'And so the chorus points to a secret law' one feels like saying to Frazer's collection of facts. I *can* represent this law, this idea, by means of an evolutionary hypothesis, or also, analogously to the schema of a plant, by means of the schema of a religious ceremony, but also by means of the arrangement of its factual content alone, in an *Übersichtliche Darstellung*. (RFGB: 133)

This 'perspicuous view' is: 'of fundamental importance' to Wittgenstein's approach and he describes it as that which: 'brings about the understanding which consists precisely in the fact that we "see the connections". Hence the importance of finding *Zwischengliedern* ("connecting links")' (PI: 133).

---

[4]See, for example, VB: 1940: 'Sometimes an expression has to be taken out of the language and sent to the cleaners. Then it can be re-introduced into service.'

These *Zwischengliedern* 'do nothing but direct the attention to the similarity, the relatedness of the *facts*'.

By the time Wittgenstein begins writing the text which will ultimately become the *Philosophical Investigations* (unpublished at the time of his death) the position of the *Übersichtliche Darstellung* has become clearer and more refined. Thus, as we have seen, we find the following key passage which develops the earlier idea of the *Remarks*:

> A main source of our misunderstandings is that we do not *übersehen* (oversee) the use of our words. – Our Grammar is lacking an *Übersichtlichkeit* (overview). – The *Übersichtliche Darstellung* produces the understanding which allows us to 'see connections'. Hence the importance of finding and inventing *Zwischengliedern*.
>
> The concept of the *Übersichtliche Darstellung* is of fundamental significance for us. It designates our *Darstellungsform* (viewpoint), the way we see things. (Is this a *Weltanschauung*?) (PI: 122)

The 'way of seeing' or 'oversee', is not however intended to engender a passive acceptance of ourselves or the world. Rather, the overview will lead, suggests Wittgenstein, to a change of attitude which will also transform our relationship with the world. As we saw earlier, for Wittgenstein, his proposal of an *Übersichtliche Darstellung* is not as another competing *Weltanschauung* with others in the post-enlightenment/scientific world (hence the phrase 'Is this a *Weltanschauung*?') but rather a new *Weltbild*, hence the similarity we pointed out earlier between Wittgenstein's approach to psychology, and analysis in particular, and that of 'psychological heretics' such as Rank.

Wittgenstein and the soul: A way of seeing

Among the biggest and perhaps most wide-ranging consequences of Wittgenstein's 'way of seeing' are the consequences it has for the notion of interiority which, as we have seen, have lain so close to the Western tradition of soul-searching from its Platonic and Augustinian roots onwards. This is nowhere more apparent than in Wittgenstein's last writings on the process of what he would call 'aspect-seeing', particularly stimulated by his prolonged reflection on Jastrow's famous 'Duck-Rabbit' diagram.

As he lived in virtual isolation at a farmhouse in Rosro near Connemara, Ireland (having resigned his professorship in Cambridge and more or less withdrawn from academic life) there are amusing stories of the great philosopher drawing the diagram in the sand of the sea-shore and then standing there for hours staring at it, much to the bemusement of his fellow villagers. In his final writings published as *Remarks on the Philosophy of Psychology*, he returns continually to the figure and how an aspect is changed in our thought and life. What fascinated him was how 'nothing and yet everything' is changed with the change of aspect as he wrote in 1948 at Rosro:

> What is incomprehensible is that *nothing*, and yet *everything*, has changed, after all. That is the only way to put it. Surely *this* way is wrong: It has not changed in *one* respect, but has in another. There would be nothing strange about that. But 'Nothing has changed' means: Although I have no right to change my report about what I saw, since I see the same things now as before – still, I am incomprehensibly compelled to report completely different things, one after the other. (RPP: 2.474)

As we look at the duck-rabbit, or indeed other parts of our perception of the world, 'a new aspect' dawns – everything has changed while nothing has changed. In his prolonged reflection on this phenomenon Wittgenstein is at pains to discount two lines of explanation. The first is what he calls 'the psychological'. This, he explains, would be to 'seek causes' for the change – which we can interpret as the neurological or reductionist search for the physical causes of the change – either in the firings of neurons or some other aspect of brain structure:

> Indeed, I confess, nothing seems more possible to me than that people some day will come to the definite opinion that there is no picture/representation in either the physiological or nervous systems which corresponds to a *particular* thought, a *particular* idea or memory. (LWP: 1.504, I have adjusted the translation slightly)

True to his later growing disillusion with the universalist claims of such 'scientism' he declares that such searching for causes is of no interest to him (LWP: 1.434).[5] For as he says himself in the *Philosophical Investigations*, by

---

[5] Interestingly this final part is deleted in the published version of the *Investigations*: 'Its causes

'giving all these examples I am not aiming at some kind of completeness, some classification of psychological concepts' (PI: 206e).

Having resisted the siren voices of neo-empirical psychology (rather like Rank and Hillman), Wittgenstein then proceeds to turn his guns on what he sees as the other chief distraction in formulating his response to the change of aspect – the lure of inwardness. As he warns: 'Do not try to analyse the experience in your self' (PI: 204e/LWP: 1.548).[6] 'Inner pictures/*Inneren Bilden*' are 'misleading, for this concept uses the "outer picture" as a model' for 'the use of the words for these concepts are no more like one another than the uses of "numeral" and "number". (And if one chose to call numbers "ideal numerals", one might produce a similar confusion)' (PI: 196e/PU: 523).[7] As I have argued elsewhere (Tyler 2011), I see one of the characteristics of Wittgenstein's style as the use of 'shock tactics' to force his reader to think for themselves. As I wrote in *The Return to the Mystical*, Wittgenstein 'prods and pokes' his reader to allow each of us trapped flies to escape our own personal 'fly-bottles'. Typical of these tactics are the use of irony (in Wittgenstein's case inherited from his master Søren Kierkegaard), exaggeration, paradox and humour. Wittgenstein's later writings are peppered with many examples of all of these and one of his most startling assertions makes its appearance in his critique of the inner:

I can know what someone else is thinking, not what I am thinking.
It is correct to say 'I know what you are thinking', and wrong to say 'I know what I am thinking'
(A whole cloud of philosophy condensed into a drop of grammar).
(PI: 222e/PU: 565)

To say the change of aspect occurs by the change of an 'inner picture' is therefore for Wittgenstein nonsensical – tautologous even:

The 'inner' is a delusion. That is: the whole complex of ideas alluded to by this word is like a painted curtain drawn in front of the scene of the actual word use. (LWP: 2.84e)

---

are of interest to psychologists, not to me' in LWP becomes 'Its causes are of interest to psychologists' in the final version of PI. Was one of his editors worried about Wittgenstein's perceived anti-psychologism here – or that his method somehow transcends psychology? As no editorial guidance was given for this decision in 1953 we cannot know.
[6] The official translation here is 'Do not try to analyse your own inner experience.'
[7] See also LWP 2.13e: 'The aspect seems to belong to the structure of the inner materialization.'

Now, if we begin to turn Wittgenstein's thoughts here onto the grand tradition of Christian reflection on the soul we have discussed in this book we immediately encounter a problem – for the tradition, as we have seen, has sometimes been obsessed with the 'inner'.[8] No better example of this can be found than in the later writings of Thomas Merton (1915–68), the twentieth century Trappist monk. The lives of the two men – Wittgenstein and Merton (like Tagore) – have striking parallels. Both born into relatively affluent and artistic families they were afforded as young men a certain freedom of education and style that probably contributed more than anything to their fiery independence of spirit and thought. Both in their twenties had a life crisis that propelled them into a complete re-evaluation of all that they had achieved and led to the contemplation of a monastic vocation. In the case of Wittgenstein this was rejected (more by his fellow monks than by Ludwig himself) and in the case of Merton embraced. Both wrote significant works as young men that shaped the philosophical and theological climates that followed them – in the case of Wittgenstein the *Tractatus Logico-Philosophicus* and in Merton's the *Seven Storey Mountain* – works, incidentally, that both men began to repudiate as they moved into middle age. Both also (like Tagore) stand on the cusp of modernity and postmodernity and reveal in their works the transition from one to another. Thus, bringing Wittgenstein up against Merton we have a confrontation between the Christian vision of the soul presented in Part I with the postmodern turn of the twentieth century.

The inner Merton

The Inner Experience (IE), published in 2003 from the manuscript of Merton's 1950s revision of his earlier *What is Contemplation* (1948), neatly encapsulates Merton's lifelong attempt to describe the nature of the contemplative life.[9] Throughout the work he appears to assume the approach to the 'inner' as a distinct 'mental realm' that Wittgenstein had so forcibly

---

[8] Although see my essay 'To Centre or Not to Centre' in Tyler 2013 where I deconstruct the notion of 'the inner' with respect to the writings of Ss Teresa of Avila and John of the Cross.
[9] Both authors share the distinction of having just as much published after their deaths as in their lifetimes. As with Wittgenstein, editors have sometimes been less than transparent about giving their reasons for certain editorial choices. However this makes studying the posthumous work more challenging and exciting for the serious research student!

critiqued in his own late writings. Take this passage from the beginning of the text for example:

> Every deeply spiritual experience, whether religious, moral, or even artistic, tends to have in it something of the presence of the interior self. Only from the inner self does any spiritual experience gain depth, reality, and a certain incommunicability. But the depth of ordinary spiritual experience only gives us a derivative sense of the inner self. It reminds us of the forgotten levels of interiority in our spiritual nature, and of our helplessness to explore them. (IE: 7)

Now much of the language here is the traditional language of the Christian contemplative tradition that we explored in Part I such as we found in, for example, St Augustine – that is, 'interiority', 'depth', 'the inner self' and 'levels of interiority'. As explained above, Wittgenstein was deeply sceptical of such metaphors, not least because he continually asked: *'Yes, but what do they mean?' 'How can we talk of psycho-physical spatial "depth" in the construct of the mental which is essentially non-spatial?'* Merton is right to point to the 'certain incommunicability' that lies in this process for the very concepts of meaning (or in Wittgensteinian terms, 'the language game') begin to break down at this point.[10] Now if Merton was to simply essay 'the inner' as a realm to be 'mysteriously approached' through contemplation without *intuiting* (I use the word here in its Kantian sense) any unease with such language our discussion of Merton could finish at this point, we could applaud the wisdom and perception of Wittgenstein and leave the mystical theology of Merton to continue languishing in its dark 'inner' prison. But, fortunately for our investigation, what *is* fascinating in Merton's late writing (and the editing of the *Inner Experience* by William Shannon allows us to read the middle-aged Merton critiquing the work of his younger self) is that Merton himself intuits that the mental language of 'inner and outer' simply won't work as a means of expressing what he has encountered in the contemplative life. These ideas are brought out forcibly in one of his last published works, *Zen and the Birds of Appetite* (ZB 1968). In this late work Merton (like Wittgenstein) takes as his target the Cartesian self:

> Modern man, in so far as he is still Cartesian … is a subject for whom his own self-awareness as a thinking, observing, measuring and

---

[10] In similar vein see Tyler 2013.

estimating 'self' is absolutely primary. It is for him the one indubitable 'reality' and all truth starts here. The more he is able to develop his consciousness as a subject over against objects, the more he can understand things in their relations to him and one another, the more he can manipulate these objects for his own interests, but also, at the same time, the more he tends to isolate himself in his own subjective person, to become a detached observer cut off from everything else in a kind of impenetrable alienated and transparent bubble which contains all reality in the form of purely subjective experience. (ZB: 22)

Here, then, we find Merton similarly teasing apart a false subject-object duality that Wittgenstein was critiquing in his later writings.[11] Modern consciousness, for Merton, becomes 'an ego-self imprisoned in its own consciousness, isolated and out of touch with other such selves in so far as they are all "things" rather than persons' (ZB: 22). So our two authors, then, share a common unease of the developing of the subject-object duality of the post-Cartesian Western empirico-scientific mindset. However the two authors do differ somewhat in their solutions to this problem. Wittgenstein prefers to lay the problem before us and give us his unendingly curious, frustrating and infuriating puzzles, cryptograms and aphorisms in order to coax each of our own dualistic Cartesian mindsets out of our individualized fly-bottles.

Within Merton's writings, on the other hand, we can find at least three attempts to crack this problem by three related, but quite different solutions (which has led, perhaps unfairly but understandably, to charges laid at Merton's feet over the years of eclecticism and syncretism).

The first is the one that occurred to Merton as a young man – his encounter on the trams of New York with the writings of Étienne Gilson, especially his *Spirit of Medieval Philosophy*. From this work he became interested in what he later characterized as 'the search for Being' as being at the root of his conversion from postmodern lost soul to reborn Trappist monk:

Underlying the subjective experience of the individual self there is an immediate experience of Being. This is totally different from an experience of self-consciousness. It is completely non-objective. It has in it none of the split and alienation that occurs when the subject

---

[11] I refer the reader here back to my discussion in the previous chapter of Hillman's 'hidden dualism'. The problem with Hillman's account of the self was that unlike Wittgenstein, and ultimately Merton, he had not intuited (or explained) the Cartesian duality that lay behind his schema: Wittgenstein's 'painted curtain'.

becomes aware of itself as a quasi-object ... In brief this form of consciousness assumes a totally different kind of self-awareness from that of the Cartesian thinking-self ... Here the individual is aware of himself as a self-to-be-dissolved in self-giving, in love, in 'letting-go', in ecstasy, in God. (ZB: 24)

This is an attitude that Merton had explored all his life following his conversion to Catholicism as a young man and developed through his long study of scholastic theology in Gethsemani monastery. However, as revealed in this late quote from *Zen*, Merton is still striving for the *healing* of a split (between self and Other) rather than the dispersal of the *illusion of a split* that Wittgenstein is pursuing in his late works.

Accordingly, it is no surprise then that Merton turned to two other sources to seek his way out of his fly-bottle – both from non-Christian traditions: in Zen Buddhism and Sufism. As well documented in Baker and Henry's *Merton and Sufism: The Untold Story* (Baker and Henry 1999), from the late 1950s onwards Merton became fascinated with the work of Sufi scholars such as Abdul Aziz, Reza Arasteh, Louis Massignon and Martin Lings (for the full correspondence see *The Hidden Ground of Love*, ed. Shannon, 1985). This culminated in a series of lectures given to the Gethsemani novices during the last two years of his life from 1966 to 1968. One constant theme in these lectures, which will take us back to Wittgenstein, is the sense that the 'change of aspect' required for Sufi (or indeed monastic) insight comes not from thinking or book-work but rather from the act of seeing itself. As he constantly tells the monks:

You can't learn it from a book, you've got to learn it by experience. And if you're learning it by experience, you need somebody else who's been through the mill to tell you what's happening to you ... And that is what Sufism is for, is to provide the situation where there is somebody around who knows the score and who can tell you. (Baker and Henry 1999: 149)[12]

But perhaps even more than Sufism (Merton's Sufi studies came somewhat later in his life and would have perhaps flowered had he lived longer), Merton's deliverance from the illusory dualism of the *cogito* lies in his study

---

[12] Baker and Henry tend to tidy up Merton's somewhat rambling style in their transcript of his lectures. I shall shortly give some of my own transcription which I have left more or less as Merton gives it.

of Zen. Unlike with his Sufi studies, Merton had over a decade to perfect his understanding of Zen – including many conversations and much correspondence with the noted Zen master D. T. Suzuki (again, see Shannon 1985). This time he was able to write out his mature thoughts on the matter in works such as *Zen and the Birds of Appetite* and the later revisions of *The Inner Experience*.

Zen-practice, the awareness of Zen-mind and the practice of *satori* clearly gave Merton the language he needed to escape from his Cartesian fly-bottle. In particular, from Zen, Merton learns the importance of stressing non-thought, seeing and experience with *satori* if realization is to happen:

> Buddhist meditation, but above all that of Zen, seeks not to *explain* but to *pay attention*, to *become aware*, to *be mindful*, in other words to develop a certain *kind of consciousness that is above and beyond deception* by verbal formulas – or by emotional excitement. (ZB: 38)

Zen therefore encourages a certain type of 'authentic metaphysical intuition which is also existential and empirical' (ZB: 38), for the Zen practitioner sees 'what is right there and does not add any comment, any interpretation, any judgement, any conclusion' (ZB: 53). Thus Zen provided a means for Merton whereby he could articulate 'a breakthrough, an explosive liberation from one-dimensional conformism, a recovery of unity which is not the suppression of opposites but a simplicity beyond opposites' (ZB: 140) – a breakthrough, or revolution, not just for the practitioner but to the whole of a culture dominated by the dead-ends of objectification and reification:

> The inner self is as secret as God and, like Him, it evades every concept that tries to seize hold of it with full possession. It is a life that cannot be held and studied as object, because it is not a 'thing'. (IE: 7)

Using the concepts of Zen, then, Merton is able to escape the fly-bottle of dualism to articulate a position not a million miles from that presented by Wittgenstein. This is no better illustrated by the very Wittgensteinian inverted commas Merton brings to his final (revised) remarks of *The Inner Experience*:

> The 'reality' through which the contemplative 'penetrates' in order to reach a contact with what is 'ultimate' in it is actually his own being, his own life. The contemplative is not one who directs a magic spiritual intuition upon other objects, but one who, begins perfectly

united in himself and recollected in the center of his own humility, enters into contact with reality by an immediacy that forgets the division between subject and object. (IE: 151)

In these last few crucial years, then, Merton was clearly struggling as much with the notions of 'inner and outer' as Wittgenstein was in his final years. In a letter to Suzuki written on 11 April 1959 he ponders when contemplating the differences between Christianity and Zen:

> The Christ we seek is within us, in our inmost self, *is* our inmost self, and yet infinitely transcends ourselves. We have to be 'found in Him' and yet be perfectly ourselves and free from the domination of any image of Him other than Himself … Christ Himself is in us as unknown and unseen. (Shannon 1985: 564)

In passages such as this it is almost as if Merton's (theological) conceptual apparatus is collapsing and it is only notions such as Zen (or Sufism) that will give him the language to present what he is experiencing in these last extraordinary years. It is striking, and a little sad, then, that in *Zen*, having referenced Wittgenstein's famous aphorism from the *Investigations* – *Don't Think, Look!* – in support of his notion that Zen 'blasts out' the preconceptions of the mind 'by using language against itself' so that 'we can see directly' (ZB: 49), he concludes *Zen* with a thin attack on what he terms 'the canonization of "ordinary speech" by linguistic analysis' (ZB: 49). Given the state of post-Wittgensteinian analytical philosophy in the academy by the time Merton wrote these words in 1968 this is perhaps not surprising. As I have argued elsewhere (Tyler 2011) the post-Wittgensteinian splitting of Wittgensteinian interpretation into various rival 'camps', coupled with some strange editorial choices on behalf of his literary executors, has led to some of the ill-informed and frankly prejudicial views that still attach to Wittgenstein's name and philosophy to this day. With the unedited state of the *Investigations* at the time of its publication in 1953 (the version which Merton would have read) and the lack of supporting material such as the *Last Writings* I have referred to in this chapter, it is perhaps unsurprising that Merton would not have found in the Austrian's writings what he was looking for. I hope to have demonstrated here that there are sufficient congruencies between their two approaches to justify my claim that both of these twentieth century masters are working in the same direction to release the Cartesian fly from its (post)-modern fly-bottle.

The postmodern soul

By placing Wittgenstein's linguistic philosophy alongside the spiritual exercises of Merton we are presented with two twentieth century masters meeting over a theological-philosophical divide. In the *Last Writings*, Wittgenstein concludes that 'experiencing a change of aspect is similar to an action' (LWP: 2.14e). The thought, sight and action of a 'change of aspect' (or better – *das Aufleuchten eines Aspekts* – 'the dawning of an aspect', RPP: 2.474) are all intimately linked (not for nothing did he consider 'In the beginning was the deed' as the epithet for the *Investigations*). Merton sees contemplation as seeing, thinking and acting too, leading to a 'level of experience that society does not really encourage and does not really want' (*Lectures to Novices*).

For Wittgenstein the aim of philosophy was to 'show the fly the way out of the fly-bottle' (PI: 309). For him philosophy could never be an abstract rarefied discipline: it had to have a *practical, ethical* dimension. The right seeing of true philosophy will bring about right action. In this respect I will conclude by saying that I believe that the Wittgensteinian *Blick*, despite Merton's reluctance to admit it, shares many characteristics with the 'Zen-Christian' mind of Merton that we have explored here. Both of them with their gestures and comments nudge us in certain directions so that in Wittgenstein's case we can begin to 'see the world aright' (T: 6.54) and in that of Merton we will establish the correct conditions to be brought into deeper contemplative relationship with God. Their comments interrupt the spontaneous, unselfconscious flow of the dualistic Cartesian mind forcing us to re-evaluate our place in the world and our attitude to it. By using language, similes and metaphors in unusual and provocative ways (as indeed Merton tells us is the role of Zen master in ZB: 34) both authors bring us back to what we knew already but were unable to express in words.[13]

Radical revolutionaries and reactive conservatives both, Wittgenstein and Merton sought throughout their troubled lives the change of aspect that would afford them the existential peace they longed for and which, I have argued here, they both finally glimpsed in their last tantalizingly incomplete, and yet strangely prophetic, writings.

---

[13] In his perceptive essay on the implications of the Wittgensteinian perspective for our understanding of the self in religious context, *The Suspicion of Suspicion: Wittgenstein and Bonhoeffer*, Rowan Williams concludes that Wittgenstein's arguments point towards a notion of 'religious interiority' that 'means the learning of patterns of behaviour that reinforce the awareness of my finite and provisional status, my being in time' (Williams 2007: 199). We shall return to this key aspect of the Wittgensteinian choreography in the final chapter.

Conclusion: *The King of the Dark Chamber*

We began this chapter with the traumatized Wittgenstein struggling to find an academic mode of speech before the bemused eyes of the Vienna Circle. As I hope to have demonstrated here, the final form his discourse would take, as evidenced in the later philosophy upon which I have drawn heavily here, is ultimately a dialectic that seeks through the choreography of what is said and what is shown to lead to the transformational 'release of the fly from the fly-bottle'. Accordingly, Wittgenstein's fascination with Tagore, and in particular *The King of the Dark Chamber*, becomes prescient for the type of academic discourse he was hoping to foster in the final decades of his life, not least his 'discourse of the soul'.[14]

The story of 'the King' is simply told. The eponymous King dwells in a dark chamber at the centre of his kingdom. No subject has seen him – some fear him, some love him and some even doubt his existence. His wife, Sudarshana, grows restless at never being able to see the King and Tagore contrasts her impatient speculations as to the nature of the King with the simple devotion of the maid-servant Surangama who is content to love the King in his darkness:

> Sudarshana: Light, light! Will the lamp never be lighted in this chamber?
> Surangama: My Queen, you can meet others in the lighted rooms; but only in this dark room can you meet your lord …
> Sudarshana: Living in this dark room you have grown to speak darkly and strangely Surangama, I cannot understand you. No, no – I cannot live without light – I am restless in the stifling darkness. (*King*: 17)

Sudarshana, representative of the restless intellect, can only be comfortable with light, form and discrimination. Surangama, on the other hand, is happy to live in the darkness with all its paradox and mystery – in her unknowing she accepts the will of her Lord, so much so that her intuitive powers can perceive the approach of the King:

> Surangama: I hear his footsteps in my heart. Serving him in this dark chamber, I have gained this new sense – I know and feel without seeing.

---

[14] "'Soul-ish" is for me not a metaphysical but a logical epithet' (LWP: 2.63e).

Finally unable to bear the strain of not seeing her Lord, Sudarshana searches him out in a pleasure garden and falls in love with an impostor, these acts lead to the destruction of the palace in fire. Entering once again the Chamber while all is fire outside Sudarshana encounters the true King but this time she has seen him and perceives him as terrifying darkness:

> Terrible, oh, it was terrible! I am afraid even to think of it again. – Oh you are dark and terrible as everlasting night! Even though I only looked on you for one dreadful instant! (*King*: 58)

As John of the Cross proposes – the vision of the Eternal King is dark and confusing as the boundary between the sayable and unsayable is crossed. For as the King states:

> The utter darkness that has today shaken you to your soul will one day be your solace and salvation. What else can my love exist for? (58/59)

Running from the encounter Queen Sudarshana pursues a destructive course not only for herself but her country (one thinks here of Wittgenstein's war traumas and his 1920s search for 'the truth'). Finally, humiliated and resigned the Queen can once again enter the Chamber. With her intellect laid low she can at last finally see the King and discourse with him openly. The 'perspicuous vision' has been restored and the play ends with the King opening the windows and doors of the Chamber to the Queen as she steps into the light.

In summary, the *King of the Dark Chamber* can be taken as an allegory for Wittgenstein's own search to articulate the truths of the spiritual life. Neither fideist, foundationalist nor fundamentalist (as I have argued) the turn of the Wittgensteinian key unlocks a whole garden of mystical discourse for us his contemporary readers.

As in the postmodern practice of psychotherapy, Wittgenstein, as we have seen, invites us to observe the foundations of possible buildings rather than trying to build one building – the *Weltbild* rather than the *Weltanschauung*. He does not (like Tagore) provide us with clever interpretations and interventions but allows the clarity of insight (*Übersichtliche Darstellung*) to be turned on the 'foundations of possible buildings'.

This post-enlightenment way of knowing (such as therapeutic discourse – to which we could add mystical discourse) requires a more interactive and immediate medium or frame of reference than could be grasped by the verification of either the Vienna Circle or what we can term 'scientism'.

Action is the closest activity available to language and such activity will be tempered by a necessary vein of humility arising from the lack of an overriding *Weltanschauug*. This is the necessary humility of the practitioner of the mystical discourse – whether contemplative or clergy, philosopher or psychotherapist.

For Wittgenstein, Tagore and Merton *change* and *transformation* are paramount. They entice, excite, goad and puzzle us. *They are not meant to leave us alone.* They pose us problems which cannot be ignored. By their nature they 'subvert'; if they do not subvert they have failed in their task. If we play their games with them they re-orientate our perceptions of reality, ourselves and our place in the world: they are primarily *performative discourses* that 'show' rather than 'say'.

In conclusion, I would like to suggest that Wittgenstein's Viennese turn not only allowed a new discourse to return to the heart of academic philosophy but also enabled us to appreciate once again the soul from a new perspective – a change of aspect that frees us from the prison of interiority and psychologistic scientism. In this respect Wittgenstein's turn mirrors that of his contemporary Otto Rank in his understanding of the dynamic and nature of psychology. We can thus see clear parallels between the two men in their suspicion of the scientization of the search for the self and their shared understanding that the self has by its nature a tendency to move away from the concretization of the empirical approach – a scepticism shared too, as we have seen, by the late Merton.

In common with Otto Rank, therefore, we find in Wittgenstein, Tagore and Merton the tools to turn once again to the mystery of the *psyche* in its encounter with the transcendent as did the early fathers and philosophers we discussed at the beginning of the book. To conclude this book's 'pursuit of the soul', I would like to turn to another German contemporary of Rank, Tagore, Merton and Wittgenstein – the Carmelite nun Edith Stein (Saint Teresa Benedicta a Cruce). My reason for ending this book with her writings is that in many respects she gathers together so many of the threads that have been woven through this book – a philosophical phenomenologist who found the answers to her (post-)modern searching in the pre-modern texts of the Christian tradition, especially in Thomas Aquinas, Dionysius, Teresa of Avila and the person with whom it all began – St Augustine. In contrast to Hillman, however, whose view I suggested at the end of Part II eventually ends up being a 'dead end', I will suggest that Stein's synthesis steers a path through competing interpretations to present a final picture of the soul that will appeal to postmodern and pre-modern perspectives alike.

CHAPTER 8
EDITH STEIN AND LOVE OF THE SOUL

'This is the truth'

On 9 August 1942 a young German Carmelite nun of Jewish descent went to her death in the killing fields of Auschwitz. Of all the saints of the confused and confusing 'short twentieth century' this nun, Edith Stein – feminist, atheist, Jew and Catholic – is one of the most complicated. Born of a devout Jewish family in Breslau, Germany, Edith developed an early love and skill in philosophy which was to remain with her throughout her life. The greatest influence on her philosophical development was the work of Edmund Husserl and the newly emerging phenomenological school. From her Jewish faith Edith turned to atheism, although always with a lively interest in the 'God question'. In the dialogue between the Orthodox bishop, Tikhon, and the enigmatic Stavrogin in Dostoyevsky's 1872 novel *The Demons*, Tikhon informs the unbelieving Stavrogin that: 'a complete atheist stands on the next-to-last upper step to the most complete faith'. This quote could have been directly applied to the young Edith. In all her atheistic questing she sensed the importance of the divine perspective for all phenomenological research. The key moment of her conversion occurred in 1921 when she stayed at the house of some friends, the Conrad-Martiuses, at their home near Bergzabern. Wanting some reading for the evening she looked through the bookshelves of her hosts and found Teresa of Avila's *Book of the Life*. She was not able to sleep that night and was completely gripped by the narrative that Teresa presented. Afterwards she would say of Teresa's book: 'This is the truth'; finally she had found what she had been looking for (see Herbstrith 1992: 65). As she would write later 'It is just the people who at first passionately embrace the world who penetrate farthest into the depths of the soul. Once God's powerful hand has freed them from its allurements, they are taken into their innermost selves' (From *Die Seelenburg* in WP: 66).

She was baptized a Christian in 1922 and began an extended study of the Church Fathers and Scripture, especially the works of St Thomas Aquinas. The next ten years were ones of teaching and work to reconcile Christian and atheist philosophy, in particular the phenomenology of her 'master' Husserl and the high scholasticism of Thomas Aquinas.

Husserl would end his days a Christian having experienced a deathbed conversion in 1938. On hearing the news, Edith, just about to take her solemn vows in the Cologne Carmel,[1] wrote to another sister: 'As regards my dear Master, I have no worries about him. To me, it has always seemed strange that God could restrict his mercy to the boundaries of the visible Church. God is truth, and whoever seeks the truth is seeking God, whether he knows it or not' (Letter 259, quoted in Herbstrith 1992: 139).

Despite her conversion to Christianity she was still a target for Nazi persecution and after the horrendous events of *Kristallnacht* on 8 November 1938 she was forced to leave Germany to seek shelter with the Carmelite community at Echt, Holland. Despite the persecution, throughout all this time Edith was able to continue her philosophico-theological writings on the interface of phenomenology and theology. What they reveal is a woman who grasped the essence of Carmelite spirituality in all its intellectual depth and existential consequence.

Since her student days Edith had been fascinated by the 'nature of empathy', and in fact had written her doctoral thesis on the subject (published as *On the Problem of Empathy*). Commenting on this interest, Roman Ingarden writes that 'What interested her most was the question of defining the possibility of mutual communication between human beings, in other words, the possibility of establishing community. This was more than a theoretical concern for her; belonging to a community was a personal necessity, something that vitally affected her identity' (Ingarden 1979: 472). Perhaps, as Edith realized, our hope as alienated, atomized, late capitalist individuals lies in the return to community as the manifestation of our essential natures as *homo empathicus*.

Like many of the thinkers we have studied throughout this book in our pursuit of the soul, language of the soul was for Stein essentially a language of union and wholeness – a cipher for the locus where body, mind, heart and spirit could be usefully identified and held in creative tension. From her early writings, then, she creates a picture of the soul where all four categories of being can be held together. As she puts it in the late commentary on Teresa of Avila's 'Interior Castle', *Die Seelenburg*, the soul is 'the middle of the whole bodily, soulish and spiritual picture that we call *human*'. In this late work she attempts a synthesis between her own phenomenological anthropology and the medieval Christian writing she had come to admire

---

[1] She entered Carmel in 1933 having considered vocations with the Dominicans and Benedictines.

so much (including, amongst others, those of Teresa of Avila, Thomas Aquinas and Dionysius the Areopagite). From Thomas she appreciates the Aristotelian notion of the soul as form of the body, whilst from Dionysius, on the other hand, she accepts the essential unknowing that lies at the heart of the self (Tagore's 'dark chamber'). This she deftly combines with what she sees as the dynamic sense of self that Teresa of Avila provides in her notion of the 'Interior Castle'. In so doing, like Wittgenstein, she breaks free from the constraints of both 'inwardness' and 'empiricism' in discussing the nature of self. As she puts it in *Endliches und Ewiges Sein*:

> The soul is often spoken as a sort of 'space' (*Raum*) with 'depth' (*Tiefe*) and 'surface' (*Oberfläche*). In such fashion belongs the picture (*Bild*) of the 'castle of the soul' (*Seelenburg*), that has outer and inner chambers and ultimately an innermost abode. The 'I' (*Ich*) inhabits this castle, and it may choose to reside in one of the outer chambers, or it may retire into an inner one. The examples cited can help us to understand the sense of these pictures (*diese Bilder*): they remain however always a necessary help (*Notbehelf*) to grasp relationships which are fully without space (*sie bleiben ja immer ein Notbehelf, um völlig unräumliche Verhältnisse zu veranschaulichen*). (EE: 398)

Over-concretization or literalism is for Stein the enemy of grasping the nature of self and, like Rank, Hillman and Wittgenstein, she understands that 'soulish' language will undermine the concretization of empirical and pseudo-scientific methods of understanding the self. As she puts it in *Ewiges and Endliches Sein*: 'the I has no life that is not the life of the soul'/'*das Ich hat kein Leben, das nicht Leben der Seele ware*' (EE: 398).

Like Rank, Wittgenstein and Hillman, Stein was increasingly unhappy with the 'psychology without soul'/'*psychologie ohne Seele*' (WP: 63) that had been growing in popularity in the German-speaking lands of the mid-twentieth century. The empiricist reductionism of the self was for Stein a grave element that threatened to destroy the unity of the self. In contrast to this movement Stein recognized a 'Life-way'/'*Lebewesen*' at the heart of the human self (WP: 65) that sought expression through what Rank would have called 'the soulish'/'*seelische*'. Only the person with a 'hot heart'/'*heisse Herz*' who had seized the world, could, she suggests (clearly in autobiographical terms but also reflecting Ss Augustine and Teresa) really appreciate the *Lebewesen* that lies at the heart of the self. Thus, she concludes, the soul 'is a personal-spiritual picture within which is expressed the innermost and most actual, the essence, from which the person's strengths and ability to change arises. Not then an unknown X that we seek to clarify through experienced facts, but something which enlightens us and can be felt whilst always remaining mysterious.'[2]

And this is exactly the point where Stein makes the same move as Augustine – that is, to see in the inner contradiction and mysterious tension of the soul a reflection of the Trinity itself. Thus, Stein's solution to the problem of the soul in postmodern context is essentially that envisaged by Augustine in *De Trinitate* and places her writing firmly in the Augustinian rather than the Plotinian tradition (of, for example, a writer like Hillman). For her, the multiplicity of perspective of the soul is held in the unity of apperception which is Christ. Christ is the unity of perception that holds together all the contradictions of the psyche. In *Endliches und Ewiges Sein* she again characterizes the 'human being'/'*menschliche Sein*' as being a composite of 'body, soul and spirit'/'*leiblich-seelisch-geistig*' (EE: 336, 7.3.1). The '*Menschengeist*' is determined 'from above'/'*von obern*' and 'from below'/'*von unten*' (cf. Freud and Jung's conscious and unconscious). Thus the soul for Stein consists of a choreography of *Geist*/spirit and *Leib*/body: 'the spiritual life of the human person rises from a dark ground. It rises like a candle-flame that illumines itself nourished by non-luminous matter.' The 'non-luminous matter' of the human body is to be distinguished (in true phenomenological fashion) from the matter which we perceive in the world around us. For, in contrast, *our* matter is matter that is *felt, experienced and innerly sensed*. This, for Stein, constitutes an essential layer and part of self – which is why she refers to it as *Leib* rather than *Körper* (338), as she says 'What distinguishes the body from a corpse is that the body is an *ensouled* corpse'/'*Was den Leib von einem blossen Körper unterscheidet, ist, dass es ein beseelter Körper ist.*' Thus, the human self, as a composite of matter and spirit, is what for Edith is determining of the term 'soul' and reflects the Trinitarian nature of God (7.9.1): '*Die Menschenseele ist nicht nur ein Mittleres zwischen Geist und Stoff, sondern ein geistiges Geschöpf, nicht nur Gebilde des Geistes, sonder bildender Geist*'/'Therefore the human soul is not a mean between spirit and matter but a spiritual creature – not only a formed structure of the spirit but a forming spirit' (EE: 7.9.1, my translation).

---

[2] '*Ist ein persönlich-geistiges Gebilde, darum ist ihr Innerstes und Eigentlichstes, ihr Wesen, aus dem ihre Kräfte und das Wechselspiel ihres Lebens entspringen, nicht nu rein unbekanntes X, das wir zur Erklärung der erfahrbaren seelischen Tatsachen annehmen, sondern etwas, was uns aufleuchten und spürbar warden kann, wenn es auch immer geheimnisvoll bleibt*' (WP: 67).

This human choreography of *Leib* and *Geist* held together in the embrace of *Seele* is for Stein the reflection in the human person of the Triune God of Christianity: 'the threefold formative power of the soul must be regarded as a tri-unity, and the same is true of the end product of its forming activity: body-soul-spirit' (EE: 6.9.10). Thus 'if we attempt to relate this tri-unity to the divine trinity, we shall discover in the soul … the image of the Father; in the body … the image of the Eternal Word; and in the spiritual life the image of the Divine Spirit' (EE: 6.9.10). If, therefore, the person can see this when 'it then opens itself in its innermost being to the influx of divine life, the soul (and through it the body) is formed into an image of the Son of God' (EE: 6.9.10).

As she would later put it in *Kreuzeswissenschaft*, the last (uncompleted) work she began in 1941 as a commentary on St John of the Cross for the 400th anniversary of his birth:

> Human beings are called upon to live in their inmost region and to have themselves as much in hand as possible only from that centre-point … It is God's mystery, which God alone can reveal to the degree that pleases him … God himself has chosen it as his dwelling. (KW: II.3b)

Whilst working on this text, in the early evening of 2 August 1942, SS officers arrived at the Echt convent where Edith was staying, demanding that she leave with her sister, Rosa, who had become an extern sister at the convent. In the shock and surprise, the whole neighbourhood came out to protest at this indecent act. In the crowd and confusion Rosa became alarmed and upset. In this distress and confusion Edith gently took her hand and said 'Come, Rosa. We're going for our people'.[3] We have fragmentary accounts of what happened to Edith next including reports from Westerbork, the Nazi holding camp in Holland for all deported Jews (where the other great Jewish mystic, Etty Hillesum, would also be held), and from guards and functionaries as her train moved slowly East to the killing fields of Auschwitz. One account, from the Dutch official Mr Wielek at Westerbork, will suffice to give a sense of Edith's last days on earth:

> The one sister who impressed me immediately, whose warm, glowing smile has never been erased from my memory, despite the disgusting

---

[3] From the *Kölner Selig- und Heiligsprechungsprozess der Dienerin Gottes Sr. Teresia Benedicta a Cruce – Edith Stein* (Cologne 1962: 92) in Herbstrith 1992: 180.

incidents I was forced to witness, is the one whom I think the Vatican may one day canonize. From the moment I met her in the camp at Westerbork … I knew: here is someone truly great. For a couple of days she lived in that hellhole, walking, talking and praying … like a saint. And she really was one. That is the only fitting way to describe this middle-aged woman who struck everyone as so young, who was so whole and honest and genuine. (Herbstrith 1992: 186)

Edith went to her death at Auschwitz; we assume it was on 9 August 1942, the day on which she is now celebrated as Saint Teresa Benedicta at the Cross since 1998.

EPILOGUE: THE SYMBOLIC LANGUAGE OF THE SOUL

As our long journey nears an end it is time to draw together a few threads from our pursuit of the soul. Fenn in his *On Losing the Soul* (1995) describes the soul as:

> Myth, mystery, essential being, and the common, ordinary, human struggle for a real, even an essential self. (1995: 1)

Whilst Bernice Martin suggests that:

> The soul represents a hypothetical point in the individual's subjectivity: the point from which it is possible to become aware of the existence of an essential self or of its possible loss and corruption. (Fenn 1995: 2)

As we conclude by reviewing the long 'pursuit of the soul' in the Christian and Platonic traditions, I hope to have demonstrated that such essentialist views of the soul by writers such as these, especially in the light of the critiques in the latter half of this book, are misguided. I have argued throughout that from Plato onwards Christian and non-Christian writers alike have recognized the dynamic contrasts that make the word 'soul' a transformational locus at the heart of the human personality.

Yet, in one respect our contemporary writers on the soul are right. Martin continues that the word soul: 'suggests to me the possibility of recognizing – hinting at – a level of discourse which accords some ultimate significance to the person beyond what can be said by the expert social scientific disciplines. The metaphysical and theological connotations of "soul" suggest a dimension of the integrity of persons, which is not fully captured by the vocabulary of "self" and "selfhood"' and 'we wish to use the term to point toward a mystery at the heart of social life' (Fenn 1995: 2–3). For one thing has become clear from our pursuit of the soul: if it is not necessarily a marker of the essential nature of self it is surely a locus for the interface of the temporal and eternal as the individual transects the transcendent and immanent. Otto Rank, as we saw, expressed an unease with the notion of psychology being the ultimate aim and resting place for the search of the self (an unease shared by his fellow heretic, James Hillman). As early as his *Will Therapy* he saw the soul-life as basically symbolic (WT: 30) and that 'the new type of humanity will only become possible when we have passed beyond the psychotherapeutic transitional stage'. Such an art will lead to a 'conquest of fear of life'. For Rank this conquest has been led in the past by respectively religion, art and science (WT: 126), none of which, for him, is now adequate to our needs – psychoanalysis will now lead humanity into the future. Some commentators have indeed speculated that Rank 'was moving toward a kind of religious psychotherapy' (Ellenberger 1981: 860). Yet my argument in this book has been, *pace* Rank and Hillman, that such a 'religious psychology' *is* possible from the perspective of Christianity. In the latter half of the book I have tried to meld the early 'pictures of the soul' from the Church Fathers to the postmodern insights of Stein, Wittgenstein and Merton. The result, I would like to suggest, is a soul-psychology that avoids the pitfalls of, on the one hand, the Charybdis of overly mechanized scientistic solutions, and on the other, the Scylla of a spiritualized 'anti-matter' that seeks a divorce of soul-language from the wholeness of personhood expressed in terms of body, heart, mind and spirit.

Thus, if we seek a conclusion to our pursuit of the soul, the conception of the Trinitarian nature of self held in the unity of Christ espoused by Stein (and ultimately Augustine) seems to come closest to the symbolic sense of self that I have argued lies at the heart of the Christian recovery of the soul. Of course, we can never discount the Plotinian counter-current in Western thought. However, as I argued in my review of Hillman's work, I think there are perhaps sufficient deficits in this account to make it of questionable application in the contemporary world.

As Rank suggests Plato also knew: the mythic is the proper discourse for the soul. For, as already stated above, a key element of psychology does not deal with facts, but with the *interpretation* of facts; this is no better shown than in the dream interpretation:

> In the dream we ourselves interpret physical and psychical states (facts), but this 'interpretation' is as little 'analysis' of 'facts' as is our analytic 'interpretation', which represents only another kind of symbolization and rationalization. (WT: 230)

Yet despite his Plotinian leanings Hillman would, I suspect, also agree with the thrust of my argument in this book that an overly scientistic psychologization of the soul misses the gossamer-light warp and woof of a performative soul-language that by its nature moves from the transcendent to the immanent and back again. As Hillman himself wrote in 1967:

> Because the soul is lost – or at least temporarily mislaid or bewildered – ministers have been forced, upon meeting a pastoral problem, to go upstairs to its neighbour, the next closest thing to soul: the mind. So the churches turn to academic and clinical psychology, to psychodynamics and psychopathology and psychiatry, in attempts to understand the mind and its workings. This has led ministers to regard troubles of the soul as mental breakdowns and cure of soul as psychotherapy. But the realm of the mind – perception, memory, mental diseases – is a realm of its own, another flat belonging to another owner who can tell us very little about the person whom the minister really wants to know, the soul. (I: 44)

And again later in 1975:

> The soul cannot be understood through psychology alone, our vision even leaves the field of psychology as it is usually thought of, and moves widely though history, philosophy and religion. (RVP: ix)

In this spirit I shall conclude our pursuit by drawing upon the critiques and arguments of the thinkers presented in the final part of this book to summarize five essential components of what I suggest a contemporary 'soul-discourse' may consist of:

1. A way of seeing

Following Wittgenstein, soul-work can be described as a 'way of seeing' that releases liberating perspectives in our day-to-day existence. In Hillman's words:

> By soul, I mean, first of all, a perspective rather than a substance, a viewpoint towards things rather than a thing itself. (RVP: x)

Thus the work of the analyst, pastor or care-worker is to cultivate the 'third position' of Wittgenstein's *Weltbild* that 'sees the foundations of possible buildings'. Each *Weltanschauung* is to be viewed from a critical perspective – including (controversially for our present times) the scientistic perspective. From this alert ambiguity the soul-maker helps us attune ourselves to the transcendent by drawing attention to our responses to the immanent. Uniquely, the soul-maker recognizes the human person as the locus of intersection of the transcendent and immanent.

2. The path of unknowing

Beginning with Plato and Plotinus we saw the essential unknowing that lies at the heart of the soul-project. Wittgenstein's showing allows us to see the limits of knowing as we understand meaning as lying on the interface of the choreography between what is said (and known) and what is unsaid (and unknown). In contradistinction to the rationalist path of knowing of the Cartesian 'I', the path of soul-making is one that must move 'under the radar' of the all-knowing rational 'I' and allow a softening of rational certainties in the light of a greater presence. Hillman termed the Freudian desire to replace 'It' with 'I' the 'strip mining of the psyche' (IV: 46) and his counter-move suggests an approach to the 'unknown thing' that gives space for the unconscious to breathe. In this respect the apophatic unknowing of the soul is simply letting the conscious know its place while the unconscious figurations reassert themselves. 'Maybe', suggests Hillman, 'they know best what is relevant to the conscious personality, rather than the unconscious personality' (IV: 46). Therefore contemporary soul-making will require as much 'unknowing' as it does 'knowing'.

3. Ambiguity and paradox

The contemporary soul-maker must live in the realm of ambiguity that is the soul's true home. Whether with a client, facing a dream or working on the self, the demands of the soul require an openness to the ambiguity that lies at the heart of the human personality. Imagination, for Hillman, becomes the place where we uniquely play with the self in its efforts to overcome the straightjacket of the post-Cartesian 'I'. For him, the world of Cartesian dualism allows 'no space for the intermediate, ambiguous and metaphorical' (RVP: xii). Rather it is the place inhabited by living subjects and dead objects. All affect is removed from the world around us. In Hillman's writing, following as we have seen Plotinus and the neo-Platonists, this place of ambiguity will become populated by the world of 'archetype' and '*daemones*'. For Christian writers such as Stein (following Augustine and Aquinas) the ambiguity of the self is held in the tension of the Trinity, where Christ becomes the unity of apperception for the individual believer. The paradox of the Trinitarian vision thus reflects the paradox that lies at the heart of human personhood.

4. The symbolic, creative and artistic

Beginning with Plato and for many of the thinkers discussed in this volume, the symbolic and mythic becomes the special locus for this ambiguous sense of self to find expression. For Hillman it is indicative of that mode of consciousness that 'recognises all realities as primarily symbolic or metaphorical' experienced through 'reflective speculation, dream, image and fantasy' (RVP: x). The symbolic sources of the soul thus lie very close to the sources of creative and artistic endeavour and thus the pursuit of the soul will often manifest itself through these means.

5. The relational and libidinal

Soul-making is at heart a relational process. In Rank's words, analysis is 'an art of love' and the relationship between the soul-seeker and soul-maker is at the heart of the matter. The Platonic tradition always emphasized the role of *eros* in this relationship. In contrast to Hillman, who sees the Christian tradition as suppressing the role of *eros*, I have argued in these final chapters that thinkers as diverse as Merton, Stein and Wittgenstein present an embodied Christian view of the self that maintains the transcendent through relationship with the bodily and libidinal. The soul is found not in flight from the body but in the very embrace of its ambiguity and libido. This is not surprising. For, as I demonstrated earlier in the book, despite Augustine's famous suspicion of 'concupiscence', there were sufficient alternative (neo-Platonic) strands of early Christian anthropology in writers such as Evagrius and Origen to preserve alternative narratives of the soul in the Christian tradition. As I have demonstrated elsewhere (Tyler 2011), the medieval traditions of the *theologia mystica* with their Dionysian emphasis were sufficient to keep this tradition alive. Despite Hillman's caricature of Christianity as a life-denying and anti-libidinal locus (and he is of course not alone here) I hope to have demonstrated here that this is far from the case and there are sufficient traces of this alternative relational and libidinal anthropology in the Christian tradition to allow a future Christian anthropology, open to the possibilities of the libidinal, to flourish. The future of the soul lies in the libidinal and relational.

Epilogue: The Symbolic Language of the Soul

The Christian soul

As we saw, Hillman's critique of Christianity is more directed to its perceived *monomania* or indeed *monism* rather than to the five functions of the soul that we have outlined above. Taking his cue from the Renaissance neo-Platonic writers such as Marsilio Ficino who want to return to a more ambiguous and polyistic sense of self, he characterizes monotheist religions such as Christianity, Judaism and Islam as the chief enemies of such a polyistic sense of self. As he puts it:

> We can do little exploration of the imaginal until we have surmounted our own egocentricity, that capital I appearing in the monotheism of consciousness (Jung), in monotheistic science and metaphysics and in the root of all: the monotheism of Christian humanism with its tolerance for but one historical, unique, divine personification. (RVP: 41)

As I have argued in an earlier chapter, I find this, what I have characterized as the 'Plotinian' view of the soul, deficient for the reasons stated. In contrast the strand of thought I have characterized as Augustinian seeks to reconcile the ambiguity of the human soul through contemplation of the Christian Trinity. For the reasons stated throughout this book I find this the most satisfactory position in which not only contemporary soul language can be grounded but also a position that holds the unity and diversity of the soul together in a necessary continuum. Using writers such as Stein and Wittgenstein, it is possible to develop a language of the soul/self that moves beyond the narrow straightjacket imposed by much language of the self – whether from a scientistic overly mechanical perspective or an unthinking credal fundamentalism. As Tertullian stated in his *Apology*: 'the soul is naturally Christian.'[4] For as Augustine recognized at the onset of the Christian project and Stein reiterated in our own times, the picture of the Trinity holds the truth of the human person in the transcendent apperception of Christ. For the Christian, Christ is able to hold together the multiple perspectives and contradictions of the *psyche* in a unity of apperception.

---

[4] '*O testimonium animae naturaliter Christianae!*'/ 'O the witness of the soul – by its very nature Christian!' (*Apology*: 17:3).

A third space

Accordingly, we end this book where we began – with the proposal of a 'third place of the soul' that can transcend narrow reductionist or transcendentalist categories of self. In such a way the realm of soul will enable psychology (and pastoral theology) to reinvest its efforts in a realm of *psyche* which is neither based on physical or empirical concerns nor the metaphysics of pure spirit. As I suggested earlier, this symbolic 'soul-work' will therefore rely on relationship, the creative and artistic and the necessary perspective of the embodied/libidinal self. Pursuing the 'way of seeing' described in this book a 'third way' is thus revealed in our search of the self that allows the ambiguous choreography of saying and showing to restore the necessary transcendental perspective to the twenty-first century self.

Conclusion

Therefore, at the end of our long 'pursuit of the soul' that has taken us to so many places, languages and sources over so many centuries, I conclude that soul-language is the language of the choreography of the transcendent and immanent. The soul, we could say, is a linguistic signifier that allows us to gaze simultaneously at the physical and spiritual realms, as so many of the authors presented here have done. Over-emphasis on one, I have suggested, at the expense of the other, whether that be overly physicalist, idealist or spiritualist, will of necessity break the delicate web of meaning with which the *logos* of the *psyche* must be spun. In contemporary terms, then, the word 'soul' is a call to hold theology and psychology together in their shared pursuit of the divine and, as such, as we have seen throughout this book, it is therefore a call to synthesis and creativity.

Having travelled through three millennia in 'soul pursuit' we can conclude that talk of the 'death of the soul' is perhaps a little premature. As we have seen, the idea of the soul has haunted human imagination since records of that imagination begin and I see no reason to believe that this vision will not continue to beguile, intrigue and infuriate us for as long as humans continue to exist.

BIBLIOGRAPHY

Primary sources

Abbreviations

CUP Cambridge University Press
DS M. Viller, F. Cavallera, J. de Guibert, A. Rayez, A. Derville, P. Lamarche, A. Solignac (eds) *Dictionnaire de Spiritualité Ascétique et Mystique Doctrine et Histoire* (Paris: Beauchesne, 1937–present)
ICS Institute of Carmelite Studies, Washington
LCL Loeb Classical Library
OUP Oxford University Press
PG J.-P. Migne (ed.) *Patrologiae Cursus Completus. Series Graeca* (Paris, 1857–66)
PL *Patrologiae Cursus Completus. Series Latina* (Paris, 1844–64)
SC *Sources Chrétiennes*, Éditions du Cerf, Paris.

The Theologians

St Augustine of Hippo
Comm Gen *Literal Commentary on Genesis/De Genesi ad litteram*
On Genesis: A Refutation of the Manichees, Unfinished Literal Commentary on Genesis, The Literal Meaning of Genesis, in *The Works of Saint Augustine: A Translation for the 21st Century,* ed. J. Rotelle, trans. E. Hill (New York: New City Press, 2002)

Conf *The Confessions*
Confessions. Trans. J. O'Donnell (Oxford: Clarendon, 1992)
St Augustine's Confessions. Trans. W. Watts. LCL (London: Heinemann, 1928)
The Confessions in *The Works of Saint Augustine: A Translation for the 21st Century,* ed. J. Rotelle, trans. M. Boulding (New York: New City Press, 1997)

Hom John *Homilies on John*
St Augustine: Tractates on the Gospel of John. Trans. J. Rettig (Washington, DC: The Catholic University of America Press, 1988)
Augustin: Homilies on the Gospel of John, Homilies on the First Epistle of John, Soliloquies (ed. P. Schaff), in *A Select Library of the Christian Church – Nicene and Post-Nicene Fathers* (Peabody, MA: Hendrickson, 1995)

Bibliography

Hom Ps *Homilies on the Psalms*
Expositions of the Psalms, in *The Works of Saint Augustine: A Translation for the 21st Century*, ed. J. Rotelle, trans. M. Boulding (New York: New City Press, 2001–2)

Trin *On the Trinity*
The Trinity, in *The Works of Saint Augustine: A Translation for the 21st Century*, ed. J. Rotelle, trans. E. Hill (New York: New City Press, 1996)

Latin texts
Corpus Christianorum, Series Latina (Turnhout: Brepols, 1955–)
Corpus Scriptorum Ecclesiasticorum Latinorum. S. Aureli Augustini, ed. J. Zycha (Prague/Vienna: F. Tempsky, 1894)

John Cassian
Conf *The Conferences*
The Conferences, ed. B. Ramsey (New York: Newman Press, 1997)
Conférences, ed. E. Pichery. SC 42, 54, 64 (Paris: Cerf, 1955–9)
Institutions Cénobitiques, ed. J.-C. Guy. SC 109 (Paris: Cerf, 1965)

Clement of Alexandria
Clément d'Alexandrie, Les Stromates, ed. A. Le Boulluec, C. Mondésert, P. Descourtieux. SC 30, 463 (Paris: Cerf, 1951/2013, 2001)

Dionysius the Areopagite
CH *On the Celestial Hierarchy*
DN *On the Divine Names*
EH *On the Ecclesiastical Hierarchy*
Ep *Epistles*
Corpus Dionysiacum, ed. B. R. Suchla, G. Heil and A. M. Ritter (Berlin: De Gruyter, 1990–1)
Dionysiaca: Recueil donnat L'ensemble des traditions latines des ouvrages attributes au Denys de l'Aréopage, ed. M. Chevalier (Paris: Desclée de Brouwer, 1937–50)
Opera Veteris ac novae translationis cum Hugonis, Alberti, Thomae et aliorum. Strassbourg: 1502 (Salisbury Cathedral: A 5.8, 1502)
Pseudo-Dionysius: The Complete Works. Trans. C. Luibheid and P. Rorem (New York: Paulist, 1987)

Eusebius
Eusebius' Ecclesiastical History: Complete and Unabridged. Trans. C. Cruse (Peabody, MA: Hendrickson, 1998)

Evagrius of Pontus
Gnos *Gnostikos*

KG *Kephalaia Gnostica*
OP *On Prayer*
OTT *On the Thoughts*
Prak *Praktikos*
Evagrius Ponticus Praktikos – The Chapters on Prayer. Cistercian Studies No. 4.
    Trans. J. Bamberger (Kalamazoo, MI: Cistercian, 1981)
Praktikos & On Prayer. Trans. S. Tugwell (Oxford: Faculty of Theology, 1987)
Évagre le Pontique, Traité Pratique ou Le Moine, ed. A. Guillaumont and
    C. Guillaumont. SC: 170 and 171 (Paris: Cerf, 1971)
Évagre le Pontique, Le Gnostique ou A celui qui est devenu digne de la science, ed.
    A. Guillaumont and C. Guillaumont. SC: 356 (Paris: Cerf, 1989)
Évagre le Pontique Sur Les Pensées, ed. A. Guillaumont and C. Guillaumont. SC:
    438 (Paris: Cerf, 1998)
Les six Centuries des 'Kephalaia Gnostica' d'Évagre le Pontique. Trans.
    A. Guillaumont. *Patrologia Orientalis* 28.1, 134 (Paris: Firmin-Didot, 1958)
PG 79 1200d-1233a, attributed to St Nil and called *De Maligris Cogitationibus*

St Jerome
A Select Library of Nicene and Post-Nicene Fathers of the Christian Church, Second
    Series, Vol. 6. *St Jerome: Letters and Select Works.* Trans. W. H. Fremantle, ed.
    Philip Schaff and Henry Wace (Edinburgh: T&T Clarke, 1996)

Thomas Merton
CF *Cassian and the Fathers: Initiation into the Monastic Tradition,* ed. P. O'Connell
    (Kalamazoo, MI: Cistercian Publications, 2005)
HGL *The Hidden Ground of Love: Letters on Religious Experience and Social
    Concern,* ed. W. Shannon (New York: Farrar, Straus, Giroux, 1985)
IE *The Inner Experience: Notes on Contemplation,* ed. W. Shannon (London: SPCK,
    2003)
SS *The Seven Storey Mountain* (London: SPCK, 1948/1990)
ZB *Zen and the Birds of Appetite* (Kentucky: The Abbey of Gethsemani, 1968)
The Lectures to Novices (audio recordings). Credence Cassettes, The National
    Catholic Reporter, USA

Origen
Comm John *Commentary on the Gospel of John*
Comm Num *Commentary on the Book of Numbers*
Comm Songs *Commentary on the Song of Songs*
Princ *On the First Principles/De Principiis*
Origène: Traité des Principes, ed. H. Crouzel and M. Simonetti. SC: 252, 253, 268,
    269, 312 (Paris: Cerf, 1978–84)
Origène: Commentaire sur le Cantique des Cantiques 1, ed. L. Brésard and
    H. Crouzel. SC: 375 (Paris: Cerf, 1991)
Origène: Commentaire sur Saint Jean V (Livres XXVIII–XXXII), ed. C. Blanc. SC:
    385 (Paris: Cerf, 1992)

Bibliography

On First Principles. Trans. G. W. Butterworth (Translation of Koetschau's Text *De Principiis*) (Gloucester, MA: Peter Smith, 1973)
Homilies on the Book of Numbers. Trans. T. Scheck (Downers Grove, IL: IVP Academic, 2009)

Edith Stein (Sister Teresa Benedicta a Cruce)
AB *Der Aufbau der Menschlichen Person: Vorlesung zur Philosophischen Anthropologie,* ed. B. Beckmann-Zöller (Freiburg: Herder, 2010)
EE *Endliches und Ewiges Sein: Versuch eines Aufsteigs zum Sinn des Seins* (Freiburg: Herder, 1986)
KF *Knowledge and Faith.* Trans. W. Redmond (Washington: ICS, 2000)
KW *Kreuzeswissenschaft* (Freiburg: Herder, 1950)
PE *On the Problem of Empathy.* Trans. W. Stein (Washington: ICS, 1989)
PPH *Philosophy of Psychology and the Humanities.* Trans. M. Baseheart and M. Sawicki (Washington: ICS, 2000)
WM *Was Ist Der Mensch? Eine Theologische Anthropologie* (Freiburg: Herder, 1994)
WP *Welt und Person: Beitrag zum christlichen Wahrheitsstrebe,* ed. L. Gelber (Freiburg: Herder, 1962)
Finite and Eternal Being. Trans. K. Reinhardt (Washington: ICS, 2002)
The Science of the Cross. Trans. J. Koeppel (Washington: ICS, 2002)

Tertullian
Tertullian: Apology, De Spectaculis, ed. T. Glover. LCL 250 (London: Heinemann, 1931)
Latin Christianity: Its Founder, Tertullian. Ante-Nicene Fathers Vol. 3, ed. A. Roberts and J. Donaldson (Peabody, MA: Hendrickson, 1995)

The Philosophers

Aristotle
De Anima. Trans. R. Hicks (Cambridge: CUP, 1950)
The Nicomachean Ethics. Trans. H. Rackham. LCL (London: Heinemann, 1934)

Friedrich Nietzsche
Friedrich Nietzsche Werke in Zwei Bänden (Munich: Carl Hanser Verlag, 1990)

Philo of Alexandria
All *Allegorical Interpretation of Genesis 2, 3.* LCL 226. Trans. F. Colson and G. Whitaker (London: Heinemann, 1929)
Conf *On the Confusion of Tongues.* LCL 227. Trans. F. Colson and G. Whitaker (London: Heinemann, 1929)
Opif *On the Account of the World's Creation Given by Moses.* LCL 226. Trans. F. Colson and G. Whitaker (London: Heinemann, 1929)

Giovanni Pico Della Mirandola
Oration on the Dignity of Man, ed. F. Borghesi, M. Papio and M. Riva (Cambridge: CUP, 2012)

Plato
Timaeus, Critias, Cleitophon, Menexenus, Epistles. LCL 234. Trans. R. Bury (London: Heinemann. 1929/1989)
Charmides. LCL 201. Trans. W. Lamb (London: Heinemann, 1927)
Phaedo, Phaedrus. LCL 36. Trans. H. Fowler (London: Heinemann, 1929/1982)
The Republic. LCL 276. Trans. P. Shorey (London: Heinemann, 1935/1970)
Plato: The Collected Dialogues Including the Letters, ed. E. Hamilton and H. Cairns (Princeton, NJ: Princeton University Press, 1961)

Plotinus
Enn *The Enneads*
Plotinus the Enneads. LCL 440–445, 468 (7 vols). Trans. A. H. Armstrong (London: Heinemann, 1966–88)
Plotinus the Enneads. Trans. S. Mackenna (London: Faber and Faber, 1969)
Plotini Opera, ed. P. Henry and H.-R. Shwyzer (Oxford: Clarendon, 1964–82)

Porphyry
On the Life of Plotinus/Vita Plotini in *Plotinus* Vol. 1, LCL 440. Trans. A. H. Armstrong (London: Heinemann, 1966)

Ludwig Wittgenstein
BEE *Wittgenstein's Nachlass: The Bergen Electronic Edition* (Oxford: OUP, 2000)
CLL *Wittgenstein's Lectures: Cambridge 1930–1932, from the Notes of John King and Desmond Lee,* ed. D Lee (Oxford: Blackwell, 1980)
CV *Culture and Value,* ed. G. von Wright and H. Nyman (Oxford: Blackwell, 1980)
LPE *Letters from Ludwig Wittgenstein with a Memoir by Paul Engelmann,* ed. B. McGuinness (Oxford: Blackwell, 1967)
LPP *Lectures on Philosophical Psychology 1946–47. From the Notes of P. Geach, K. Shah and A. Jackson,* ed. P. Geach (London: Harvester, 1988)
LWP *Last Writings on the Philosophy of Psychology,* ed. G. E. M. Anscombe and G. H. von Wright (Oxford: Blackwell, 1982)
NB *Notebooks 1914–1916.* Trans. G. E. M. Anscombe (Oxford: Blackwell, 1984)
OC *On Certainty,* ed. G. E. M. Anscombe and G. H. von Wright (Oxford: Blackwell, 1969)
PI *Philosophical Investigations,* ed. G. E. M. Anscombe and R. Rhees (Oxford: Blackwell, 1958)
PU *Philosophische Untersuchungen* in *Werkausgabe in 8 Bände,* Vol. 1 (Frankfurt am Main: Suhrkamp, 1993)
RFGB *Remarks on Frazer's Golden Bough,* reprinted in *Philosophical Occasions 1912–1951,* ed. J. C. Klagge and A. Nordmann (Cambridge: Hackett, 1993)

Bibliography

RPP *Remarks on the Philosophy of Psychology,* ed. G. H. von Wright and H. Nyman (Oxford: Blackwell, 1980)
T *Tractatus Logico-Philosophicus.* Trans. D. F. Pears and B. McGuinness (London: Routledge and Kegan Paul, 1961)
VB *Vermischte Bemerkungen* in Volume 8: *Werkausgabe in 8 Bände* (Frankfurt am Main: Suhrkamp, 1993)
W *Werkausgabe in 8 Bände* (Frankfurt am Main: Suhrkamp, 1993)
Z *Zettel,* ed. G. E. M. Anscombe and G. H. von Wright (Oxford: Blackwell, 1967)

The Psychologists

Sigmund Freud
GW *Gesammelte Werke in Achtzehn Bänden mit einem Nachtragsband,* ed.
  A. Freud, E. Bibring, W. Hoffer, E. Kris and O. Isakower (Frankfurt am Main: Fischer Verlag, 1960–8)
SE *Standard Edition of the Complete Psychological Works of Sigmund Freud.* Trans.
  J. Strachey (London: The Hogarth Press). Including:
  The Question of Lay Analysis. Vol. 20. 1926/1959
  A Difficulty in the Path of Psycho-Analysis. Vol. 17. 1917/50
  New Introductory Lectures. Vol. 22. 1933
  The Future of an Illusion. Vol. 21. 1927
Sigmund Freud, Oskar Pfister: Briefe 1909–1939 (Frankfurt am Main: Fischer Verlag, 1963)
Psycho-analysis and Faith: The Letters of Sigmund Freud and Oskar Pfister, ed.
  H. Meng and E. Freud. Trans. E. Mosbacher (London: The Hogarth Press, 1963)
The Freud/Jung Letters: The Correspondence between Sigmund Freud and C. G. Jung,
  ed. W. McGuire. Trans. R. Manheim and R. Hull (Princeton, NJ: Princeton University Press, 1974)
The Penguin Freud Library. Trans. J. Strachey (London: Penguin, 1991)

James Hillman
HY *We've Had a Hundred Years of Psychotherapy and the World's Getting Worse.*
  With M. Ventura (New York: Harper, 1992)
I *Insearch: Psychology and Religion* (Woodstock: Spring Publications, 1967/1994)
IV *Inter Views: Conversations with Laura Pozzo on Psychotherapy, Biography, Love, Soul, the Gods, Animals, Dreams, Imagination, Work, Cities and the State of Culture* (Dallax, TX: Spring Publications, 1983)
LD *Lament of the Dead: Psychology after Jung's Red Book,* ed. S. Shamdasani (New York: W. W. Norton, 2013)
MA *The Myth of Analysis: Three Essays in Archetypal Psychology* (Evanston: Northwestern University Press, 1972)
PP (Ed.) *Puer Papers* (Dallas, TX: Spring Publications, 1991)
RVP *Re-Visioning Psychology* (New York: Harper, 1975/1992)

SC *The Soul's Code: In Search of Character and Calling* (New York: Random House, 1996)
SS *Suicide and the Soul* (Dallas, TX: Spring Publications, 1964/1997)

Carl Jung

CW *The Collected Works of C. G. Jung.* Trans. and revised by R. Hull and H. Baynes (London: Routledge, 1971/1999)
RB *The Red Book: Liber Novus,* ed. S. Shamdasani (London: Norton & Co. 2009)
Briefe 1906–1961, ed. A Jaffé (Freiburg im Breisgau: Walter, 1972/3)
Memories, Dreams, Reflections, ed. A. Jaffé (London: Vintage, 1963/1989)

Otto Rank

AL *A Psychology of Difference: The American Lectures,* ed. R. Kramer (Princeton, NJ: Princeton University Press, 1996)
BePs *Beyond Psychoanalysis.* 1928 in Kramer 1996
BP *Beyond Psychology* (New York: Dover, 1958)
MP *Modern Psychology and Social Change.* 1938 in Kramer 1996
PG *Psychoanalysis as General Psychology.* 1924 in Kramer 1996
PS *Psychology and the Soul: A Study of the Origin, Conceptual Evolution and Nature of the Soul.* Trans. G. Richter and E. Liebermann (Baltimore: John Hopkins University Press, 1930/1998)
SL *The Significance of the Love Life.* 1927 in Kramer 1996
Sp *Speech at First International Congress on Mental Hygiene.* 1930 in Kramer 1996
SP *Seelenglaube und Psychologie* (Leipzig: Franz Deuticke, 1930)
TB *The Trauma of Birth.* Trans. J. Lieberman (New York: Dover, 1924/1993)
WT and TR *Will Therapy and Truth and Reality.* Trans. J. Taft (New York: Alfred Knopf, 1950). Originally vols 2 and 3 (1936) *Technik der Psychoanalyse* (Vol. 2: *Die Analytische Reaktion in Ihren Konstruktiven Elementen,* Vol. 3: *Die Analyse des Analytikers u seiner Rolle in der Gesamtsituation*)
YL *The Yale Lecture (The Psychological Approach to Personal Problems).* 1929 in Kramer 1996

Church Documents and Scripture

Decrees of the Ecumenical Councils, ed. N. Tanner (Cambridge: CUP, 1990)
Les Conciles Oecuméniques De Nicée à Latran V. Vol. 2 *Les Décrets,* ed. G. Alberigo (Paris: Les Éditions du Cerf, 1994)
The Documents of Vatican II, ed. W. Abbott (London: Geoffrey Chapman, 1966)
Fides et Ratio. Encyclical Letter of St John Paul II (London: Catholic Truth Society, 1998)
Catechism of the Catholic Church (CCC) (London: Continuum, 1994)
Scripture Quotations from the *New Revised Standard Version* (London: Harper, 2007) with modifications as necessary

Bibliography

References to the Nag Hammadi texts from *The Nag Hammadi Library: Definitive Translation of the Gnostic Scriptures,* ed. J. Robinson (Brill, 2002)

Other works

Armstrong, A. H. 'Salvation, Plotinian and Christian' in *The Downside Review,* 75, No. 240 (1957)

Armstrong, A. H. *St Augustine and Christian Platonism.* Villanova: Villanova University Press, 1967

Armstrong, A. H. *Plotinian and Christian Studies.* London: Variorum, 1979

Baker, R. and Henry, G. (ed.) *Merton and Sufism: The Untold Story.* Louisville: Fons Vitae, 1999

Barnhart, R. (ed.) *Barnhart Dictionary of Etymology.* New York: H. W. Wilson, 1988

Berchman, R. *From Philo to Origen: Middle Platonism in Transition.* Chico, CA: Scholars, 1984

Bettleheim, B. *Freud and Man's Soul.* London: Penguin, 1982/2001

Bishop, P. *The Dionysian Self: C. G. Jung's Reception of Friedrich Nietzsche.* Berlin: Walter de Gruyter, 1995

Boardman, T. 'The Enigma of Canon XI: The "Abolition" of the Spirit – The Year 869 & Its Significance in the Destiny of Europe' in *New View* (Spring 2008)

Capps, D. 'Enrapt Spirits and the Melancholy Soul: The Locus of Division in the Christian Self and American Society' in *On Losing the Soul: Essays in the Social Psychology of Religion*, eds. R. Fenn and D. Capps. New York: State University of New York Press, 1995

Cary, P. *Augustine's Invention of the Inner Self: The Legacy of a Christian Platonist.* Oxford: OUP, 2000

Clack, B. *Freud on the Couch: A Critical Introduction to the Father of Psychoanalysis.* London: Oneworld, 2013

Cook, C. *Spirituality, Theology and Mental Health.* London: SCM, 2013

Cook, C., A. Powell and A. Sims. *Spirituality and Psychiatry.* London: RC Psych Publications, 2009

Cremer, H. *Biblico-Theological Lexicon of New Testament Greek.* Trans. W. Urwick. Edinburgh: T&T Clark, 1895

Crouse, R. D. 'Paucis Mutatis Verbis: St Augustine's Platonism' in R. Dodaro and G. Lawless, *Augustine and His Critics: Essays in Honour of Gerald Bonner.* London: Routledge, 2000

Davis, R. *Jung, Freud and Hillman: Three Depth Psychologies in Context.* London: Praeger, 2003

Dodaro, R. and G. Lawless. *Augustine and His Critics: Essays in Honour of Gerald Bonner.* London: Routledge, 2000

Dostoyevsky, F. *The Demons.* Trans. R. Maguire. London: Penguin, 2008

Dysinger, L. *Psalmody and Prayer in the Writings of Evagrius Ponticus.* Oxford: OUP, 2005

Dysinger, L. *Themes in Evagrius,* 2014, available online: http://www.ldysinger.com/ Evagrius/07_Antirrhet/00a_start.htm (accessed 21 August 2014)

Ellenberger, H. *The Discovery of the Unconscious: The History and Evolution of Dynamic Psychiatry.* New York: Basic Books, 1981

Fenn, R. and D. Capps (eds). *On Losing the Soul: Essays in the Social Psychology of Religion.* New York: State University of New York Press, 1995

Foucault, M. (ed. P. Rabinow). *The Foucault Reader.* London: Penguin, 1991

Genova, J. *Wittgenstein: A Way of Seeing.* London: Routledge, 1995

Gilson, E. *The Spirit of Medieval Philosophy.* New York: C. Scribner's, 1940

Gomez, L. *The Freud Wars: An Introduction to the Philosophy of Psychoanalysis.* London: Routledge, 2005

Hadot, P. *Philosophy as a Way of Life: Spiritual Exercises from Socrates to Foucault.* Oxford: Blackwell, 1995

Herbstrith, W. *Edith Stein: The Untold Story of the Philosopher and Mystic who Lost her Life in the Death Camps of Auschwitz.* Trans. B. Bonowitz. San Francisco: Ignatius, 1992

St John Paul II. *Crossing the Threshold of Hope.* London: Jonathan Cape, 1994

Kelly, J. N. D. *St Jerome: His Life, Writings and Controversies.* London: Hendrickson, 1998

Kenney, J. P. *The Mysticism of Saint Augustine: Rereading the* Confessions. London: Routledge, 2005

Kenney, J. P. *Contemplation and Classical Christianity: A Study in Augustine.* Oxford: OUP, 2013

Kidel, M. 'James Hillman Obituary' in *The Guardian,* 21 December 2011

Klein, E. *A Comprehensive Etymological Dictionary of the English Language.* Amsterdam: Elsevier Scientific Publishing, 1971

Konstantinovsky, J. *Evagrius Ponticus: The Making of a Gnostic.* Farnham: Ashgate, 2009

Lamb, M. 'Eternity Creates and Redeems Time: A Key to Augustine's *Confessions* within a Theology of History' in *Divine Creation in Ancient, Medieval and Early Modern Thought: Essays Presented to the Rev'd Dr Robert D. Crouse,* eds. M. Treschow, W. Otten and W. Hannam, Leiden: Brill, 2007

Leemans, E. A. *Studie over den wijsgeer Numenius van Apamea met uitgave der fragmenten* in *Memoires de l'Academie Royale de Belgique.* Vol. 37, Pt. 2. Brussels: Palaise des Academies, 1937

Liddell, H. and R. Scott. *A Greek-English Lexicon.* Oxford: Clarendon Press, 1996

Liebermann, E. J. *Acts of Will: the Life and Work of Otto Rank.* New York: The Free Press, 1985

Lorenz, H. 'Plato on the Soul' in *The Oxford Handbook of Plato,* ed. G. Fine. Oxford: OUP, 2008

Louth, A. *Denys the Areopagite,* London: Geoffrey Chapman, 1989

Louth, A. *The Origins of the Christian Mystical Tradition: From Plato to Denys.* Oxford: OUP, 2007/1981

McGinn, B. *The Presence of God: A History of Western Christian Mysticism. Vol I: The Foundations of Mysticism.* London: SCM, 1991

McGinn, B. 'Humans as *Imago Dei*: Mystical Anthropology Then and Now' in

Bibliography

Sources of Transformation: Revitilizing Christian Spirituality, eds. P. M. Tyler and E. Howells. London: Continuum, 2010

McGuinness, B. *Wittgenstein: A Life. The Young Ludwig (1889–1921).* London: Penguin, 1988

Miller, F. 'The Platonic Soul' in *A Companion to Plato,* ed. H. Benson. Oxford: Blackwell, 2006

Monk, R. *Ludwig Wittgenstein – The Duty of Genius.* London: Jonathan Cape, 1990

Nedo, M. and M. Ranchetti. *Ludwig Wittgenstein: Sein Leben in Bildern und Texten.* Frankfurt am Main: Suhrkamp, 1983

O'Connell, R. *The Origin of the Soul in St Augustine's Later Works.* New York: Fordham University Press, 1987

O'Connell, R. *Augustine's Confessions.* Oxford: Clarendon Press, 1992

O'Daly, G. *Platonism Pagan and Christian: Studies in Plotinus and Augustine.* Aldershot: Ashgate, 2001

O'Meara, D. *Introduction to the Enneads.* Oxford: Clarendon, 1995

Onians, R. *The Origins of European Thought about the Body, the Mind, the Soul, the World, Time and Fate.* Cambridge: CUP, 1951

Proceedings of the First International Congress on Mental Hygiene. Ed. Ruth Shonle Cavan in *American Journal of Sociology.* Vol. 41, No. 1 (July 1935), pp. 131–2

Rhees, R. *Recollections of Wittgenstein.* Oxford: Oxford Paperback, 1987

Russell, D. *The Life and Ideas of James Hillman,* Vol. 1: *The Making of a Psychologist.* New York: Helios, 2013

Scull, A. *Madness in Civilisation: A Cultural History of Insanity from the Bible to Freud, from the Madhouse to Modern Medicine.* London: Thames and Hudson, 2015

Slater, G. Introduction to *Senex and Puer, Uniform Edition of the Writings of James Hillman,* Vol. 3. Putnam: Spring Publications, 2005

Spengler, O. *Der Untergang des Abendlandes: Umrisse einer Morphologie der Weltgeschichte.* Munich: C. H. Beck'sche Verlag, 1923

Spengler, O. *The Decline of the West: Form and Actuality.* Trans. C. F. Atkinson. London: George Allen and Unwin, 1926

Tacey, D. 'Twisting and Turning with James Hillman: From Anima to World Soul, from Academia to Pop' in *Post-Jungians Today,* ed. A. Casement. London: Routledge, 1998

Tagore, R. *The King of the Dark Chamber.* New Delhi: Rupa, 2002

Tauber, A. *Freud: the Reluctant Philosopher.* Princeton: Princeton University Press, 2010

Taylor, C. *Sources of the Self: The Making of the Modern Identity.* Cambridge: CUP, 1989

Trapè, A. 'VI. Saint Augustine' in *Patrology,* Vol. 4, *The Golden Age of Latin Patristic Literature from the Council of Nicea to the Council of Chalcedon,* ed. A. Di Berardino. Westminster: Christian Classics, 1986

Treschow, M., W. Otten and W. Hannam (eds). *Divine Creation in Ancient, Medieval and Early Modern Thought: Essays Presented to the Rev'd Dr Robert D. Crouse.* Leiden: Brill, 2007

Tripolitis, A. *The Doctrine of the Soul in the Thought of Plotinus and Origen.* New York: Libra, 1978

Tyler, P. M. *The Way of Ecstasy: Praying with Teresa of Avila.* Norwich: Canterbury Press, 1997

Tyler, P. M. *Sources of Transformation: Revitilizing Christian Spirituality,* eds. P. M. Tyler and E. Howells. London: Continuum, 2010

Tyler, P. M. *St John of the Cross: Outstanding Christian Thinker.* London: Continuum, 2010a

Tyler, P. M. *The Return to the Mystical: Ludwig Wittgenstein, Teresa of Avila and the Christian Mystical Tradition.* London: Continuum, 2011

Tyler, P. M. 'To Centre or Not to Centre: Ss. Teresa of Avila and John of the Cross and the "Centre of the Soul"' in *Christian Mysticism and Incarnational Theology – Between Transcendence and Immanence,* eds. L. Nelstrop and S. Podmore. Surrey: Ashgate, 2013

Tyler, P. M. *Teresa of Avila: Doctor of the Soul.* London: Bloomsbury, 2013a

Tyler, P. M. *Picturing the Soul: Revisioning Psychotherapy and Spiritual Direction.* Bangalore: Dharmaram, 2014

Tyler, P. M. 'Carl Jung: Friend or Foe of Christianity?' in *Vinayasadhana: Dharmaram Journal of Psycho-Spiritual Formation.* Vol. VI, No. 1 (January 2015)

Von Balthasar, H. U. *Herrlichkeit: Eine theologische Ästhetik.* (Einsiedeln: Johannes Verlag, 1961–1969). Trans. 'The Glory of the Lord: A Theological Aesthetic', eds Fessio, J. and Riches, J., trans. Davies, O., Louth, A., Sayward, J., Simon, M., McNeil, B., McDonagh, F., Riches, J., Leiva-Merikakis, E. and Williams, R., Edinburgh: T&T Clarke, 1982–1989

Waismann, F. *The Principles of Linguistic Philosophy,* ed. R Harre. London: Macmillan, 1965

White, D. *The Lost Knowledge of Christ: Contemporary Spirituality, Christian Cosmology and the Arts.* Collegeville, Minnesota: The Liturgical Press, 2015

Williams, R. *Wrestling with Angels: Conversations in Modern Theology,* ed M. Higton. London: SCM, 2007

Yates, F. *The Art of Memory.* Chicago: University of Chicago Press, 1966

Zoja, L. 'Analysis and Tragedy' in A. Casement (ed.) *Post-Jungians Today: Key Papers in Contemporary Analytical Psychology.* London: Routledge, 1998

Zoja, L. *Cultivating the Soul.* London: Free Association, 2005

INDEX

Index

Index

Index